For Bennett—my trusted brother,
sometimes teacher, and always friend

COERCION

ains. They say polyuns
u than saturated fat. Th
a rock prove there wa
r children's test score
sus was a direct descei
y you can earn fifteen t
ur spare time. They sa
d LSD can lead to suici
n. They say homosexua
arned trait. They say th
lity. They say people ca
ing. They say people
pnosis that they wou
ey say Prozac allevia
utual funds are the be
ey say computers can
y you haven't met your
en's test scores are dec
lirect descendent of Kii
rn fifteen say human b
their brains. They say
r for you than saturat
uiggles in a rock pro
ars. They our children'
ey say Jesus was a d
avid. They say you can
rs a week in your spare
ads to LSD, and LSD ca
e corner of son. They s
ronmentally learned tr
r homosexuality. They
ged to do anything. The
ing under hypnosis th
nscious. They say Pro
ey say mutual funds a
stment. They say co
eather. They say you ha
ey our children's test
y Jesus was a direct o
ey say you can earn f
st scores are declining
ct descendent of King
rn fifteen say human

COERCION

Why We Listen to What "They" Say

Douglas Rushkoff

RIVERHEAD BOOKS

A MEMBER OF PENGUIN PUTNAM INC.

NEW YORK 1999

Riverhead Books
a member of Penguin Putnam Inc.
375 Hudson Street
New York, NY 10014

Library of Congress Cataloging-in-Publication Data
Rushkoff, Douglas.
    Coercion : why we listen to what "they" say /
      by Douglas Rushkoff.
      p.   cm.
    Includes bibliographical references.
    ISBN 1-57322-115-5
    1. Mass media—Influence.   2. Persuasion (Psychology)
      I. Title.
  P94.R87 1999
  302.23—dc21   99-18230 CIP

Printed in the United States of America

10 9 8 7 6 5 4 3 2 1

This book is printed on acid-free paper. ∞

BOOK DESIGN BY LOVEDOG STUDIO

CONTENTS

COERCION

They Say

They say human beings use only ten percent of their brains. They say polyunsaturated fat is better for you than saturated fat. They say that tiny squiggles in a rock prove there once was life on Mars. They say our children's test scores are declining. They say Jesus was a direct descendant of King David. They say you can earn $15,000 a week in your spare time. They say marijuana leads to LSD, and LSD can lead to suicide. They say the corner office is a position of power. They say the elderly should get flu shots this season. They say homosexuality is an environmentally learned trait. They say there's a gene for homosexuality. They say people can be hypnotized to do anything. They say people won't do anything under hypnosis that they wouldn't do when conscious. They say Prozac alleviates depression. They say mutual funds are the best long-term investment. They say computers can predict the weather. They say you haven't met your deductible.

Who, exactly, are "they," and why do they say so much? More amazing, why do we listen to them?

We each have our own "theys"—the bosses, experts, and authorities (both real and imaginary) who seem to dictate our lives, decide our fates, and create our futures. In the best of circumstances they can make us feel safe, the way parents do. They make our decisions for us. They do our thinking for us. We don't have to worry about our next move—it has already been decided on our behalf, and in our best interests. Or so we hope.

For not everyone to whom we surrender ourselves is deserving of our trust. The pretty young "sales associate" at the Gap may not be the best judge of how that pair of blue jeans looks on us, or of which belt we should wear to a job interview. Even though she seems genuinely concerned with our well-being, we must not forget that she's been trained in the art of the "upsell" and is herself under the influence of a barrage of incentives conceived at corporate headquarters. One scheme leads her to compete with her colleagues on the sales floor for daily prizes, while another threatens penalties or termination if she does not meet a certain quota of multiple-item sales by the end of the week. The coercive techniques inflicted on her, and the ones she in turn inflicts on us, are the products of years of painstaking research into methods of influencing human behavior.

The justifiably cynical among us have come to expect this sort of treatment from the professional people in our lives. When we walk into a shopping mall, we understand that we will be subjected to certain forms of influence. We recognize that retail sales are about the bottom line, and that to stay in business, shop owners depend upon our behaving in a predictable and somewhat malleable fashion. If instructing a salesgirl to unfasten the second button of her blouse may garner a larger volume of sales, the store manager owes it to himself and his superiors and their shareholders to do so. And, chances are, it will work.

But these techniques are rapidly spreading from the sales floor and the television screen to almost every other aspect of our daily experience. Whether we are strolling through Times Square, exploring the Internet, or even just trying to make friends at the local bar, we are under constant scrutiny and con-stant assault by a professional class of hidden persuaders. In most cases, if the coercion works according to plan, we don't even realize it has been used.

It's not always easy to determine when we have surrendered our judgment to someone else. The better and more sophisti-cated the manipulation, the less aware of it we are. For example, have you ever attended a sporting event, rock concert, or politi-cal convention in one frame of mind, but found yourself inex-plicably swept away by the emotion of the crowd? How many times have you walked into a mall to buy a single pair of shoes, only to find yourself purchasing an entire outfit, several books, and a few CDs before you made your way back to the parking lot?

Have you ever picked up the phone, realized the caller was from an organization you'd never considered supporting, and gone ahead and pledged a sum of money or bought a magazine subscription? How did that automobile salesman get you to pay more than you'd planned to for a car, and add more features than you wanted, even though you came armed with your *Con-sumer Reports*?

Why do the advertisements in fashion magazines make us feel inadequate, and after they do, why do we feel compelled to buy the products advertised anyway? How can we feel we're so aware of the effects of advertising and marketing, yet still suc-cumb to them?

Why are our kids tattooing themselves with the Nike "swoosh" icon? Are they part of a corporate cult? If young people today are supposed to be beyond the reach of old-fashioned marketing, then why do they feel the need to find their identity in a brand of sneakers?

No matter how many coercive techniques we come to recog-nize, new ones are always being developed that we don't. Once we've become immune to the forceful "hard sell" techniques of the traditional car dealer, a high-paid influence consultant develops a new brand with an entirely new image—like the Saturn, whose dealers use friendly "soft sell" techniques to accomplish the same thing, more subtly. Media-savvy young people have learned to reject advertising that tries too hard to make its product look "cool." In response, companies now produce decidedly "uncool" advertisements, which appeal to the cynical viewer who thinks he can remain unswayed. "Image is nothing. Thirst is everything," Sprite advertisers confess to their hype-weary target market. Our attempts to stay one step ahead of coercers merely provokes them to develop even more advanced, less visible, and, arguably, more pernicious methods of persuasion.

Corporations and consumers are in a coercive arms race. Every effort we make to regain authority over our actions is met by an even greater effort to usurp it.

If we stop to think about this invisible hand working on our perceptions and behavior, we can easily become paranoid. Although we cannot always point to the evidence, when we become aware that our actions are being influenced by forces beyond our control—we shop in malls that have been designed by psychologists, and experience the effects of their architecture and color schemes on our purchasing behaviors—we can't help but feel a little edgy. No matter how discreetly camouflaged the coercion, we sense that it's leading us to move and act ever so slightly against our wills. We may not want to admit consciously to ourselves that the floor plan of the shopping center has made us lose our bearings, but we are disoriented all the same. We don't know exactly how to get back to the car, and we will have to walk past twenty more stores before we find an exit.

In order to maintain the illusion of our own authority, we repress the urge to panic. Unfortunately, the more we stifle that little voice telling us we are in danger, the more we repress our ability to resist. We deny what we are feeling, and we disconnect further from what remains of our free will. As a result, we become even better targets for those who would direct our actions.

I was not always predisposed to think this way. On the contrary, for years I believed that we were winning the war against those who would shape our wills. Through the eighties and early nineties, I cheered as cable television, video games, the personal computer, and the Internet seemed to offer the promise of a new relationship to the mainstream media and a chance to undermine its coercive nature. Home-video cameras demystified for us the process by which news is reported, and public-access channels gave everyone an opportunity to broadcast his version of what was going on in the world. C-SPAN revealed to us the pompous rhetoric of our elected representatives, as well as the embarrassing fact that they usually address an empty chamber.

The low cost of video production and the increase in available channels gave rise to countless tabloid television shows. Like their print counterparts, these programs broadcast stories that more established news agencies would have held back—which in turn gave rise to a whole new set of journalistic standards and an unleashing of alternative news sources and outlets. Tabloid and Internet journalists were the first to publish everything from Clinton's trysts with Gennifer Flowers and Monica Lewinsky to Prince Charles's dirty phone calls with Camilla Parker Bowles. *Time* and *Newsweek* have simply struggled to keep up with the rising tide.

Internet discussion groups and bulletin boards gave us a new forum in which to discuss the information that was important to us. Online, we could access the latest word on new AIDS or cancer treatments, and then question our doctors (or our stingy HMOs) about a course of treatment. Even if all we intended to do was shop, the Internet gave us the ability to conduct instant price and feature comparisons, and to talk to others about a product before we bought it.

Meanwhile, young computer hackers had gotten their hands on the control panel of our electronic society. Bank records and other personal data that formerly were accessible only to credit bureaus and loan officers were now within the reach of any skilled fourteen-year-old. As a result, our privacy finally became an issue to be discussed publicly. We became aware of how information about us was being gathered, bought, and sold without our consent, and we supported activists, organizations, and candidates who promised to enact policies to prevent this invasion.

The Internet made us more aware of the process by which news and public relations are created and disseminated. As we gained access to press releases and corporate data, we have witnessed firsthand how public relations experts are allowed to write the evening news. In the early nineties, there was a participant of an electronic bulletin board who would post the transcripts of local news shows and then compare them, word for word, with the prepared press releases of the companies or individuals concerned. The results were embarrassingly similar, with whole paragraphs lifted directly from press release to newscaster's script.

As the coercive effects of mainstream media became more self-evident, media awareness led to a revival of cultural literacy. Our ability to see through the shameless greed of televangelists changed the way we related to the ritual surrounding the collection plate. Our ability to deconstruct the political process as it took place on TV gave rise to independent, homespun candidates like Ross Perot and Jerry Brown, whose campaigns promised direct access and accountability.

In the meantime, television programs like "Beavis and Butthead" and "The Simpsons" were deconstructing the rest of the mediaspace for our children. With Bart as their role model, the generation growing up in the last decade has maintained a guarded relationship to the media and marketing techniques that have fooled their parents. While his dad, Homer, was suckered by every beer promotion, Bart struggled to maintain his skateboarder's aloofness and dexterity. Through Bart, our kids learned to remain moving targets.

As a happy witness to what was taking place in our culture, I began to write books celebrating our liberation through the tools of new media. *Cyberia* applauded the scientists, hackers, and spiritualists who were determined to design a better society with these new tools. The technological revolution seemed to me a populist renaissance through which real people would wake from centuries of heartless manipulation. Hierarchy and social control soon would be things of the past as every individual came to realize his or her role in the unfolding of civilization. I saw my vision confirmed as the Internet rose in popularity, and as the once-ridiculed nerds of Silicon Valley began to engineer the communications infrastructure for the world's business community. The Internet would not fade into obscurity like CB radio. It was here to stay. Our culture was hardwiring itself together.

I became fascinated and inspired by the organic and responsive qualities of this new mediaspace. Just as our chaos mathematicians and quantum physicists had suggested, we were venturing into uncharted cultural turf, where huge systemwide changes could be provoked by the tiniest actions. In a system as dynamic as the weather, we learned, a single butterfly flapping its wings in Brazil could lead to a hurricane in New York. So, too, was the awesome power that "feedback and iteration" offered every member of a networked whole. Now that the media had become such a system, the beating of a black man by white policemen in Los Angeles, amplified throughout our mediated culture via a single, replicated, and endlessly broadcast camcorder tape, could lead to rioting in a dozen American cities.

Spurred on by these developments, in the early nineties I wrote an optimistic treatise on the new possibilities of an organic mediaspace. I proposed that provocative ideas could be launched in the form of mutant media packages—or "viruses"—by anyone who had a video camera or Internet connection. Thanks to the spread of commercial broadcasting, almost everyone in the world had been given access to the media in one form or another. What the people who put all those wires and TV satellites in place didn't realize was that electrons travel in both directions. Home media like camcorders, faxes, and Internet connections were empowering all of us to launch our ideas into the mediaspace.

Huge, well-funded, mainstream publicity campaigns were becoming obsolete. Now, anyone could launch an idea that would spread by itself if it were packaged in a new, unrecognizable form of media. Mutant media got attention because it was strange. And there's nothing the media likes more than to cover new forms of itself. The Rodney King tape proliferated as much because it demonstrated the power of a new technology—the camcorder—as for the image contained within it. One of the reasons why the O. J. Simpson story became the biggest trial in history was because it began with a mutant media event: the nationally televised spectacle of the Bronco chase, during which Los Angeles TV viewers ran outside and literally onto their own TV screens as the motorcade drove by. Similarly, the media stunts of ACT UP activists, Earth First "eco-terrorists," Greenpeace, and even unorthodox political candidates received worldwide attention simply by launching their campaigns through media viruses.

The hegemony of Hearst and Murdoch were over. We had entered an age where the only limiting factor was an idea's ability to provoke us through its novel dissemination. An idea no longer depended on the authority of its originator—it would spread and replicate if it challenged our faulty assumptions. In an almost Darwinian battle for survival, only the fittest ideas would win out. These new, mutated forms of media were promoting our cultural evolution, empowering real people, and giving a voice to those who never before had access to the global stage.

Best of all, young people were the ones leading the charge. Adults were immigrants to the new realm of interactive media, but kids raised with joysticks in their hands were natives. They spoke the language of new media and public relations better than the adults who were attempting to coerce them. What media can you use to manipulate a kid when he is already more media literate than you are? He will see through any clunky attempt to persuade him with meaningless associations and hired role models. By the time this generation came into adulthood, I believed, the age of manipulation would be over.

Once I'd published a book announcing that we'd entered the final days of the marketing wars, I began to get phone calls from politicians, media companies, advertisers, and even the United Nations, anxious for me to explain the new rules of the interactive age. I saw little harm in taking their money just to tell them that the genie was out of the bottle. I felt like an evangelist, spreading the news that the public had grown too media savvy to be fleeced any further. The only alternative left for public-relations people and advertisers was to tell the truth. Those promoting good ideas or making useful products would succeed; the rest would perish.

At first I found it easy to dismiss the writings of naysayer cyber critics like Jerry Manders, Paul Virilio, and Neil Postman, who attacked the notion that the new media had made a positive shift in the balance of power—culturally, economically, or otherwise. There was just too much evidence to the contrary. Although I had some sense that there were people out there attempting to deploy these same innovations coercively, I believed that acknowledging their efforts would only feed their power. If we ignored them, they would go away.

My optimism—and my willingness to consort with the enemy—was met with a number of personal attacks as well. One morning in November 1996, I woke up to a *New York Times* article describing me as a Gen-X guru who sold youth culture's secrets to media companies for upward of $7,500 per hour. Many of my friends and readers wondered how I could have betrayed the "movement," and wrote me to voice their disapproval. Alternative newspapers who had supported me in the past now called me a sellout. Mentors like virtual-community maker Howard Rheingold and Electronic Frontiers Foundation chairman Mitch Kapor warned me that my uncritical enthusiasm might be blinding me to very real threats to the civic revival we were all working for.

"Vigilance is a dangerous thing," I wrote at the time. I was convinced that a guarded approach to the development of new media would only slow things down, giving our would-be oppressors and manipulators a chance to catch up. And even if I was no better than the scores of "cool hunters" who hoped to cash in on corporate confusion about the changing priorities and sentiments of youth culture, since the ideas I promoted were empowering ones, I couldn't see the harm. I told executives at Sony to design a video game console that allowed kids to create their own video games. I told the people developing content for TCI's new interactive television network to make programs that gave viewers the chance to broadcast their own news stories. I told phone companies that the way to please their customers was to stop treating them like criminals whenever they were late with a payment.

I went to conferences and sat on panels alongside my media-hacking heroes like Michael Moore, the director of the GMbashing documentary *Roger and Me,* and Stewart Brand, one of the original band of Ken Kesey's Merry Pranksters. I delivered keynote addresses to thousands of advertising executives and television programmers, telling them to admit to themselves that their monopoly over the public will was over. The older executives threw up their arms in disgust, while the younger ones transcribed my every word. I couldn't have been more pleased. I felt at least partly responsible for dismantling the engines of propaganda and demilitarizing the coercive arms race. Better yet, I was making good money for doing so. My books were hitting best-seller lists, and my speaking and consulting fees were going through the roof—even if they never quite reached the fabled $7,500 per hour.

I guess it was too good to be true.

In the summer of 1997, I was invited to speak about my book *Media Virus* at a convention of "account planners" (advertising's version of anthropologist-researchers) sponsored by the American Association of Advertising Agencies. I packed up my laptop and headed for Sheraton Bal Harbour in Miami to spread the good news. The conference theme was "Mutant Media/Mutant Ideas," itself a play on the ideas in my book. Had the advertisers come to recognize that their power was dwindling?

Hardly. These friendly, well-dressed, and articulate people had bought and read my book—but for a reason very different from the one I'd had for writing it. They were eager to learn all about the mutant mediaspace, but only in order to figure out ways of creating advertisements that were themselves media viruses! *Media Virus* had become a best-seller not because so many activists, public-access producers, or computer hackers were reading it, but because it was now a standard text in the science of public relations. My work was being taught in advertising school.

Before I had the chance to put on my name tag, a young creative executive asked me what it was like working on the Calvin Klein jeans campaign—the one in which teenagers were photographed in a setting made to look like a porn-movie audition.

"It was a media virus," he congratulated me. "The campaign got more publicity because of the protests! It made Calvin look cool because his ads were taken off the air!" True enough, the campaign became the lead story on the evening news once "family advocates" targeted the ads for their exploitation of young people. They never could have bought as much airtime as they received for free. But I had nothing to do with the scheme's conception.

I assured him that I had never met with the Calvin Klein people, but it was no use. He was convinced they had based their work on my book, and there was no changing his mind. Had they? I certainly hoped not.

The succession of featured speakers soon proved my worst fears. With titles like "Mutants Produce Bounty" and "Giving Birth to Mutant Ideas in a Commercial Context," each presenter sought to regain the ground lost to the chaos-thriving hackers who had taken over the mediaspace. The conference's purpose was to upgrade the advertising industry's weapons systems to the new style of war.

I was flattered—and flabbergasted. I felt honored to be appreciated, but horrified by the application of my work. No sooner had I proclaimed the revolution than it was co-opted by the enemy. And I had aided and abetted them.

It was at that moment, in the Bal Harbour hotel ballroom, that I decided to write this book. With my newfound access to the corridors of Madison Avenue and beyond, I would become a double agent—attending meetings, taking notes, analyzing tactics, and then reporting my findings.

For the past two years, I have been studying the ways marketers, politicians, religious leaders, and coercive forces of all kinds influence everyday decisions. I have sat in on strategy sessions with television, advertising, and marketing executives, and read countless documents by professionals in government, law enforcement, the military, and business. I've cozied up to automobile salesmen and multilevel marketers to pry from them their secrets.

What I've learned in my two-year odyssey is that however advanced the tools being used to sway us, the fundamental principles responsible for their effectiveness remain the same. Coercers are like hunters: They can don better camouflage, learn better ways to scent their prey, develop longer-range bullets and more accurate sights, but they still need to find their quarry and then figure out which way it's moving so they can "lead" with the gun barrel and hit it. Sonar, radar, and night-vision specs will only increase their efficiency and compensate for their prey's own increasing skill in evasion.

The prey's only true advantages are its instinct and its familiarity with its environment. Just as a deer "knows" when it is in the hunter's sights, we know on some level when we are being targeted and coerced. The more complex, technological, and invisible coercion gets, the harder it is for us to rely on this instinct. We are lured away from our natural environment and are more likely to depend on directions from our shepherds or the motions of the herd to gain our bearings. As soon as we become familiar with the new terrain—be it the mall, the television dial, or the Internet—it is the goal of the coercion strategists to make it unfamiliar again, or to lure us somewhere else.

The rapid change we have experienced in the past several decades as we have moved from the postwar boom through the space age and into the computer age has provided ample opportunity for our coercers to retool and rearm themselves. Even when a new technology, like the Internet, appears to offer us a chance to reclaim our mediaspace in the name of community or civic responsibility, it fast becomes a new resource for the direct marketer, the demographics researcher, and the traditional advertiser.

Worst of all, the acceleration of the arms race between us and our coercers deteriorates the foundations of civil society. Telemarketers make us afraid to answer the phone in the evening. Salesmen bearing free gifts (with strings attached) make us reluctant to accept presents from our neighbors. Greedy televangelists twisting Bible passages into sales pitches, and church charity drives employing state-of-the-art fund-raising techniques make us wary of religion. Our president's foreign policy is channeled through spin doctors before it reaches Congress or the people, leading to widespread cynicism about the political process. Our sporting events are so crowded with product promotions that we can't root for a team without cheering a corporate logo. Our movements through department stores are videotaped and analyzed so that shelves and displays can be rearranged to steer us toward an optimum volume of more expensive purchases. Scientists study the influences of colors, sounds, and smells on our likelihood of buying.

It's not a conspiracy against us, exactly; it is simply a science that has gotten out of control.

In a desperate attempt to use any tool available to keep up with our rapidly growing arsenal of filters, marketing professionals turned to high technology. They invented the personalized discount card at the local supermarket, which is used to create a database of our purchasing decisions. This information is bought and sold without our knowledge to direct marketers, who customize the offers filling our mailboxes to match our individual psychological profiles. Home-shopping channels adjust the pacing of sales pitches, the graphics on the screen, and prices of products based on computer analyses of our moment-to-moment responses to their offers, in real time, automatically.

The automation of coercive practices is a threat more menacing than any sort of human manipulators. For unlike with real human interaction, the coercer himself is nowhere to be found. There is no man behind the curtain. He has become invisible.

And yet, even when the coercer has vanished into the machinery, we still have the ability to recognize when we are being influenced and to lessen the effect of these techniques, however they originate. There are ways to deconstruct the subtle messages and cues coming at us from every direction. No matter how advanced and convoluted these styles of coercion get, they still rely on the same fundamental techniques of tracking, disorientation, redirection, and capture. Restoring our instinctual capacity to sense what we want, regardless of what we're told, is within our reach.

For instance, as you read the words on this page, consider what is being done *to* you. Picture yourself reading this book, and consider your relationship to the author. Should the fact that my words have been bound in a book give them more authority than if you had heard them on the bus from a stranger?

Already you have been exposed to a battery of coercive techniques. In fact, everything you have read so far has been concocted to demonstrate the main techniques I'll be exposing in this book.

The opening paragraph, mixing humor with terror, combined a rhythmic assault with the fear-inducing creation of a powerful "they" that means to shape our destiny. The humor disarmed you just enough for the next barb.

Then came a list of rhetorical questions. Of course the answers were already built-in, but they gave you the illusion of interactivity. Like the responsive readings in a church service, they made you feel like you were actively participating in a deductive process, even though the script had already been written and you had no power to change it.

I asked you to personalize the dilemma I had been describing. I asked you to consider the authorities in your own life that act upon you in unwanted ways so that you would personally identify with the threats to your well-being. You were no longer just reading about a problem; you were now in the middle of it.

Once roped in, you could be subjected to standard fear-mongering. I personified the enemy as teams of psychologists, working late into the night to devise plans for shopping malls that thwart your natural cognitive processes. These devils hope to disconnect you from your own soul, I implied.

Then came simple presupposition. I suggested what would happen if you read on. "As we'll see," I claimed, presupposing that you will soon see things as I do. I stated it as an inevitability.

What better time to establish my own expertise? I enumerated my qualifications—how I have spent years studying the coercive techniques of leading industry experts, and how I have written books on the effect of media on human consciousness.

After the tone had been set, I was free to engage you in one of the oldest coercive techniques of them all: the story. You were meant to identify with my plight—how my optimistic naïveté about media and culture led me into the clutches of the advertising industry, turning my own work against its purpose. Like a spin doctor relating the tale of a downed jet or sexually deviant politician, I confessed my sins—exaggerated them, even—to turn a disaster into an opportunity for redemption. The comeback kid.

Sadly, my story is true; the point is that I've used the saga to gain your trust and engage you in my fight. The technique is simple. Create or present a character with whom someone can identify, then put that character into jeopardy. If the reader has followed the character into danger, he will look to the storyteller for a rescue, however preposterous. The storyteller alone has the ability to relieve the reader's anxiety, if he chooses to. And the

relief I offered was to go to war against our new enemy: the coercers, who, like hunters, mean to track us down and kill us.

Then, just to avoid appearing too forceful, I briefly backed in
the other direction. "It's not a conspiracy," I retreated, "just a
science that has gotten out of control." I encouraged you to
relax by telling you there was no conspiracy, but then I impli-
cated the entire scientific and hi-tech community in the automated conspiracy against humanity.

Once you were reduced by my story to the role of a passive
spectator in a state of mild captivation, I could lead you down to
the next level of vulnerability: trance. I asked you to envision
yourself reading the book in your hands right now. Like a hypnotist asking you to watch your breath, I employed a standard
trance-induction technique called "disassociation": You are no
longer simply reading this book, but picturing yourself reading
the book. By separating your awareness from your actions, you
become the observer of your own story. Your experience of voli-
tion is reduced to what a New Age psychotherapist would call a
"guided visualization." From the perspective of coercion technicians who call themselves "neuro-linguistic programmers" (hyp-
notists who use the habits of the nervous system to reprogram
our thought processes), this state of consciousness renders you
quite vulnerable. The moment you frame your own awareness
within a second level of self-consciousness is the moment your
mind is most up for grabs.

Then I set upon the establishment of an elusive goal—what
can be called the "pyramid" technique—in which I promised
you that there are ways to escape from the tyranny of our social
programmers, if only you follow the course I am about to lay
out in this text. Like a cult leader, I presented myself and my text
as the key to your awakening and freedom.

Finally came the section we are up to now. I appear to disarm
myself by revealing all the tactics I have used so far. I am your

friend because I'm disclosing what I am doing to you. I am pulling back the curtain, showing you how the trick is done. You're in on it now. In fact, we're in this together. *Wink wink, nudge nudge.* You're safe because you have an ironic distance from the coercive techniques I'm employing. All of them, that is, except *this* one.

Are you on your guard yet? Does it feel good? Of course not. The point is not to make you paranoid. My purpose is to help us get free of coercion, not simply live in reaction to it—especially if that reaction is to succumb to a constant state of suspicion. It wouldn't be a fun way to go through life. Believe me—researching and writing this book has brought me there more than once. Besides, suspicious people are some of the most easily manipulated. Ironically, perhaps, the more fun you're having in life, the more satisfied you are with yourself, the harder a target you are to reach.

The fact is, *everything* is coercive. Even something as minute as the way I put the word "everything" in italics is meant to influence you. There's nothing wrong with attempting to sway others to our own way of thinking, especially if we truly believe we are right. It's how relationships, families, businesses, and societies improve themselves. If someone has a better idea for how to dig a hole, elect a leader, or raise happy children, it's up to that person to convince us why he's right.

Using what influence we have is not in itself a destructive thing. The problem arises when the style and force of a person's or institution's influence outweighs the merits of whatever it is they're trying to get us to do. For example, through carefully managed public relations, a chemical company can convince voters that a proposition is intended to protect the environment, even though it loosens regulations on toxic-waste disposal. A crafty car salesman can make us think he is our friend, that he's conspiring with us against his dealership's manager, even though all he is really doing is working to pad his own commission. A fund-raiser can appeal to our religious inclinations while actually persuading us to donate to a political cause with which we might not agree.

The techniques of coercion have advanced so far over the past several decades that we no longer live in a world where the best man wins. It's a world where the person who has made us *believe* he is the best man wins. Advertisers have dispensed with the idea of promoting a product's attributes in favor of marketing the product's image. This image is conceived by marketing psychologists quite independently of the product itself, and usually has more to do with a target market than the item being sold.

All too often, the decisions we make as individuals and as a society are directed by people who may not have our best interests at heart. To influence us, they disable our capacity to make reasoned judgments and appeal to deeper, perhaps unresolved, and certainly unrelated issues. By understanding the unconscious processes we use to make our choices of what to buy, where to eat, whom to respect, and how to feel, clever influence professionals can sidestep our critical faculties and compel us to act however they please. We are disconnected from our own rational, moral, or emotional decision-making abilities. We respond automatically, unconsciously, and often toward our own further disempowerment. The less we are satisfied by our decisions, the more easily manipulated we become.

To restore our own ability to act willfully, we must accept that we are the ones actively submitting to the influence of others. We are influenced because, on some level, we want to be.

Almost all the techniques of coercion I have studied take advantage of one or more of our healthy psychological or social behaviors. For example, parents are the first real authorities in our lives. Mom and Dad are the first "they." In most cases, they are highly deserving of our respect. Our survival depends on it. By admiring and imitating our parents' behaviors, we learn basic life skills. By trusting in their authority, we are free to explore the world around us without fear. We surrender authority to our parents, and they protect us from harm.

We instinctually long for our parents' approval, and they instinctually reward us with praise when we make progress. Learning to stand, walk, speak, or ride a bicycle is not so much a quest for independence as it is an effort to earn our parents' praise. The authority they exercise over our lives is absolute, and absolutely essential.

Growing up, we transfer this authority to our teachers and ministers. Again, this process is altogether healthy. A wider array of role models allows the developing child to learn a variety of coping skills and behaviors. In this manner, we are socialized and eventually initiated into our parents' world. We become adults, capable of making our own decisions.

But sometimes, even as adults, we find ourselves feeling like children again: helpless and desperate for approval from above. Certain people can make us feel like children simply through the intonations of their voices, the styles of their clothing, the manners in which they regard us, or the ways they position their desks at work. A voice on a loudspeaker or over an intercom can command instant authority. A man in a police uniform can lead us to speak an octave higher than we normally do.

Textbooks on employee management, salesmanship, and interrogation all detail precise methods for eliciting childhood emotional states. The technique is called "induced regression," and it exploits the remnants of our natural childhood urges so that the subject "transfers" parental authority onto the practitioner. Or, to say it another way, it's a technique to create a new "they." Our built-in instinct to respect authority is exploited by people who, for one reason or another, need us to revert to our obedient and praise-seeking childhood state of mind.

There are hundreds of natural and healthy cognitive processes that can be exploited by those who understand them. As individuals hoping to regain a sense of authority over our own lives, we need not purge ourselves of our psychological traits so that they cannot be tapped. We liberate ourselves from coercion not by denying our underlying social and emotional needs—we do so by reclaiming them.

For instance, fund-raisers and salespeople commonly give the prospective donor or customer a free gift. Many charities send us sets of greeting cards along with their pleas for financial assistance, while insurance salespeople give away calendars or appointment books. Are they giving us these things out of the goodness of their hearts? Of course not. They are trying to provoke a sense of obligation in us. Once we accept the gift, a transaction has been initiated. We owe the giver something. If we use the gift without paying anything, we feel a little guilty. Accepting a gift or favor obligates us to return one. Why? Because the development of a set of social and financial obligations is part of what allowed us to form communities in the first place. I help you build your barn today, and you help me swat locusts off my crop next summer. This relationship isn't as mercenary as it sounds. Mutual need, obligation, and reciprocity over time are the bases of any community. Survival depends on them.

Today, we still give gifts as a way of establishing social rapport. When someone moves into our neighborhood, we may bring them food or something to make their adjustment easier. Unless the new neighbors are deeply neurotic about accumulating social obligations, they are thankful to be welcomed. The fact that we have permitted them to owe us something is itself a gift. We have initiated them into the fabric of community relationships.

Enclosing a free gift in a solicitation for donations is meant to capitalize on this evolved set of behaviors. The technique has become so overused by now that it rarely works. We might feel guilty about it. We might throw out the free greeting cards rather than use them, just so we don't have to be reminded about the animals that are suffering without our financial support every time we send a greeting. But most of us won't be swayed enough by the offering to open our checkbooks. We just resent it.

This resentment actually erodes the community spirit on which the manipulative technique is based. We are now suspicious of people who offer us gifts. A stranger who gives us something must want something in return. We are reluctant to perform acts of goodwill ourselves lest we provoke paranoia in the recipients.

The most destructive side effect of coercive techniques is that they prey upon our best instincts and compromise our ability to employ them when we want to. Some of us are simply suckered. Others are made uncomfortable. The most sophisticated and wary of us are made increasingly paranoid and antisocial.

Today, P. T. Barnum's famous insight on suckers can be extended: Currently there are three levels of response to coercion, which exist simultaneously in our culture. Some of us are readily fooled by the simplest of manipulative techniques. These people, who I call the "Traditionalists," are the sort of folks who are emotionally moved by politicians' speeches, dedicated to their local sports teams, and ready to believe that government agencies would prevent us from being duped by misleading advertisements.

The next group—who marketers like to call "sophisticated" audiences—feels they understand how the media hope to manipulate them. These "Cool Kids" respond to coercive techniques that acknowledge their ironic detachment. Their television re-

mote controls and video game controllers have changed their relationship to the television tube. They like to deconstruct every
image that is piped into their homes. But they fall for the *wink
wink, nudge nudge* plea of the modern advertiser or salesperson
who appeals to their media-savvy wit. As long as the coercer admits with a sideways glance that he's coercing, the Cool Kid is
likely to take the bait. He is being rewarded for his ironic attitude.

The last group has graduated from the culture of cool and is
just plain fed up with everything that has a trace of manipulation. The "New Simpletons" want straightforward, no-nonsense
explanations for what they're supposed to buy or do. They like
salespeople that dispense with jargon and just tell it how it is.
They buy Saturns so they won't have to negotiate, and they like
plain-speaking pain-reliever commercials that simply say "This
drug works." They go to the Price Club and Home Depot and
order computers over the World Wide Web, basing their decisions on RAM, megahertz, and price.

The existence of these three very different reactions to coercion in one culture at the same time is making life hard for advertisers, marketers, and public-relations experts. To appeal to
one sensibility is to alienate both the others. (On the other hand,
a homespun message meant for New Simpletons may at first attract but ultimately confuse Traditionalists.) No matter how well
the advertisers define the "target market," the rest of us are still
exposed to the same messages. Two-thirds of us are unaffected.
And the people who have made a profession of manipulating us
are scared.

That's why we have a unique opportunity to disarm our manipulators and to restore the social interactions that their efforts—and our complicity—have eroded over time. More
important, we can put an end to the coercive arms race that is
fast absorbing so much of our time and resources.

These realizations are just as valuable to advertisers and public-relations experts as they are to us. None of the influence professionals I spoke and worked with while writing this book actually likes the direction that the compliance industry has taken. Many of them suffer from migraines or insomnia and pay high bills for psychotherapy and prescription drugs. They would like nothing better than to exchange the guilt-inspiring drudgery of manipulation for the joy of real communication. Many of them want the race to end.

If we accept that salesmanship, advertising, the telephone, lesson plans, and rituals all are really just ways of mediating human interaction, then this book ultimately amounts to a course in media literacy. For these and most other media, though originally forms of communication, have been turned into avenues of behavior and thought control. In order to make them truly interactive media once again, we must determine what it is we wish to communicate ourselves. This process is complex, requiring real thought and patient determination.

The United States is the only developed nation in the world that does not mandate media literacy as part of its public-school curriculum. There are reasons why. Media literacy is dangerous—not to the individuals who gain it, but to the people and institutions that depend on our *not* having it. Once we master the tools of media literacy, we cannot apply them selectively. If we learn the techniques that an advertiser uses to fool us, we have also learned the techniques that a government uses. If we demystify the role of our hi-tech pundits, we may demystify the role of our priests as well.

We also run the risk of succumbing to full-blown paranoia. Once we gain the ability to perceive the coercive forces acting on us every day from seemingly innocent sources, it will be difficult not to see the work of an influence professional behind every magazine cover. (It's probably there, but that's beside the point.)

Once coercive techniques are put into practice, they have a tendency to sustain themselves and multiply. Although someone may have intentionally concocted the technique at some point in the past, chances are it has been on automatic pilot ever since. And once we've programmed these techniques into our computerized marketplace, there's no turning back. On whichever side of the electric fence we find ourselves—as the coercer or the coercee—we are equally victimized, and equally to blame.

That's why it would be foolish for us to personify the forces behind our culture's rampant coercive efforts. The chairman of the board is just as victimized by his shareholders and the quarterly bottom line as we are by his public-relations specialists. The art of manipulation has become so prevalent that it drives our culture forward more than any of its best agents do. It is more constructive to think of the coercive forces in our society as part of a big machine that has gotten out of control. As we become more conscious of how it works, we can begin to dismantle it.

We are living through end-stage propaganda, a culture which has been subjected to so much assertion of authority—so much programming—that it exhibits pathological symptoms. Those of us who have been coerced into submission find ourselves feeling powerless, passive, or depressed, and we may even resort to medication. Those of us compelled to resist these authorities tend to become suspicious and cynical. We believe "they" are real and allied against us. "They" have become the enemy.

They're not. As one of the people who has been paid to come up with new strategies for manipulation, I can assure you: they're just us.

CHAPTER ONE

Hand-to-Hand

The customer has a split second of insanity. The mind
goes blank, the body paralyzes, the eyes get glassy.

—*A retired automobile salesman*

"When you're wearing a thousand-dollar suit," Mort Spivas
tells me as he lights a Havana cigar, "you project a different
aura. And then people treat you differently. You exude confidence. And if you feel confident, you'll *act* confident."

Mort Spivas (I've changed his name) has just won a "regional
salesman" award from a distributor of mechanical beds, and he
has invited a few of his best friends to celebrate his success in the
cigar lounge of Windows on the World, high atop Manhattan's
World Trade Center. I've known Mort for about five years, and
in that time he has sold all kinds of things—real estate, used
cars, hair-replacement procedures, and summer-camp con-
tracts—with varying success. Those of us sipping Scotch together have stuck with him through hard days—I even lent him a
few hundred bucks for rent and groceries once, after a real-estate

deal went south—and this little celebration is his way of saying thanks.

Mort is a master of interpersonal relationships. He has read countless books and taken dozens of seminars on selling, self-esteem, the spirituality of money, and the secrets of negotiating. No matter how bad things get, Mort always seems to maintain his faith in his ability to pitch almost anything and then close the deal. He believes he can get himself out of any predicament. And you get the feeling that if you hang around Mort long enough, he'll do the same for you. His enthusiasm is contagious. Sometimes mysteriously so.

"If you can figure out what a person wants, and then make what you have into that thing, you'll always sell them," Mort likes to say. He appears to have proven his point. On this clear September night, looking out over the Hudson River, Mort Spivas—who, in his mid-thirties, is one of the youngest people ever to win his company's "regional salesman" award—is, quite literally, on top of the world.

About eight weeks later, very late into the night of a record-breaking East Coast snowstorm, my phone rings.

"I'm at the hospital," Mort confesses in an embarrassed, broken voice. He doesn't want me to hear him this way. "They won't let me out unless a friend comes to get me."

The next morning I manage to get to Queens, check my friend out of the emergency room, and transport him back to his fourth-story walk-up in Astoria. The doctors have assured Mort that the chest pains he experienced while shoveling snow the night before were only stress-related. His EKG looks fine, but the ambulance trip and ER ordeal have shaken Mort up pretty badly, so I use the snow as an excuse to stay with him for the next two days.

Only then do I learn about the darker side of Mort's surefire selling strategies, and the toll they are taking on his customers and himself.

"As soon as I saw the address on the prospect card, I knew it was going to be trouble," Spivas tells me as he prepares two egg-white-only omelets. (Not even a heart attack would keep him from being a good host.) "People don't buy two-thousand-dollar beds in the South Bronx, but it was the only location I had time to reach before the storm hit, and they had an Italian name, so I gave it a shot."

Salesmen know that a pitch is only as good as the prospect, so they try to figure out as much as they can about the name on the response card before they invest an afternoon in anyone. The bed company he works for runs ads with an 800 number to call for more information. Respondents are sent a promotional videotape and then called on by a salesman for a follow-up visit—the close.

Mort deftly dices some onions and peppers, then spreads them out in a pan of simmering oil as he continues his tale. He parked his beat-up Oldsmobile in front of the tenement (he takes the Lexus only to the suburbs) and paid a twelve-year-old in the street two bucks to watch it for him as went inside to meet his marks. He left his thousand-dollar suit at home, too—less for fear of being mugged than out of a desire not to intimidate his lower-middle-class prospects.

"You've got to match yourself to the customer," Mort explains. "Maybe be one notch better off, but never more than that. You want to be well-off enough for them to want to be your friend, but close enough to be their equal. People want to trust you." He trails off into silence for a moment, losing himself in his cooking. Mort knows he has been regularly betraying the trust he so painstakingly works to gain.

"When I got in I could tell the wife was the one who called.

They were old. Seventies, maybe. The guy just looked at me sus-
piciously with his arms crossed. I knew to either draw the husband in or get rid of him completely and hope the wife was
allowed to sign a check." Mort says he immediately went into
one of his well-practiced routines. To gain the husband's trust,
he set himself up as the couple's advocate.

He told them, "One of our shifty salesmen got your card, but
when I saw the neighborhood—the place my own grandmother
grew up—I took it from him and did the call myself, even
though this is a long drive from my regular region. It was more
important to me that you didn't get screwed, if you'll pardon my
French, than that you buy a bed."

Apparently this tactic worked, because the husband followed
his wife and the salesman into the kitchen for the pitch. Mort
pulled out an order form and put it on the table. He didn't refer
to it for a long time. He just left it there, as if it would be dealt
with inevitably. Instead, he explained what the other, more devious salesman would have done. He showed them a picture of the
bed that "Arnie" would have sold them: the $2,100 "special"
that gets pitched to people who live in zip codes where they
think they can pull a fast one. Poor craftsmanship, a shorter
warranty, but a higher profit margin. A bed not even manufactured in the United States!

The wife *tsk*'ed and shook her head, but the husband, un-
moved, hadn't uncrossed his arms. Worse, he had put one finger
over his mouth—a sure sign, according to the many body language books Mort has read, that the husband did not believe
him. Time for a self-deprecating detail.

"But Arnie's jokes would have been a lot better than mine,
ma'am, I can assure you of that."

"We didn't call for jokes," the old lady said with a laugh. "We
called about beds." She absentmindedly brushed her hand across
the order form—a telltale sign she was ready to buy, and a

tempting opening for a "trial close," Mort thought to himself. But with the husband on shaky ground, it was too much of a risk. According to the negotiating books, you get only two shots at a close, and Mort wanted to make sure he was in a better position. So he changed tacks.

"Is that your son?" he asked, motioning to a photo taped to the refrigerator. The old man seemed pleased.

"Our *grand*son," he answered proudly.

"No!" Mort feigned disbelief as he touched the old woman's hand, securing it more firmly on the sales form in the process. "Why, he must be twenty, at least!" He rose to get a better look at the picture, as well as the husband, who had maneuvered himself behind Mort's chair. Never lose track of your prospect, the experts advise.

"He's a water-sports enthusiast, huh?" Mort asked. Neither of the grandparents replied, but Mort forged ahead with the old friendship-making technique of pretending he was interested in water sports, too. "I haven't been up to my parents' lake house in months. I'd love to get back on a parasail. Does your grandson parasail?"

"He used to," replied the man. "I think he did. But he hasn't done anything like that since the accident."

Oops. Mort was about to change course, when the old woman continued.

"He had an accident water-skiing," she said sadly. "Four years ago. Fractured a vertebra."

"Oh my," Mort said. "Is he okay now?"

"He's in a wheelchair," the old man said, walking out to the living room.

Mort was in a tough position. He threw himself on the old woman's mercy, apologizing profusely. If she felt sorry enough for him, he'd still accomplish his original purpose of drawing her out.

"You couldn't have known," she reassured him. Mort surmised from the way she put her tongue to her upper teeth and looked down and to the right that she had more to say but that her rational left brain was holding her back. She wanted a confidante. People make friends by sharing confidences. They need to talk. He took a shot in the dark.

"How is your husband doing with it?" Mort asked, motioning subtly with his eyes toward the old man, who was already flipping through the dial on the TV set.

"He's holding on to the pain, if you know what I mean."

"I know exactly what you mean," Mort responded compassionately. He had found his sales hook.

Mort pauses for a moment to carefully fold over the first of his omelets as he explains to me that his own faux pas revealed a dynamic between the couple to be exploited. The husband was holding on to his pain, and the wife sought to relieve it. The mechanical bed would make a perfect metaphor for her struggle. The old man's resistance to buying the bed could now be generalized, by a perceptive salesman, into the husband's whole problem. By convincing her husband to buy a more comfortable, more flexible bed, the old woman could start him on the road to recovery. His decision to buy the bed was more important for him than the bed itself. It would amount to a symbolic act of caring for himself.

"He's got to think of himself, too," Mort began.

"I know," the old woman agreed, getting up and escorting Mort to the bedroom. She spoke loud enough for the husband to hear over the television set.

"He doesn't have a good back, and look at what he's sleeping on." Mort pulled back the bedcover to reveal the frame beneath. He was shocked. Not only was it a mechanical bed manufactured by his own company's fiercest competitor, but it was the best bed on the market. However, the mattress on top was not the correct one for a mechanical bed with two separate elevation controls. It was a one-piece mattress that would slip off the frame whenever one side or the other was raised. In theory, all the couple needed to do was buy a set of hinged mattresses from the company that made the bed, and they'd have a better system than anything Spivas could offer them.

"Who sold you this?!" Mort asked in horror.

"The people who moved out upstairs," she said. "But it hasn't worked—"

"I know." Mort nodded. He invented reasons to get rid of it, all lies. "That company's beds are the worst. The mattresses can even slip right off the frame. It's very dangerous. You shouldn't even plug it in. There've been reports of fires."

"Did you hear that?" she shouted out to her husband. "Fires!"

"Tell him what Eddie said!" the husband shouted back.

Eddie, the couple's son-in-law, had informed them of the bed's real problem. He told them to buy the appropriate mattress from the original bed manufacturer and everything would be okay.

"If only that were true," Mort lied. "These companies make things so cheap these days that you can't replace individual parts. Did you ever try to fix your VCR? It's cheaper to get a whole new bed." Mort used his new weapon. "He shouldn't be sleeping on a patched-together piece of mechanical crap, anyway, if you'll excuse my language." He paused meaningfully. "How long has he been suffering?"

"Too long," she said, looking up and to the left.

"That's the sign I was waiting for," Mort tells me as he flips the first completed omelet from the frying pan onto a warm, waiting plate in the oven. "Up and to left means she's accessing her emotional memories, and very impressionable."

By the time all three were gathered once again around the kitchen table, Mort had sold the wife on his company's best bed, but the husband was unsure. Time for an old trick he'd developed during his days on the used-car lot. He told the old man that he was down at the warehouse yesterday, where he saw two improperly labeled mattresses. Their serial numbers indicated that they were standard mattresses, but he could plainly see that they had heating units installed—an $800 value.

He made a call on his cellular phone to his "buddy at the warehouse" to find out whether those mattresses were still available. Miraculously, only one had been sold. The other—well, Arnie had put dibs on it, but if Mort had a signed sale he'd release it to him.

Mort put his hand over the mouthpiece and related the information to his prospects. Of course the whole call was a ruse—all the beds come with heating as part of the standard package. But Mort made it clear that if they didn't grab this bed right now, they'd lose out to Arnie. Convinced he was getting something for nothing, and anxious to beat Mort's slimy competitor, the old man quickly agreed to the sale and signed on the line.

Spivas had already milked the couple for $3,800, but he wasn't through with them yet. If he could get them to agree to pay for the bed on installment, he would double his commission. The old man was already trying to write a check, so Mort had to act fast.

"I'm supposed to take that check and go home," Mort confided, "but I'd feel terrible if I let the company get away with it." He had their attention, now. "The rich folks we sell to all use the payment plan because they know how much they're saving. We're not supposed to mention this anywhere but Westchester, but you don't have to pay for the bed today, or even this year."

The old man didn't like to buy on credit, he explained.

"How much do you make a year on your investments?" Mort asked. "I don't mean to get too personal, but if you'll let me, I can show you how to make the bed pay for itself."

"I make about twenty percent," the man told him, smiling.

Mort knew from his car-dealing days that most people lie about how much interest they earn. "I'll be generous," he told the man. "Let's say you make just ten percent a year on your money. With an interest rate of only six percent, the loan on this bed earns you four percent on your money every year. The math is simple."

Mort demonstrated through a long and confusing set of numbers that the couple could earn more interest by keeping their money in savings and paying for the bed on the installment plan. Between the loan fee and a balloon payment at the end of the five-year loan—technically a lease on the bed—the couple would end up paying an exorbitant fee for the privilege of layaway. But Mort's calculations thoroughly baffled the old man into submission. To preserve his sense of dignity in front of his wife, he agreed to a payment schedule and savings scheme that he did not fully understand.

Mort had sold more than $5,000 of bedding and financing for a product he told me was worth roughly $2,500. Although all the paperwork was signed and a team of expert "customer service" representatives were ready with an arsenal of strategies in case the couple changed their minds, Mort had a simple method for insuring that the sale would be final. From his case he pulled out a large, zippered, plastic bag. Inside it was a twenty-five-dollar "cottony" quilted pad, which he presented to the couple as a token of his appreciation for their order.

"I want to make sure you're happy with the order before I leave," he said. "If you want to change your mind, we can rip this up right now."

"No, no," the old lady protested, taking the gift. "You've been a great help to both of us."

And with that little exchange, Mort reduced the probability of cancellation by eighty percent, according to one of his influence books.

On the way home, however, it wasn't fear of the couple's buyer's remorse that plagued him, but rather his own seller's remorse. Normally, he would have been overjoyed. He had converted a highly improbable prospect into a $1,500 commission, and he was going to make it home before the snowstorm hit. But as he waited to pay his toll on the Triborough Bridge, he was besieged by his own guilt. He couldn't get the image of the couple's wheelchair-bound grandson out of his head. He imagined himself confronted at the Pearly Gates by every customer he had suckered in his ten years of coercive selling.

When he got up to the toll booth, he paid double, instructing the collector to let the next car pass through for free. Not even this little gesture could assuage his guilt. Instead, it made him question all of his real-life relationships. Did he have any genuine friends at all, or had he merely "won" them through his well-honed trickery? By the time Mort got home, he was in the midst of an anxiety attack. He couldn't think of a single friend he hadn't gained through some method or other he had gleaned from a sales class or psychology book, and as the snow began to blanket Astoria in white, Mort felt his world closing in on him. He got out a shovel and tried to dig himself out. When his downstairs neighbors saw him standing in the snow, his hands to his chest, they made him take a cab to the hospital.

"The whole time, the title of that Dale Carnegie book kept going through my head: *How to Win Friends and Influence People*," Mort tells me as he finally serves me my omelet. "That's what I'd done. I'd won friends by influencing people. Then fucked them over."

Mort hadn't suffered a heart attack. No, the best regional salesman had had an attack of conscience.

Get Him in the Box

Perhaps Mort shouldn't have been so hard on himself. He didn't invent the techniques he was inflicting so skillfully on the old couple from the Bronx. Most of them had been used, in one form or another, since Dale Carnegie's day and long before.

In fact, Carnegie's 1936 classic has sold more than 15,000,000 copies, and is still considered the Bible in the art of hand-to-hand coercion. Written as the country was emerging from a devastating depression, the book has four main sections, which serve as a template to exploiting the basic emotional needs of human beings in order to manipulate them: Fundamental Techniques in Handling People, Six Ways to Make People Like You, How to Win People to Your Way of Thinking, and How to Change People Without Giving Offense or Arousing Resentment.

Carnegie's primer on coercion has provided the basis for decades of much more advanced research into personality assessment and behavioral control. With each new discovery in psychology, neurology, and cognition comes a corresponding leap in the influence industry's ability to hone its own techniques. While more complex than the examples elucidated by Carnegie in 1936, the methods developed by automobile companies, customer-service experts, and even CIA interrogators are simply more scientific, better camouflaged, and precisely tuned versions of Carnegie's classics.

The hundreds of interpersonal coercive techniques developed since Carnegie's day all still rely on his basic premise that people can be *handled, made* to like you, *won* over, and ultimately *changed* without their knowledge. Human beings are reduced to manageable personality types, and friendship is reduced to a precondition for manipulation. The illusion of an interpersonal social bond puts a target off-guard. Once sufficiently lulled into a false sense of security, the new "friend" can be subjected to more directly coercive techniques without activating his natural defense mechanisms.

By elevating the coercive process to a philosophy of life, books like Carnegie's legitimize people-handling. It's a set of techniques so well proven that the U.S. Central Intelligence Agency includes it in its interrogation manual. The CIA's "Kubark" manual, written in 1963, was designed to help their operatives elicit confessions and intelligence from detainees.[1] There are no references to rubber hoses or electric shocks. Apparently the mind games of salesmen like Spivas work better than overt torture.

The CIA structures its noncoercive interrogations in four main parts, loosely corresponding to each section of Dale Carnegie's book and to Spivas's final sale of a mechanical bed. Before the first phase even begins, the agents use whatever knowledge they have of the subject to assign an appropriate interrogator to his case. The subject's nationality, military training, and "hostility level" are the primary criteria for choosing an interrogator who is most likely to develop "a genuine insight into the source's character and motives . . . because it is considered basic to the establishment of rapport." This advance work is called "screening."

Although Spivas lied about taking the old Italian couple's card from the nefarious but imaginary Arnie, his superiors had assigned the prospects to him based on their zip code and preliminary answers to the telephone operator's questions. In the first phase of questioning, a CIA interrogator works to generate "an initial assumption of good will," or, as Carnegie puts it, to "win a friend." The CIA manual suggests appearing genuinely concerned about the subject's feelings, developing a mutual set of goals, or defining a common enemy as a means to developing the illusion of friendship. The opening is about listening, assessing, acknowledging, and befriending.

The manual instructs interrogators not to steer the subject toward any topic in particular—least of all the information he is trying to extract—and to "gain a deeper understanding of the source as an individual . . . " It continues, "Sometimes seemingly rambling monologues about personal matters are preludes to significant admissions." CIA experience has shown that many people cannot bring themselves to provide information that puts them in an unfavorable light until, through a lengthy "prefatory rationalization," they feel that they can make the interrogators understand why they acted as they did.

Spivas won his targets as friends by telling them how he rescued them from their common enemy, Arnie, how his grandparents used to live in the same neighborhood, and by empathizing about their grandson's tragedy. Instead of driving his prospects toward the sale, he slowed them down and provoked them to speak about deeper emotional issues. Thus he had more to work with later, when he wanted to make his prospects pick the more expensive bed and payment plan.

Like the salesman, the CIA interrogator watches for subtle reactions that might be revealing, and for "nonverbal" communications like gestures, posture, blushing, sweat, or a visible pulse in the neck or throat. Unnatural pauses indicate that questions are getting close to "sensitive areas."

The "opening" also begins the process through which the subject's own world and values are replaced by those of the interrogator. As the minutes, hours, or days go by, the "sights and sounds of an outside world fade away, [and] its significance is replaced by the interrogation room, its two occupants, and the dynamic relationship between them," which is why interrogation rooms are generally devoid of windows and free of all reference to the outside world, including time of day and day of the week.

The subject becomes completely dependent on the interrogator for all external stimuli and, accordingly, his sense of self. The CIA has observed that when people are detained in such conditions for several days, they begin to experience symptoms of "superstition, intense love of any other living thing, perceiving inanimate objects as alive, hallucinations, and delusions." Although a salesman like Spivas doesn't have the luxury of a closed interrogation room in which to imprison his prospect, he can work toward building dependency by painting a picture of the rest of the bed-sales universe—Arnie and the warehouse, for example—as a dark and dangerous place. The salesman must appear like the only friendly face in an otherwise hostile world. Old people living alone are usually the most susceptible to this technique.

In the second stage of interrogation, "reconnaissance," the interrogator gently directs the subject toward more sensitive areas—topics the interrogator has chosen through his observation of the subject's body language and tone of voice. For Spivas, this was the moment he went into the bedroom, saw the bed, and asked how long the husband had been suffering.

Now the salesman moves toward the close, or what the CIA interrogator would call "extracting a confession." The use of language and leading sentences is extremely important at this stage. The CIA recommends against using questions like "Do you know anything about Plant X?" because this kind of phrasing will most likely lead to a negative answer. Instead, they suggest more presumptive questions, like "Do you have any friends who work at Plant X?"

If a good rapport has been established early on, this more direct manipulation usually yields excellent results. The focus has been taken off the subject's resistance to revealing information and has shifted to his personal psychological longings. An expert interrogator can lead his subjects to the rationalization that their confessions are satisfying a greater mutual goal. Since the relationship with the interrogator is the only way the subject has of judging his progress toward that goal, the better that relationship gets, the better he feels about himself.

The CIA offers a list of tricks to help the interrogator in this difficult psychological maneuver. They are all designed to disrupt a person's familiar emotional associations and to lead him into a state of confusion. "When this aim is achieved," the manual explains, "resistance is seriously impaired. There is an interval—which may be extremely brief—of suspended animation, a kind of psychological shock or paralysis . . . that explodes the world that is familiar to the subject as well as his image of himself within that world. Experienced interrogators recognize this effect when it appears and know that at this moment the source is far more open to suggestion."

The great majority of coercive techniques are aimed at generating that same moment of disorientation. Once a person's rational faculties have been compromised, he is ripe for manipulation.

Hand-to-hand coercion specialists stage "psychodramas" to achieve this effect. The CIA has names for each scenario they role play. In "Nobody Loves You," the subject is told that other detainees are denouncing him maliciously. "The Witness" leads the detainee to believe that someone else is confessing. A secretary simply emerges from the "witness's" interrogation room and pretends to type reports from her notes. As she does, she asks the subject how to spell certain words "closely linked to the activity of which he is accused." Then the interrogator emerges and tells the frightened subject he is not needed anymore. A desperate confession usually follows. "Ivan Is a Dope" involves making the hostile agent's boss or organization look like they don't care about him: "Sell the agent the idea that the interrogator, not his old service, represents his true friend."

In a scenario called "Spinoza and Mortimer Snerd," the interrogator asks lofty and confusing questions for which the subject could not possibly have answers. By the time the interrogator asks a question that the subject does know, he is relieved to be able to answer correctly. In "The Staged Escape," interrogators pretend to be agents from the prisoner's own country. They "kill" the captors, bring the prisoner to "safety," then ask him to tell them what he did *not* reveal to the enemy. For "Alice in Wonderland," interrogators ask silly nonsensical questions and use bizarre vocal inflections that make the prisoner think he is hallucinating. In "Under the Spell," subjects are convinced they have been successfully hypnotized. The interrogator suggests to the subject that his arm is about to become very warm. What the subject does not know is that the arm of his chair has been heated. If the subject believes a great force is controlling him, he has an excuse to surrender.

The "Mutt and Jeff" routine is just a version of the good-cop/bad-cop technique employed by the boys on "NYPD Blue." The CIA manual describes the script:

> The angry interrogator accuses the subject of . . . offenses, any offenses, especially those that are heinous or demeaning. During the harangue, the friendly, quiet interrogator breaks in to say, "Wait a minute, Jim. Take it easy." The angry interrogator . . . says, "I'm going to take a break, have a couple of stiff drinks. But I'll be back at two—and you, you bum, you better be ready to talk."

After the "bad cop" is gone, the "good cop" offers the prisoner a "fair chance to tell his side of the story . . ."

Spivas's little psychodrama took place when he pretended to call his warehouse to see if the "mislabeled" bed was still available. The moment of confusion occurred when he put his hand over the mouthpiece of the phone and asked the couple what they wanted to do. They were no longer in their own kitchen, deciding to buy a bed. They were transported, emotionally and psychologically, to a fictional warehouse with a mislabeled bed. Spivas then used a variation on "Alice in Wonderland" to confuse the old man into opting for a payment plan.

Because of his young age relative to his prospects, Spivas couldn't use the CIA's most powerful confusion technique, induced regression. Based on Sigmund Freud's method for inducing childlike states during psychoanalysis, the questioner is to remain sympathetic and understanding, and wait for the patient to discuss early-life experiences. The CIA manual instructs that "routine questions about schoolteachers, for example, will lead the subject to reveal a good deal of how he feels about his parents, superiors, and others of emotional consequence to him because of associative links in his mind."

The subject who focuses on his past will eventually revert to a childlike, helpless state in which he transfers parental authority to the questioner. As the handbook puts it, even when more manipulative techniques are required, they are "in essence methods of inducing regression of the personality to whatever earlier and weaker level is required for the dissolution of resistance and the inculcation of dependence." Interrogators also induce regression by strictly controlling the environment. They retard and advance clocks, serve meals at odd times, and alter the lights erratically— anything to make the subject feel helpless in an environment that is out of his control.

Once transference is achieved, the interrogator assumes a fatherly demeanor. The parent figure presents the subject with a way out—a face-saving solution. "Whether the excuse is that others have already confessed ('All the other boys are doing it'), that the interrogatee had a chance to redeem himself ('You're really a good boy at heart'), or that he can't help himself ('They made you do it'), the effective rationalization, the one the source will jump at, is likely to be . . . an adult's version of the excuses of childhood."

The final stage of interrogation and sales, "the conclusion," is, of course, necessary only for subjects who have survived the interrogation. The objective of this stage is to secure "ongoing cooperation" by convincing the subject that he has not been duped. The subject must not be allowed to know he has been exposed to these techniques, lest he attack the agency later in court. Also he might be a useful source at some later time. By bringing the subject out of regression slowly, and making him feel good about his confession, the agency can depend on his future business.

Spivas was well aware of the necessity for this fourth and final stage. That's why he gave his customers the quilted pad and offered them a chance to back out of the deal precisely as they were accepting the gift. The physical object confirms the contract symbolically and serves as a tangible reminder that the couple has been given an opportunity to change their minds.

System Selling—Car Dealers

The influence techniques promoted by Dale Carnegie and refined by the CIA have been adapted and upgraded by a wide variety of industries. Unlike Spivas, who depends on his wiles to induce disorientation, regression, transference, and compliance, specialists in larger businesses like retailing, marketing, and, perhaps most of all, automotive sales have learned to systematize the tools of the hand-to-hand coercer for more effective use. Today, car salesmen work from prepared scripts that are revised and improved based on our increasing resistance to their methodology.

It amounts to a tactical war between America and its automotive industry.

While traveling salesmen and government operatives depend on their own limited experiences and the insights of psychologists, car dealers are the beneficiaries of corporate-sponsored research. It's a big business, one that dwarfs mechanical bed salesmen and counterespionage agents alike. The millions of us who have been through the car-buying process serve as the massive experimental sample on which the system is refined. If too many of us learn to resist a particular technique, that method is reworked and then camouflaged into a new one.

Car salesmen are indoctrinated to their dealerships' selling systems through video and audio cassettes, customized literature, and live seminars. Jim Miller (not his real name), a retired automobile salesman who worked at a number of different dealerships in his thirty-year career, agreed to reveal the secrets of his trade.

The seventy-year-old Southerner handed me a large cardboard carton filled with the materials he had collected throughout his career. Among his favorites were a series of seminars on videotape called "Mike Kay's Peak Power"[2] and a set of printed materials prepared by a company called "Markham Technologies, Inc.," both of which he received from the dealerships where he's worked. The last place Miller was hired to sell cars developed a system of selling based solely on a book ostensibly aimed at helping consumers *avoid* the tricks of car dealers, Remar Sutton's *Don't Get Taken Every Time*.[3] That's when he decided to retire.

"It was like a war," Miller explained. "The smarter the customers got, the worse the manuals would get. They'd make it look like we were doing something nicer or more open, but it was the same old thing, better hidden." The devious beauty of car-selling systems is that they are so well scripted that the salesman hardly needs to make any conscious decisions during his pitch. Unlike Spivas, who relied on his own cunning to engage each of his customers in an emotional interaction, car dealers need only to master the selling system.

In car sales, like CIA interrogations, direct contact with a subject is preceded by an assessment procedure. Larger dealerships assign particular salesmen to each kind of customer. Single females will be assigned to the handsomest young salesman, while married couples—notoriously the most suspicious buyers—will be assigned to an intentionally disheveled and honest-looking salesman. Dealers prefer to conduct routine prescreening interviews over the phone with prospective buyers in order to more precisely match them with an appropriate salesman and script.

The "approach" is everything. The salesman needs to create that same sense of goodwill that interrogators earn in the opening moments of an interview. One standard technique is to approach a customer while he's examining a particular car on the lot. As Remar Sutton's sample scenario goes: "Boy, I'm glad I saw you! The guys have been trying to sell that car to someone for a month. It's just not a car you would want to own." *A car salesman telling me not to buy a car? This guy must be honest. I'm glad he got assigned to me.*

Now, the salesman's job is the same as the interrogator's: to become the customer's friend. As Mike Kay explains on the first tape in his series, "Be friendly, nice. Give them space. Find common ground. Make the customer laugh. If you can do that they will have trust in you." If the customer is in the insurance business, the salesman should mention that he has a brother in the insurance business—whether he does or doesn't. Remember how Spivas pretended to be a water-sports enthusiast when he saw the picture on his prospect's refrigerator?

According to Jim Miller, the establishment of a friendship

serves a multitude of purposes. Ideally, under the pretense of creating a bond, the salesman will be able to determine the prospect's marital status, his income range, his self-image, and, of course, his likelihood of buying a car. In the same way that the CIA interrogator assesses his subject's "psychologic-emotional and geographic-cultural typographies," the car dealer gathers information during the "preapproach" in a process called "blueprinting."

The key piece of information to be obtained during blueprinting is the customer's Dominant Buying Motive, or DBM. The DBM is never the need for a particular car, but the basic human need to be heard. Salesmen are instructed not to steer the conversation at all—especially not toward the subject of cars—but simply to listen. One of Miller's manuals explains, "Each person's strongest need is probably the need to be understood. Buying is ninety percent emotional." Thus a good salesman initially avoids the subject of cars and engines and, through what appears to be friendship, gets to the heart of the matter: the prospect's emotional life. He is attempting to help his customer rationalize how the purchase of a car will solve deeper psychological needs.

In car sales, the prospect's DBM could be anything from looking cool to his friends to demonstrating to his wife who is in charge of the family money. The more information the salesman has gathered about the customer, the more primal a motive he can address. Whatever the case, once a bond has been established and the DBM identified, the customer is ready for the car dealer's version of reconnaissance, otherwise known as the test drive.

Bringing a customer to this stage requires leading him toward a decision of what kind of car he'd like to drive. Car salesmen use the same linguistic rules as CIA interrogators. As Miller put it, "Do not ask any question that will lead to a yes or no answer, like 'Would you like to take a test drive?' Just ask him 'Which one would like to take for a drive?'" His language presupposes your actions.

Once the salesman has the customer inside a new car, he will take advantage of the car's pristine interior to change the prospect's relationship to his own sorry excuse for a car. Car dealer Remar Sutton warns prospective buyers, "Don't let him 'reinforce' you. That's a nice technique that goes something like this: 'How does the ride compare to your present car, Mr. Smith? . . . It's a quiet car, isn't it? . . . How do the seats feel? aren't they comfortable? Just like an armchair?'" Once he has led the customer to feel dissatisfied about his own car and the life it represents, he can attempt to put the customer in that same state of suspended animation that the CIA interrogator looks out for.

As Miller explained, "Somewhere during that demo drive, while you're making your trial close—not asking for the sale yet—you ask him, in these exact words, 'Is this the type of vehicle you would like to own?' It happens. And anyone will tell you this, the vacuum cleaner salesman, the carpet salesman—the customer has a split second of insanity. The mind goes blank, the body paralyzes, the eyes get glassy, dilated. And you'd be surprised how many people have an accident at just that moment! Ask any car dealer. We always joke about it."

How could a single question provoke such an extreme response? Partly because it relies on disassociation. The customer is already in a vehicle, being asked to imagine himself owning the same type of vehicle. It's the same as if I asked you if this is the kind of book you can imagine yourself reading. Your current situation is reframed in fantasy. It creates a momentary confusion, or disassociation, from the activity you're involved in. That's why so many drivers crash. They are no longer just driving the car but imagining themselves driving the car. It is a momentary loss of awareness, during which the customer's defense mechanisms and rational processes are disabled.

If the customer answers no, he is brought back to the dealership and either upgraded or downgraded to a vehicle that better suits his needs. Then the process begins again. If he answers yes, then he is brought back inside for the third stage, "extracting a confession"—or, in salesman-speak, "the close."

Even the way the customer is shown around the dealership is meant to elicit compliance. He is told where to go, how to walk, when to sit. One training manual instructs the salesman to give the customer coffee whether he wants it or not. "Don't ask him if he wants a cup of coffee—just ask him how he takes it." In this way, the customer is trained to obey and, given his fear and disorientation in the sales environment, he welcomes the commands and their implied invitation for him to regress into the safety of childhood.

Invariably, the close takes place in a carefully controlled environment, often under video surveillance. There are no windows, and the customer has little connection to the real world. The salesman is the only familiar face in this environment—the only connection to the real world and that test drive in the open air. He's the one who understands why the customer's wife insists on a safe car with a hatchback, and how annoying that is.

The prospect has been told that the reason he's been brought to this room is to figure out "how we're going to get you driving that car." He may even be led to believe his first offer on the car has been accepted already—that the negotiation is over. But it has barely started. Now the salesman brings in the tough guy: the manager or "closer." Thus begins the automobile industry's own sophisticated version of the "Mutt and Jeff" routine.

The customer probably didn't notice the manager at first. He's the guy standing by the customer's old trade-in, running his hands along its dented exterior and picking off loose paint in an old psyche-out called "dehossing." As Miller described it, "Dehossing is nothing more than a mind game. Put your finger on the tires and test the tread, any blemish at all. Just pause, scratch your head, don't say anything, but let them know you found something not perfect about their car. Dehoss them. Lower their expectations."

In many cases, the manager delays direct involvement with the prospect for a long time. He's the "heavy" but can often be more effective by remaining out of sight. Your salesman becomes the ally, putting together a deal memo and then rushing off to have it approved by the manager. In reality, the salesman might never even talk to the manager at all. As Remar Sutton reveals, "You sign an order, give the salesman your deposit, and sit there while he goes off to fight for you, to get the manager to approve your offer. This guy is really on your side, you think. In truth, however, your salesman is probably in the lounge with the other guys having a Coke."

Invariably, he returns only to say that his manager just won't let him sell a car this cheaply. Most people expect to be bumped up at this juncture and readily agree to paying a little more, taking a few extras, or signing an extended-service plan. The customer looks to the salesman as an advocate and ally who has already made the case to the omniscient boss, who already knows the true condition of that lousy trade-in. The prospect can refuse to raise his offer, but once he does, he will be treated like a prisoner of war. The salesman will leave to "reason" with the manager, while the customer must sit alone for a long time in a bare, fluorescent-lit room. The CIA employs the same technique: "A source who refuses to talk can be placed in unpleasant solitary confinement for a time. Then a friendly soul treats him to an unexpected walk in the woods . . . both Germans and the Chinese have used this trick effectively."

"When I come back," Miller told me, "I'll bring him a cup of coffee and tell him how I'm risking my job by fighting so hard on his behalf. I admire his trade-in, but my manager is a stickler. I don't mind making no commission because he's such a nice guy and we have so much in common. But my manager can't let a car go off the lot for this price—he has overhead and dealer's costs. Besides, someone else is now making an offer on the same car, and it's higher than ours. I might even get people from the accounting department to stand by the car and pretend they're customers making an offer on it."

If the customer remains intransigent, the salesman will initiate the "switch." That is, he'll bring in the manager or deal closer, who has already been watching on closed-circuit television. He has the unfair advantage of knowing how the prospect negotiates, what his priorities are, and what relationship he's developed with the salesman. His only communication so far has been big rejection stamps on the poor salesman's deal memos—themselves tested in focus groups for their ability to intimidate. Now the man with the big stamp is standing between you and your car, everything that car has been made to represent, and the salesman who is your friend.

Managers are instructed to feign annoyance with their salesmen for putting them in this position. The prospective buyer is made to feel that he is jeopardizing his new friend's job. In essence, an Oedipal triangle has been set up with the customer, the dealer, and the manager playing the roles of child, mother, and father respectively. It's up to the customer and dealer to dupe mean old Dad.

Miller would make "hand signals and winks," pretending to communicate to the customer without the manager's knowledge. "The manager knows to leave the room for a brief moment, when I'll confide how the manager has made some error in his calculation and doesn't realize what he's done. 'Sign quickly before he changes his—' Then the manager comes back." With a salesman like Miller chuckling discreetly, the customer signs the deal before the manager can figure out that he's been "fooled."

The deal is signed, the financing is approved, but the ruse doesn't end there. Just as the CIA engages stage four, so, too, the dealer works the "conclusion." The customer must continue to be made to feel that he got a good deal. The salesman will not grab the contract and lick his lips. He'll slap the buyer on the shoulder and congratulate him on his negotiating skill. He'll talk about the guy yesterday who paid a thousand dollars more for the same car, and without even getting an in-dash CD player.

Then he'll take the buyer to the service department and try to sell him an extended warranty. After all, like Dale Carnegie says, the fourth step in influencing people is to "change people without arousing resentment." That's why he won't call the customer a moron until he's out of earshot and on his way home.

Are You Being Served?

Not every car-selling system is as overtly coercive as the one Jim Miller mastered, and for good reason: Faced with increasingly aggressive sales techniques, many of us are loath to enter a car dealership at all. Reacting to this sentiment, in the early nineties General Motors launched the Saturn, a fixed-sticker-price vehicle known more for the friendly environment and manner in which it is sold than its attributes as a car.

The Saturn has succeeded because many people are willing to forfeit the best negotiable price for the satisfaction of knowing they haven't succumbed to coercive techniques. We pay a premium to be spared a humiliating trauma. The reformed car dealer hasn't given up on coercive selling; he is merely appealing to our own reformed Dominant Buying Motive—in this case, the desire not to get screwed.

Television commercials for the Saturn evoke regression and transference, but in a friendlier, positive light. New buyers are welcomed into the "Saturn family" by a roomful of loving dealers who applaud the purchase decision in the manner of a twelve-step group greeting a newly reformed alcoholic to their fold. We are still meant to see ourselves as helpless consumers, but we are also to view our new adoptive parents as more genuinely benevolent than our old ones.

The subtle communication in "good guy" strategies is that it is the dealer's prerogative to dispense with the hard sell. We are still at his mercy and should be thankful that he has relinquished his absolute authority over us. In this sense, the soft sell that so many businesses are proud to have instituted would not be possible were it not for the lingering threat of the hard sell.

Many modern retail outlets exploit increasingly refined versions of the soft sell, replacing overtly coercive sales techniques with what could loosely be called "customer service." Salesmen become "sales associates" or, better, "consultants," whose job is to advise and educate the customers about the store's product lines. In reality, customer service is simply the most efficient and transparent way to direct our actions in the modern, consumer-savvy marketplace. As the United Colors of Benetton manager's workshop literature states, today "customer service [is] the path of least resistance."[4]

One of the most memorable episodes of the 1960s television series "The Twilight Zone" hinges on just such a distinction. An advanced race of friendly aliens visits Earth, promising to bring us great advancements and prosperity. They invite human beings to visit their home planet, where we are to be treated like kings and queens. A scientist manages to obtain one of the aliens' books but is able to translate only its title: *To Serve Man.* After thousands of people board spaceships to the alien planet, he is able to decipher the rest of the text. It turns out to be a cookbook.

Similarly, customer service is often less a way to serve our interests than to prepare us for the slaughter. Under the pretext of coming to our aid, the sales consultant merely aids his or her employer in emptying our wallets and getting us to come back for more.

Unlike career car salesmen, who are painstakingly instructed in the art of selling by their distributors, most of the young employees of stores like Gap and Benetton appear oblivious to the way their selling systems work. Even as they were following a script, Jim Miller and his colleagues knew *why* they were employing the techniques they used. Because of the size and complexity of an automobile purchase, it is still important that car dealers have some awareness of how their selling systems actually function.

The more refined a selling system, however, the less the ground troops practicing it need to know about its tactics. In fact, the less they *should* know about it. In large retail chains, the employees are treated like walk-ins off the street, which many of them are. Many chain stores even have a policy of searching employees before they leave work for the day, to make sure they haven't stolen any merchandise.

Modern customer-service models depend first and foremost on convincing the salespeople that they are acting in our best interests. As the manual used by Benetton for training their sales representatives insists, "Selling is actually a way of serving others. By helping your customers find what they want and need, you are creating solutions to existing problems." Stores employing the customer-service model must begin by coercing their salespeople into believing that they are engaged in an altruistic act. If they feel guilty about what they are doing, they must look within themselves for new, positive rationales. In Benetton's language, "Objections are symptoms of deeper reservations."

A woman I'll call Marcie, who rose to the level of store manager at a United Colors of Benetton in a shopping mall in the Midwest, was responsible for overseeing her own branch's redesign—"there are three different looks to choose from"—but apparently chose the wrong style. Her store was closed within two years after she took charge. She was transferred to another branch as an assistant manager, but left when she suffered a stress-related illness. She still takes great pride in her work for Benetton, and she bears no resentment toward the company. She is convinced that her failure resulted from her own inability to live up to the goals she set for herself with the help of her superiors.

"Either my 'goal set' was too high, or my ability to effect change was too low," she told me over the telephone from her home, without a hint of irony in her voice. When I finally convinced her to send me the materials from her management training courses, I discovered the source of her Benetton-speak: the United Colors of Benetton "Customer Service and Sales Training" modules.

According to Marcie, Benetton invented the selling system that has come to be associated with Gap stores: systematized colors, open shelves, constant folding, and gentle pressure at the changing rooms to "add on" accessories. By the early nineties, however, as Gap, Banana Republic, and The Limited threatened to put Benetton out of business in the United States, the retailer redoubled its efforts. Nothing would be left to chance. Every employee, from sales associate up to regional manager, would be indoctrinated into the new selling system, conceived and directed by corporate headquarters.

The training modules reveal how carefully Benetton hopes to program their sales associates. The course is filled with mnemonic devices for memorizing the kinds of techniques that men like Spivas perform improvisationally. "Be interested, not interesting," dictates the way sales associates are to focus on the customers' needs rather than their own attributes. The company's name forms the spine of this precision-oriented training.

Understand the need for strong customer service.
Negotiate incentives.
Instruct.
Talk about concerns.
Empowerment.
Direct Sales and service efforts.
Care for your customer.
Orient them to the store and Observe their actions.
Listen to their needs.
Offer solutions and merchandise selections.
Relate to the customers.
Serve in the best way possible.
Benefits of customer service.
Energize yourself and the staff.
Notice the changes.
Evaluate the effectiveness.
Teach new skills.
Target new goals.
Organize efforts to meet new goals.
Next steps for proactive program.

This cheery list is from the training module developed for managers, not just new employees off the street. It is a Stepford Wife approach to customer service, where every thought and every action of the employees is dictated by a singsong acronym. Only the middle word, *colors,* refers directly to the selling system applied to the customer. The rest is about managing fellow employees and making everyone adhere to the overall program.

"We'd have meetings every week where we could talk about morale and I could help everyone evaluate their effectiveness and target new goals," Marcie explains in language eerily reminiscent of the training module. "Our sales associates really were empowered to make a difference in people's lives, to meet their needs." Marcie came to believe that her job as manager wasn't simply to adhere to the rules but to promote them enthusiastically. Marcie made sure that her colleagues would evaluate one another's effectiveness, so that lapses in procedure or the confidence with which it is carried out could be addressed at the next meeting.

"But obviously I didn't do enough," she confessed. "The system works when it's applied right. I just didn't do it properly or with the right energy."

What makes Marcie's saga so heartbreaking is her willingness to blame her illness and the failure of her mall outlet on her own deficiencies. She learned how to rationalize her failures this way from Benetton. The third sales module in the company's training program explains that one of the main obstacles to good selling is a faulty belief system. "A 'belief' is not something we think about," the module insists, "it is what we think 'with.'" The course teaches that unsuccessful salespeople most often suffer from "a belief that selling is unnatural for them" or from "a fear of asking customers to buy."

The chain-store employees I spoke with were not nearly as devoted to their selling systems as Marcie was. While the managers of chain stores are indoctrinated with lofty goals and motivational acronyms, the lower sales associates are trained through incentive and fear.

One twenty-four-year-old who worked at a Gap in Philadelphia for a little more than a year was so panic-stricken after our taped interview that she returned two hours later to give back the fifty dollars she had been paid in exchange for the cassette. Her reticence to speak about her time with Gap was typical. "Are you sure they won't find out who told you?" more than one former Gap employee asked me.

Gap maintains a high level of secrecy about its sales methods. Salespeople are brought to training facilities where they watch videotapes that never leave the building—presumably to avoid an embarrassing exposure of their methods. Fortunately, enough employees remembered the sales drills they were taught for me to piece together the overall strategy.

Becoming a Gap employee is akin to landing a spot as a contestant on a game show. Every day brings another contest, with its own awards and penalties. A complex system of points per sale earns free T-shirts and jeans for employees who move the highest volume of merchandise in the least amount of time. Another program encourages salespeople to focus on the upsell by rewarding the employee who has completed the greatest number of three-item sales. Anyone who sells more than a certain dollar amount to a single customer gets his or her name in the company newsletter.

Before they hit the sales floor, all new Gap employees spend at least a half day watching videotapes that teach them the art of customer service as developed by corporate headquarters. The complete system of selling, called GAP-ACT, has six parts.

1. Greet the customer within the first 30 seconds.
2. Approach and ask "Can I help you?"
3. Provide product information.
4. Add-ons. Suggest more buys.
5. Close sale honestly. If it looks bad, say so.
6. Thank customer.

To ensure compliance with this six-step mandate, Gap sends undercover agents called "secret shoppers" to each store, who pretend to be typical customers. Employees who are caught leaving out any of the steps are reported to, and then reprimanded by, their managers.

The Greeting officially assigns a salesperson to the customer. It is also meant to prevent shoplifting. According to Gap's 1996 Loss Prevention Workbook, "Greet each customer and make eye contact. Shoplifters do not want the attention of store employees." Once greeted by a human being, the customer is no longer relating to an institution but to a person. To steal something, or even to leave without buying anything, is a rejection of that new relationship.

The Approach has actually evolved in many areas from the simple "Can I help you?" to the more suggestive "How may I help you?" or "What size would you like to see that in?" As a store manager from Florida explained, "The one question gives the customer a chance to say no. The other assumes that the customer needs help."

Providing product information helps the customer learn to trust his sales consultant. Lines like "That's fifteen-percent wool and should be washed in cold water," or "Those sweaters are very popular on college campuses right now" are meant to communicate more about the reliability and knowledge of the salesperson than the quality of the product. If the customer gets used to hearing facts from a salesperson, he or she will be more likely to believe suggestions about coordinating additional items. It's all customer service.

Employees are encouraged to develop their own styles of promoting Add-ons, based on proven techniques. The most popular method is to stress the urgency of the additional purchase: "We just got in some belts that would go great with those jeans." Employees are also instructed to ask whether the garments being

purchased are for a "special occasion." The more the sales associate knows about how and where you intend to wear the item,
the more easily he or she can suggest add-ons.

Add-on techniques are most aggressively pitched while the
customer is in the changing room. The official rule of thumb is
"five in and two out." This means that the salesperson gets the
customer to bring five items into the changing room and makes
sure he buys at least two of them. If the customer has brought
only two items to the changing area, he will be allowed in—but
before the customer can emerge, the sales associate should have
gathered at least three other items from the floor for him to try
on as well.

Closing the sale is clear enough. But none of the employees I
spoke with practiced the second part of that mandate, which is
to tell customers if something does not look good. Several sales
associates confessed to me that contrary to the official videos,
their store managers told them to lie. "When they come out of
the dressing room, we compliment them no matter what," one
employee explained. "Some of the salespeople felt uncomfortable about this, like they were lying, but we were supposed to
compliment them. Say how well clothes fit them, particularly if
you didn't have the next size."

Thanking with sincerity is the easiest part, especially if the
GAP-ACT system worked and the employee was able to generate another three-item sale toward his quota.

The two Gap managers I spoke with readily admitted that
they hire the most attractive sales representatives they can find.
"If I'm attracted to her," one manager said, "then the customer
will be, too." Young men are assigned to female customers, and
young women to the males. Each salesperson develops his or her
own method of working sex appeal. "I kind of tilt my head to
the side and stare at the guy's butt," one salesgirl bragged of her
jeans-selling method. "Then, as soon as he notices I'm looking, I

quickly glance away and pretend to be caught. I can hold my breath and get my face all flushed. It works every time."

Such innovations on the GAP-ACT theme give young sales associates the sense that they are not merely following a prescribed formula but applying their own personalized systems of selling. Since employees are competing with one another for rewards, it behooves them to develop skills that will distinguish their performances from those of their peers. Meanwhile, who benefits most from the self-motivation that this incentive/punishment system encourages? Gap itself, not its employees.

By creating an ambience of customer service and a basic sense of trust, companies using the soft sell fool us into believing they have abandoned the cruelest coercive practices of their predecessors, when all they've really done is replaced them with kinder-*looking* ones and shifted the direct abuse onto their salespeople. When a complete sales system is so finely honed that it can be taught in its entirety in a single afternoon, it renders employees fairly expendable. Investment in training each individual is kept to a minimum, and the skill level required to enact the selling system is low enough for the average high school student to be able to carry it off.

For many of the thousands of young men and women trained in this fashion every year, guilt-free performance of their duties depends on their taking perverse pride in what they have learned about how people can be manipulated. The very qualities we used to hate about used-car salesmen are frequently being instilled in our children when they take new jobs. As this skewed view of human nature spills out into the general population, we tend to see one another as marks. The spread of coercive selling systems will only threaten our very definition of friendship. As Spivas learned, when you behave this way for too long, friends become nothing more than people you win into your own sphere of influence.

The Ties That Bind

Sales techniques exploit our social-survival skills. Whether inducing a psychoanalytic-style regression or just tickling our egos, the methods salespeople use to increase our spending capitalize on essentially healthy human behaviors. If an attractive member of the opposite sex indicates interest, we benefit by responding in kind if we are available. As sales techniques escape the sales floor and reach into our personal lives, much more potent and manipulative forms of people-handling become commonplace. Salesmen masquerade as our friends, taking advantage of what's left of our best instincts. Meanwhile, our social, civic, and religious leaders have adopted the tools of the salesman in order to capture our interest or generate funds for their causes. As both spheres intersect, camaraderie and coercion become indistinguishable. Salesmen pretend they are our friends, while our friends relate to us as salesmen.

Established social dynamics provide professional hand-to-hand coercion artists with the most fertile ground for influencing our behaviors. Once recognized, any predictable pattern of behavior can be reverse-engineered to give the coercer tremendous and unearned leverage in eliciting our compliance. For example, social gatherings offer us real and ritualized ways to help one another. Companies that understand the dynamic underlying our social gatherings have learned to turn them to their advantage. The results make a Tupperware party sound like fun by comparison.

A real estate company called AMREP, in fact, exploited the dynamics underlying social gatherings so effectively that the Federal Trade Commission intervened to stop them from using dinner parties as coercive selling situations.

According to AMREP's own descriptions of the parties,[5] two or three real couples and one sales representative would be seated at each table. After a half hour or so of "socializing," during which attendants were prodded to drink alcohol, the sales pitch would begin. By seating more than one couple at each table, AMREP could pit them against one another as they battled for social status. A couple who decided to buy a property would be treated like wealthy and decisive people. Those choosing not to buy would be addressed as if they were wavering not just on this but on *all* the important decisions in their lives.

Salesmen were given scripted answers to every conceivable objection, and they were taught to view the customers as enemies to be conquered. As one AMREP sales manager told his underlings, "These people who come to our party [are like] you against the Green Bay Packers. We serve them with an organized offense against a disorganized defense. We can kill them. We could walk all over them. And we do." As the FTC argued, the customer's "'defense' [was] affirmatively 'disorganized' by a social setting where 'wining and dining' [was] not just a figure of speech. Indeed, in contrast to the salesman—who [was] specifically warned by his sales training manual *not* to drink alcoholic beverages in sales situations—prospects [were] regularly served alcoholic beverages."

By trying to cover our own need or greed with a social veneer, we make ourselves vulnerable to coercion. We run to a free dinner offered by some real-estate salesperson, happily consume as much complimentary alcohol as we can, and merely succeed in undermining our ability to make a rational decision. Because we refuse to accept responsibility for the fact that all we wanted was free food and drink, we have what the AMREP people would call a "disorganized defense." If we want a free dinner, we had better just admit it to ourselves.

AMREP used social coercion as the foundation for their formula of selling but by no means limited their repertoire to just this. They combined hand-to-hand coercion with the power of spectacle. Court documents cited the sales manager's instructions to his troops before one dinner: "When the speaker says 'Thank you very much,' you applaud loud and clear. Let's practice it right now: 'Thank you very much.' [Applaud]. Loud and clear because that puts money in your pockets. You create in that room an electricity. You create an aura that the people cannot understand. When they walk into that room they have a feeling of something happening and they want to get in on it. . . . You bring the people to emotion, to the peak of emotion, and then you sign them up. . . . It's like making love."

It's *like* making love, but it certainly yields different results. By sacrificing our social lives to a free dinner, then pretending that we are attending a genuine social event, we have rendered ourselves incapable of responding rationally to the salesman's ploys.

Here is the new recipe for hand-to-hand coercion outside the sales environment: Exploit the behaviors we have developed to make friends or build community, and do so in a way that makes it embarrassing for us to say anything about it. It involves more than just inviting prospects to a party; it means watching them, manipulating them, and even hypnotizing them once they get there.

Follow the Leader

Many of our social behaviors are based on underlying psychological impulses that are themselves healthy and natural responses to real needs and situations. Psychologists have determined that these impulses originate in the structure and function of the brain itself. Because so many of them operate on an unconscious level, however, we are not generally aware of when or how they are being activated. As a result, the most advanced forms of hand-to-hand coercion today strike at these organic neural processes. And more people are using them to their advantage, and our collective detriment, every day.

Body language is the easiest coercion technique to learn and master. There are countless texts and seminars offering instruction on how to use gesture and movement to gain an edge. Ken Delmar offers classes that teach techniques outlined in his book, *Winning Moves.*[6] A film producer by trade, Delmar has created seminars that work like acting classes, in which salespeople and businesspeople are told how to effect various emotional responses in their targets. He encourages his students to "get into character" by looking in the mirror and imitating their own facial expressions and gestures. First, students elicit the gesture, and then they fill it with the necessary sincerity. His students struggle to sell themselves on the idea that their product or service is good, even if they know it is flawed. They need to fool themselves, at least temporarily, if they ever expect to fool their clients.

Delmar has deconstructed the way human beings walk, talk, and act in a variety of situations in order for his students to re-create these patterns of behavior willfully. "Assume a power posture," he suggests. "Your posture is almost military but not stiff and uncomfortable-looking."

Clothing can also be manipulated to change a prospect's psychological responses. For example, Delmar tells his students never to enter an office with outerwear still on. "You do not want to accentuate your image as an invading outsider." The handshake takes years to master. Delmar suggests putting one's left hand on the prospect's right arm or forearm during the shake in order to gain the greatest psychological control, and not to be surprised or disappointed when the prospect pulls back ever so slightly. This retreat simply shows that the intimidation tactic has worked properly. Human behavior is reduced to a set of predictable reflexes.

Body language works in both directions. The salesman who uses his own body to influence us is also watching our every move for signs of our underlying emotional states. If a prospect flicks lint off his clothes, for example, the salesperson is to take this action as a sign of irritation. If the prospect places his finger between the upper lip and the nose—as the old man did to Spivas—the sender of that signal not only doubts you but is convinced you are exaggerating or just plain lying.

The observation and subsequent exploitation of body language goes way beyond the simple interpretation of gestures. Anyone with a decent sense of intuition can tell that when a person crosses his arms, he is expressing displeasure or incredulity. Today's compliance professionals have turned such observations into a science. Sales-training literature teaches how to interpret pupil dilation, breathing rates, and skin tone for signals of underlying emotional states.

A branch of behavioral psychology developed in the 1970s called "neuro-linguistic programming" not only provides a scientific basis for the neural origins of gestural responses but teaches its practitioners how to program people through them. As defined by its founders in their seminal work, *Neuro-linguistic Programming*, "NLP offers specific techniques by which a practitioner may usefully organize and re-organize his or her subjective experience or the experiences of a client in order to define and subsequently secure any behavioral outcome."[7] It works by breaking down emotional or rational processes to their component parts so that people, usually patients of NLP therapists, can better understand the step-by-step processes by which they function.

For a simple example, let's say a person is highly skilled at throwing a football, but terrible at rock climbing. A neuro-linguistic programmer will help this client become more aware of the processes he uses to organize the experience of football throwing so that he can apply these same processes to rock climbing. The client will be urged to recall how he breathes, where he looks, and what he imagines when he is throwing a football. He will then attempt to use the same sub-behavioral patterns and images the next time he climbs a rock. NLP is the practice of unpacking human behavior into communicable sequences and then repacking them so that they can be used else-where. It brings subconscious processes into conscious aware-ness so they can be used as building blocks for new behaviors.

NLP has proven itself a useful tool for individuals and their therapists. Tony Robbins has made a career of popularizing the techniques in his "Absolute Power" seminars and books. By breaking down their thought processes into their sensory com-ponents, people are privy to the inner workings of their own neurology, and empowered to redirect it. It's really just a combi-nation of self-awareness and self-hypnosis. Unfortunately, there's very little to prevent someone else from becoming privy to our inner workings through the same tools, and then to hypnotize us the same way. NLP allows skilled programmers to affect our be-haviors without our knowledge or consent.

Neuro-linguistic programmers watch our bodies and our words for how they betray our cerebral functioning. For exam-ple, if a person uses visual language to describe his thoughts, the programmer knows which part of the brain is being accessed. A phrase as seemingly unrevealing as "I see this deal a different way" reveals that the subject is constructing a visual image, which accesses the logical faculties of the brain. If the same sub-ject had said "That sounds interesting, but . . ." he is indicating the use of auditory faculties, which are more closely connected with creative and emotional reasoning.

Programmers can reach similar conclusions by watching our eye movements. The brain is divided into two hemispheres: The left hemisphere controls the right side of the body and deals with logical, rational functions; the right hemisphere controls the left side of the body and is believed to carry out creative and emotional tasks. If I ask you to add 127 and 667 in your head, chances are you will look up and to the right—because you are accessing the left hemisphere of your brain. If I ask you to think about how you felt the first time you made love, you will probably look up and to the left.

NLP books call these eye motions "accessing cues." NLP practitioners use these cues to understand more about us than our words might indicate, however well we have attempted to edit ourselves. If a car salesman asks if you like a more expensive model better than a cheaper one and you look to the right before answering no, he knows you're lying.

Much more deviously, programmers can exploit these visual accessing cues to enhance their powers of persuasion. According to the principles of NLP, neural cues work in both directions. Thus, if a person looking to the left is accessing emotional centers in the brain, then a salesperson should stand to your left when he wants to appeal to your emotions. If he wants to appeal to your rational sensibilities, he will stand to your right. (Try sitting on the right side of a movie theater. You will be forced to look toward the left to see the screen, and you will be more likely to engage emotionally. Sit on the left for documentaries.) By properly positioning your eyes, the coercer can access the part of your brain that suits his needs.

The work of the most influential hypnotist of modern times, Milton Erickson, though developed quite intuitively during the early part of this century, has been reinterpreted by neuro-linguistic programmers for its power to tap and exploit the precursors to human behavior. While Erickson may have wanted simply to help fat people eat less or asthmatics breathe in peace, programmers use his techniques to influence our behaviors toward their own ends.

Erickson exploited cognitive processes to access a patient's subconscious. He found that by nesting ideas inside other ones, he could bypass his subject's defense mechanisms. A simple technique called "linguistic presupposition" amply demonstrates the power of this style of hypnosis. Once the master hypnotist was asked to treat the most misbehaved delinquent at a boys' school. All he said to the boy was "Will you be surprised tomorrow afternoon when you are completely transformed into a well-behaved student?" The boy answered, "Hell, yes." And, indeed, he was surprised when he turned into a well-behaved student. Erickson did not ask the boy whether or not his behavior would change; he simply asked whether he would be surprised when it did. By answering yes, the boy accepted the presupposition of his change. It's the same technique that salespeople use when they ask, "How may I help you?" presupposing the customer's need for assistance.

Neuro-linguistic programmers also use disassociation to achieve the same results. By nesting one story or idea inside another, a programmer can bypass our rational defense mechanisms. In the moment that we move from one frame of awareness to another, we are no longer able to determine the veracity of the nested concept. Like the customer on a test drive who's asked if the car he's driving is one he can picture himself owning, we're presented with a frame within a frame. We are distracted by one picture and made vulnerable to the other.

Ronald Reagan's speechwriters were well aware of this technique when they gave him an anecdote to tell during the 1980 presidential debates. In his closing statement, Reagan began telling a story about driving up the California coastline with his wife, Nancy. During the drive, Reagan explained, he looked up into the night sky and thought back to another time. . . . Apparently the technique worked so well that Reagan soon lost track of his place in the story. If you look back at videotape of the debate, you can see the moment where Reagan's eyes go blank. He disoriented himself and had to fumble his way to a nonsensical conclusion. Had Reagan been told of the technique he was using, he may not have fallen prey to its manipulative power.

Another induction technique, called "pacing and leading," calls for the programmer to mirror your gestures, breathing rate, and style of language. We naturally do these things when we are feeling empathy toward another human being—but this technique also can be used to create the illusion of an empathetic relationship. If you are physically and emotionally closed off to a salesman, he might mirror your crossed arms and legs, use the same kinds of adjectives you do, and synchronize his breathing to your own. In other words, he can pace your behavior. Two human beings become one synchronized organism.

Once he feels he has established a natural bond, the programmer leads you where he wants you to go. He will slowly uncross his arms, which gives you the subtle cue to do the same. If you follow his motion, you will have adopted a more open posture and thus, according to the principles of NLP, a more open mind. When the programmer has determined that he is in the lead, he will begin to change the rate of your breathing to a more enthusiastic rhythm, and direct your pessimistic language toward more optimistic word choices.

Unfortunately, this potent human-programming technology—which really should be restricted to the psychotherapist's office—has moved from the interrogation rooms and negotiating tables where it was first practiced into the arsenals of door-to-door salespeople and car dealers. From there, it trickles down to the street.

We use the best techniques of the salesman on one another.

Our coworkers wear "power ties" and color schemes designed to provoke fear in their colleagues. Women in bars are subjected to pickup lines culled from books based on NLP. Beggars on subway cars, and children on church-fund drives use the same sorts of hand-to-hand strategies developed for Avon ladies.

The danger is not that we will overly influence one another with stealth apparel or behavior but that we are focused on influencing others at all. A person who cares more about his power-tie selection and the way it hangs over the conference table than about the substance of a board meeting will not be very effective at his real job. Moreover, we begin to approach our fellow workers, parishioners, and even our lovers as targets to be exploited—people who Dale Carnegie would have us "handle."

Because it takes place in real time between real people, hand-to-hand coercion is the most direct form of influence and forms the basis for most other less direct styles of persuasion. The techniques we have just explored are emblematic of coercion in general, and find their way into spectacle, advertising, even architecture and direct mail. In whatever milieu coercion is practiced, the routine follows the same basic steps: Generate disorientation, induce regression, and then become the target's transferred parent figure. In the hands of public-relations specialists, "blueprinting" becomes the science of polling. The identification of a good mark, in the marketer's language, is called "research and demographics." To an advertiser, pacing and leading is simply the mirroring and magnification of a target market's desires. Disassociation, in the hands of a spin doctor, is just good, nested storytelling.

We have been reduced to marks and manipulators in an ongoing power game that is fast replacing living interaction. For the more automated our coercive techniques become, the more we risk becoming automatons ourselves. Worse, by systematizing and standardizing coercive techniques, those who develop these strategies relieve the practitioners of individual responsibility for their actions. They are simply doing their jobs.

Even Mort Spivas, who came to think of his chest pains as a "divine intervention" aimed at curbing his own devious practices, quickly discovered how to exercise his talents in a way that didn't challenge his revised moral code. Just four weeks after he quit selling mechanical beds, he became a distributor for a company that makes magnets with "magic" healing properties.

"Sure, I still use what I learned as a salesman," he admitted to me while demonstrating a magnetized insole for my shoe. "But I do it for the customer's own good. These magnets change people's lives. Besides, better me than someone else selling a *bad* product." Like so many others who feel compelled to practice hand-to-hand coercion, Spivas has rationalized his reliance on people-handling techniques with the spiritual integrity of his purpose and the coercive environment in which we have found ourselves. Everybody's doing it.

By engaging him in an interview under the pretext of sampling his products, I did pretty much the same thing, too.

CHAPTER TWO

Atmospherics

> **We want you to get lost.**
> —*Tim Magill, Designer, Mall of America*

As *The New York Times* remarked on the opening of Niketown on Manhattan's Fifty-seventh Street:

> The merchandise is secondary to the experience of being in this store, an experience that bears more than a passing resemblance to a visit to a theme park. Niketown is a fantasy environment, one part nostalgia to two parts high-tech, and it exists to bedazzle the consumer, to give its merchandise sex appeal and establish Nike as the essence not just of athletic wear but also of our culture and a way of life.[1]

With 66,000 square feet of space on five floors, Niketown is as much a museum dedicated to the art of the sports shoe as it is a store. Giant screens automatically descend at regular intervals to play inspirational films about athletes using Nike products. A huge clock in the shape of a scoreboard counts down the minutes before the next showing. The third floor boasts a map of the entire route of the New York City Marathon, set in a terrazzo tile mosaic. Photos of athletes cover a fifty-foot-high wall, and computers offer interactive access to the legend of Nike footwear.

Spectacular technology enhances sport shoe purchasing, too. An "Ngage" machine with infrared lighting automatically determines the exact size of a customer's foot. Once a customer selects a style, it is transported to the sales floor through a complex of tubes emanating from a mysterious location below.

"We are not building a store for entertainment," Nike's vice president of design, Gordon Thompson, told industry journal *Chain Store Age* in 1997, "as much as creating an environment for people who are inspired by athletes and who love sports."[2] Fortunately for Nike, younger buyers raised in malls have no need for such rationalizations. Devoted customers see the flagship theme store as a way of getting closer to the source of the products they desire. Simply knowing they should visit the official Nike store during a vacation to New York means they have read the right magazines and will gain exclusive access to the latest styles—ones they believe are unavailable at the local mall. They have cut out the "middle man."

Of course, the function of Niketown on the buyer's psyche is the same as for any theme store. If the customer is successfully seduced by the ideals of the athletic atmosphere, he will want to make himself just a little worthier of it. Here, it means a new pair of the latest Nikes. Like any well-planned theme store, Niketown is a theater set that transforms the customer into an actor whose only role is buy.

The creation of coercive environments such as these depends on two concurrently functioning devices. First, the place itself must have an overarching theme that serves to simultaneously excite and disorient the patron. Once confused or overwhelmed, the customer will be subjected to the second phase of the attack: sensory stimulus—colors, smells, and sounds—designed to influence his movements, his focus, and his temperament. The thematic element of this two-pronged attack is usually overt and instantly recognizable, while the more subtle manipulation of our individual senses is understood only by the laboratory technicians implementing them. A well-designed space broadcasts its overall theme as directly as possible, giving us a way to understand and even welcome its emotional effect. This design is merely a ruse, however, setting the stage for a less obvious battery of coercive techniques.

When we walk into a Gothic cathedral, for example, we invite the building to inspire us. We understand and accept that the huge, pointed arches symbolically reach to the heavens. We want to stare in awe at the colossal stained-glass panels. We hope to be set aglow by the colored shafts of light that slowly trace the floor while we pray. When the pipe organ starts up, the entire building acts like a resonating chamber, filling us with master composers' odes to divinity. When we enter, the external world disappears and we are transported into another. We lose our sense of bearing and become vulnerable to the second battery of psychological tricks.

These structures utilize more subtle design features that only an art-history student would be able to discern. Most of us are unaware, for example, that the shadowy band of arches and columns beneath the highest set of windows is called the "triforium," or that its architectural purpose is to evoke fear. It is an optical trick: Filled with slightly hidden doorways on inaccessible balconies—often leading nowhere at all—the triforium draws our eyes but provides us with no answers. It is meant to remind us of secret cabals within the church, and the mysterious knowledge they possess.

The miraculous architecture and its more subtle coercive cues quite forcibly convince us of the power of the religious institution to which it was dedicated.

In the Middle Ages, the coercive power of architecture was so well appreciated, in fact, that builders formed secret societies dedicated to keeping these technologies to themselves. Very few people understood how a vaulted arch was actually constructed, or why it defied gravity. Architects and the institutions they served maintained their authority by keeping this information guarded—the same way technology companies protect hi-tech secrets today.

Our association of the architectural with the mystical can have as much influence on us as the architecture itself. Such a belief explains why Michael Ovitz, as chairman of the ultrapowerful Creative Arts Agency in the late 1980s, made a point of publicizing his use of architectural techniques as a means of gaining a psychological edge. He commissioned the celebrated architect I. M. Pei to design a new home for the agency in Beverly Hills. "The last thing I wanted for this agency was a trendy L.A.-style building that would date in a decade," Ovitz told the *Los Angeles Times*.[3] "I wanted an I. M. Pei signature design straight from his own hands, and I got exactly what I was after." At an exorbitant $25 million, the building was meant to communicate something: In a business where most people are judged only by their last deal, Michael Ovitz intended to prove through architecture that he had built a solid foundation beneath the landscape of Hollywood ephemera. He was here to stay.

For the ground-breaking ceremony, Ovitz hired a Chinese feng shui master, who blessed the site by sprinkling rice and wine on the foundation. Feng shui is an ancient environmental art that employs everything from astrology to chi (life force) to determine the proper positions of walls, windows, plants, and furniture. Ovitz also let it slip into various interviews that he admired the art himself and knew of its secret power. His own office would be arranged in strict accordance with feng shui principles.

Imagine you are meeting with a famous Hollywood executive in his office after hearing of his dedication to the art of feng shui. A copy of Sun Tzu's *The Art of War*—the Bible of negotiating tactics—sits on a coffee table. Whether or not any of these techniques actually work, our mere awareness that they are being practiced is enough to set us on edge. Simply knowing that a space—be it a Gothic church, the National Mall in Washington, D.C., or a Hollywood talent agency—has been plotted out by Masons or feng shui masters according to tested rules can "psych" us into believing we are powerless to resist its coercive effects. It gives us an excuse to submit to someone else's terms.

This fetishizing of space is the rationale behind any well-planned environment. A seamless decor takes you out of your own territory and into a fictional world, where someone or something else calls the shots. You feel as if you are thrown on-stage in the middle of a play and you must somehow figure out how to fit into the script. The easiest way to get through it is to look for cues—themselves even subtler directives toward someone else's goals.

Environmental themes for shoppers evolved over the past century as retailers sought to put the spiritual drives associated with classic architecture in the service of their businesses. They hoped to turn shopping into a new religion.

Until close to 1900, most merchants peddled their wares with little regard to atmosphere. They might have jockeyed for better positions for their carts in the farmer's markets, or stacked cans of dry goods in neat, attractive rows, but for the most part the goods themselves were what mattered. A customer would go to Joe's fruit stand because his cherries were sweeter or less expensive than Pete's.

As America entered the twentieth century, however, consumption evolved from simple survival into a cultural ethic. As William Leach details in his book *Land of Desire,* a mood of optimism swept the nation as Protestantism accommodated the more ecumenical values of our capitalist society.[4] Calvinism proposed that a man in a state of grace need not shun physical comfort—in fact, worldly success may be an indication of his divine nature. Our religious institutions, our government, and our media all cooperated with big business to enact this new American Way.

The thematically enhanced department store first arose in the late 1890s, less in a deliberate attempt to thwart our natures than in an appeal to our newfound spirit of consumption. These were temples to the art of retailing. Though many psychological theories were developing simultaneously, the main innovations in store design at this time were made in direct response to the religion of shopping.

Frank Baum, the author of *The Wonderful Wizard of Oz,* believed that the retail environment, like Oz itself, could help people realize their deepest desires. As if in a dream, taboos would be lifted and consumers could express themselves through the art of consumption. In his role as America's first retail art director, Baum was hired by department stores to create lavish, dreamlike environments where this consumption could take place. Baum enabled Americans to enact their utopian dream of a commercial paradise.

Much in the way a theater designer uses spectacular sets to capture an audience's attention, Baum discovered that electric lighting and elaborate display cases could "arouse in the observer the cupidity and longing to possess the goods." He spoke of tastefully displaying single objects, adjusting lighting, and deepening the windows. He sought to stage spectacles: "Suggest possibilities of color and sumptuous display that would delight the heart of an Oriental."[5]

Window displays became as important to the department store as stained glass was to the church. Designers began using larger-size panes and fitted them with mirrors. People were encouraged to marvel at the displays. Professional window gazers were hired to stand in front of stores and gawk demonstratively.

As Leach points out, glass had as much of a symbolic effect on customers as a practical one. It whetted the appetite because the items encased within it could not be touched. "Glass was a symbol of the merchant's unilateral power in a capitalist society to refuse goods to anyone in need, to close off access without being condemned as cruel and immoral . . . At the same time, the pictures behind the glass enticed the viewer." Glass became the transparent barrier to the rewards of heaven. Not coincidentally, kleptomania rose to epidemic levels.

This first real retail "theme," perfected by Baum in the early 1900s, was the ambiance of pure affluence. The workers and inventory were hidden in the bowels of the building. The rest was a stage set dedicated to the depiction of opulence. Stores were adorned with chandeliers, bronze fixtures, marble floors, and huge atriums with glowing glass domes. These were palaces engineered deliberately to arouse feelings of class inferiority in the customers who entered them. They had names like Rainbow House and Palace of Fashion. Customers came for the spectacle, and left either feeling unworthy or carrying lighter wallets.

By 1912, almost every major department store was using the affluence theme to draw customers, and it began to lose its effect. To maintain a psychological edge, store designers turned to more advanced themes that could elicit more targeted consumption desires.

Having succeeded in staging elaborate Christmas spectacles in the children's department, retail giant John Wanamaker understood the power of creating a specific theme for a specific purpose. In 1914, he decided to transform his seasonal success into a year-round strategy, and he dedicated the entire fourth floor of his New York store to a self-contained toy department. Murals, colored lights, dragons, and comic sculptures formed a theatrical universe where children could lose themselves in a toy-filled fantasy.

Over the next few decades, stores like Macy's and Gimbel's joined Wanamaker in the quest to create individual departments that matched the psychology of their clientele. Bridal shops within dress departments were among the first to be conceived, since a bride's aspirations are so readily discerned. A Cinderella-theme bridal shop compelled a young woman to compensate for the less-than-storybook reality of her upcoming matrimony by spending money. Men's departments, furniture, and bedding soon followed. Each department was a world unto itself—an architecturally rendered dream with the singular purpose of stimulating desire and unworthiness.

In a kind of primitive version of demographic categorization, the departments of stores elicited impulsive buying from their target markets. Whether the store owners developed this strategy purposefully, designers soon came to recognize the tremendous psychological effects of their theme environments on the customers' ability to make rational decisions about purchases. On the surface, this trend didn't look like such a bad thing. Fantasy worlds kept people believing in and maintaining a culture of free enterprise. If occasional excursions into theme environments also had the effect of reinforcing class aspirations, then so be it. At least people were striving toward something and had a sense of optimism about where they were going. And such optimism would drive the economy—or so the rationale went.

Although the Depression and World War II put the development of theme stores on hold for a few decades, the postwar boom of planned communities created a new need for theme environments. As the middle class moved out to the suburbs, America became a society ever more dependent on the retail simulation. So up rose strip malls and shopping centers, steak houses and Chinese restaurants, each with its own themes. The self-contained black-lacquered and paper-lanterned world of a suburban Chinese restaurant may bear no more relation to China than the horseshoes on the wall of a steak house have to cattle ranching, but such simulacra gave weary suburbanites ways to identify their experiences. As Ada Louise Huxtable complains in her insightful critique of suburbia, *The Unreal America,* the otherwise formless limbo of suburban life was (and, perhaps, still is) characterized only by visits to these miniature theme parks.[6] There was nowhere else to go.

The rise of theme environments celebrated our growing sense that we, as Americans, could design any future that we were capable of envisioning. Though merchants certainly understood that their exciting themes had a positive effect on their sales quotas, they didn't consider the psychological power of these techniques until the very early 1970s.

In 1973, a series of seminal essays by Northwestern University professor of marketing Philip Kotler, proclaiming the arrival of the new science of atmospherics, was published in the *Journal of Retailing.*

Atmospheres are a factor present in every buying situation. Until recently, atmospheres developed casually or organically. Atmospherics, however, is the conscious planning of atmospheres to contribute to the buyer's purchasing propensity. As other marketing tools become neutralized in the competitive battle, atmospherics is likely to play a growing role in the unending search of firms for differential advantage.[7]

Theme stores would never be the same. The race was on to create environments capable of drawing customers away from competitors and then manipulating them once they were within the store. The technique that had been so successful first in turning consumption into an expression of spirituality and then in turning the suburban wasteland into a theme park would now be systematized to maximize our spending.

Marketers appealing directly to their customers' emotions specifically ignored the utilitarian attributes of the products they were selling. Countless articles in marketing journals scolded retailers who wasted their time and energy extolling the attributes of a particular item. As one shoe retailer argued in a 1970 issue of the *Journal of Footwear Management,* "People no longer buy shoes to keep their feet warm and dry. . . . Buying shoes has become an emotional experience. Our business now is selling excitement rather than shoes."[8] The author goes on to stress the importance of matching the fantasy environment to the specific world associated with the brand of shoes being sold. In his case, it was the classically styled Nunn-Bush line, for which he chose the theme of a Victorian English club: "Customers relax in leather-covered seats beneath tinkling chandeliers. Goblets of red wine and piped-in sitar music stimulate the buying hormones."

Retailers no longer pretended they were simply selling their products in the best possible light. They were doing more than just associating their wares with a desirable lifestyle. They were creating atmospheres that triggered an emotional need: to be part of a world that was different from everyday reality. This distinction is key. Salespeople were no longer focusing on the attributes of the product but of the customers.

Once this shift in focus caught on, every conceivable retail industry had its own environmental tactics painstakingly researched by atmospherics experts. Antique dealers were coached to create artificial impressions of chaos, for example, with items strewn about the store in a disorganized mess. Customers were supposed to believe they had stumbled upon buried treasure.

Meanwhile, the shopkeeper was coached to maintain a disheveled appearance and to pretend he couldn't keep track of his inventory or its true worth. The atmosphere of disorder and the owner's bumbling performance simulated the barn of a senile old furniture collector in Vermont and convinced customers that they had found a precious item amid the jumble—precisely their antique-hunting fantasy.

The Birth of the Mall

The development of these competing theme stores along our nation's suburban roadways had an unforeseen effect: It further alienated suburban patrons from any sense of the community or civic life they had left behind in the city. It took a whole day in the car to visit just two or three of these simulated Meccas, leaving at least one family member dissatisfied. Worse, the only public space encountered between shopping experiences was the highway. Consumption had become desocializing.

Austrian architect Victor Gruen had foreseen the impending loss of cultural values that America would suffer as a result of the decentralized shopping experience, and he envisioned a way to re-create Main Street and the civility it encouraged. His innovation, what we now call the shopping mall, was first introduced in 1956 to an affluent suburb of Minneapolis called Southdale. The Southdale Center brought together dozens of different retailers under one climate-controlled roof. Gruen believed malls could be "more than selling machines." His original plans for Southdale included a post office, a library, and club meeting rooms. Little did Gruen realize that his vision would be co-opted by people he would one day call "fast-buck promoters and speculators" who exploited the self-contained atmosphere of the shopping mall for its purely commercial, and coercive, potential.

By grouping stores together into a single, comfortable, indoor structure, mall developers capitalized on the consumption habits of suburban Americans. With a single car trip, the entire family could be brought to a range of theme environments that appealed to each of their predilections.

Studies conducted on mallgoers revealed six main reasons why they go there to shop. Amazingly, none applied directly to convenience. The first factor luring mall patrons was the attractiveness of the mall itself. They went to the mall to behold the mall. The second was a sense of escape. Stimulated by sound and light, customers were distracted from their daily worries. Lonely people felt they could go to the mall to alleviate their feelings of isolation. The third was the desire to explore. The density of separate shops gave shoppers the opportunity to wander through environments and sample products from stores they wouldn't have chosen to visit otherwise. The fourth was the pleasurable state of absorption and the absence of a sense of time. The fifth was the ability to find out what was new. Mallgoers in remote areas could learn what people were wearing in big cities and what new technologies might have been developed. The sixth was the social environment. Unlike freestanding stores, malls had food courts and small squares where interaction was possible. Young people would gather at the mall after school because it was the only place that offered any entertainment.

By the mid-1990s, seventy-five percent of Americans went to the mall at least once a month, and malls accounted for fifty percent of all retail sales. Mall designers pored over research to create structures and environments that addressed the psychological needs of their customers while stimulating their desire to make purchases. The designers decided that despite their sometimes stunning architecture, malls should be timeless and bland on the interior. Thus most malls are painted neutral tones and styled in uniform and uninteresting ways. Mall leases often will specify the strict palette to which the storeowner must conform.

Disorientation keeps customers inside the mall. Many malls utilize hexagonal floor plans, which have been proven to be among the most difficult to navigate. Once inside such a mall, the patron must traverse a complicated set of hallways arranged at intentionally confusing angles. "We want you to get lost," explained Tim Magill, one of the designers of Minneapolis's giant Mall of America on its opening day. A shopper doesn't turn right at the fountain—he *veers* to the right. Every turn disorients him further, until he no longer knows in which direction the exit is to be found. Consistent temperature and lighting maintain a sense of limbo. Without the cue of changing daylight, patrons have no way to gauge the passage of time.

All of these atmospheric considerations are calculated to induce what has become known as the "Gruen Transfer"—the moment when a person changes from a customer with a particular product in mind to an undirected impulse buyer. In spite of Gruen's original intentions, his invention of the self-contained shopping environment gave retailers unprecedented freedom in their ability to manipulate the disoriented consumer.

Like the regression and transference that occur in hand-to-hand coercion, in which the confused prospect transfers authority onto the salesman, the Gruen Transfer turns mall consumers into lost children wandering the corridors and looking for direction. Once the Gruen Transfer entered the retailer's common vocabulary, so, too, did the assumption that mall patrons could be treated like the subjects of zoological research. Articles in the *Journal of Retailing* from the early 1990s describe consumer activity in terms of "habitat preferences," "ecological research," and "migration."[9]

As Americans grew accustomed to the mall, many of us also grew wary of its monotony and artificiality. The aggressively dehumanizing designs became overwhelming, and the primitive application of the Gruen Transfer reduced the entertainment value of shopping below our level of tolerance. The promise of the mall as a social substitute for Main Street was revealed to be a farce. Educated city dwellers and wealthy suburbanites found it increasingly difficult to rationalize a weekly trip to the mall as an enriching experience for themselves or their growing children.

For this disenchanted group, developers came up with a counterattack: dressing up the theme for the mall in authentic cultural history. Dilapidated landmarks like Boston's Quincy Market and New York's South Street Seaport were revitalized as shopping centers, both with enough evidence of their historic significance to attract guilty intellectuals. Urban customers yearning for a sense of authenticity were treated to "shoppes" offering handmade kites and food packaged by mock cottage industries. Like an ice cream vendor discovering flavors for the first time, mall developers realized that the Gruen Transfer needn't be divorced from an overarching theme. In fact, the rendering of an all-encompassing and historically justified theme mall could go even further to dislocate patrons from any sense of familiarity.

These landmark malls, just like tourist traps Mystic Seaport and Sturbridge Village, exploit their own historic authenticity for effective theme marketing. They disorient the customers by immersing them in a painstakingly realized artificial environment. Next, they present the dream of a better life—in this case, the simplicity of the pilgrims or the heartiness of whalers. Finally, they stimulate an unconscious desire to incorporate these values into the shopper's daily life through purchases. The patron thinks he is visiting a museum; in reality, he's in a mall.

Theme restaurants work on a similar principle. Dedicated to the tourist dollar, they offer access to seemingly authentic recreations of exclusive worlds. The Hard Rock Café is decorated with the real guitars and drumsticks of famous musicians. Planet Hollywood displays genuine costumes and props from favorite Hollywood films. The Harley-Davidson Café and the Motown Café both mythologize their namesake brands with elaborate installations in which antique motorcycles or wax figures of pop legends are idolized on altars. Contemporary permutations of the theme-mall technique, these total environments now adorn the high-traffic tourist areas of many major world cities. Burly doormen use ropes to keep customers waiting in lines outside, even when tables are available. Lucky admittees are meant to believe they have earned access to an exclusive environment and might soon brush elbows with a famous rock star or film celebrity. That these restaurants collect as much profit from T-shirt sales as from menu items attests to the power of thematic marketing to provoke impulse buying.

Major brands like Nike, Disney, Ralph Lauren, Diesel, and Warner Brothers, whose own themes have long stimulated sales through media and advertising, were the next to capitalize on thematic atmospherics by creating what they like to call "flagship" stores. Not content to have their products merely occupy space in someone else's retail environment, they erected monuments to their own brands that accomplished in physical space what their advertising did in the media.

The prevalence and overwhelmingly dominating style of these overtly thematic retail environments, like the self-contained Niketown universe in which sound, sight, and theme conspire against every sense, have inspired something of a back-to-basics mentality in customers. Conscious of the millions of dollars being spent on store environments, many people feel as if they will get better value shopping in an environment stripped down to its bare essentials. What they may not realize is that these stores, too, are meticulously engineered to exploit just such a state of mind.

Many of today's consumers recognize flagship stores as an extension of the hype-filled mediaspace from which they long to retreat. For them, retailers have engineered the ultimate superstore theme: the *un*-theme—an atmosphere designed to look as if the retailer has absolutely no atmospheric considerations at all. Megastores like Builders Emporium, Ikea, Price Club, Costco, and Bed Bath and Beyond all present themselves as warehouses devoted to one thing only: value. We are to believe we are buying products wholesale, and the inconveniences we must endure are merely evidence of the store's authenticity. The displays are designed to look like industrial shelving, stacked high with unopened wooden crates. Forklifts with flashing lights and loud beeping noises confront us in the aisles. We must use dollies instead of pedestrian-grade shopping carts, as if we were building contractors. Salespeople are nowhere to be found—but why should they be? *We're* supposed to be experts who know exactly what we've come for.

The un-theme superstore simulates the rational buying experience that has been overtly repressed in other, more patently coercive shopping environments. While passing themselves off as a welcome relief from savvy marketers, superstores exploit a customer's desire to think of himself as an educated, no-nonsense consumer. These stores are temples to the idea that a practical and reasoned approach to consumption will be rewarded with fine products at the best prices.

At many of these stores, a membership card is required for entry. Though membership often involves little more than filling out a few forms and demonstrating that you have a business, a union affiliation, or even just a job, it gives the customer a sense that he has gained access to the inner circle of professional consumers. Membership is the sacred province of educated consumers, of people who have dispensed with the endless assaults on their emotions and resorted to their hard-earned wisdom.

But how do you really feel in a superstore? Do you feel truly confident as you try to make sense of in-sink garbage disposal strategies? Do you know whether horsepower or flow rate is the more significant statistic? Is thread count or fiber content the more important factor in determining the quality of a pillowcase? And what about the pillow itself? Does down, down-Dacron, or new fiberfill stand up the best to damp weather conditions?

Superstores rely on our inability to answer these kinds of questions fully. A few, like Ikea, have learned to exacerbate this effect, taking our confusion one step further by forcing us to follow a one-way path through the store. Like rats in a maze, we pursue the path prescribed for us by the store's designers, picking up a bathroom appliance here and a set of venetian blinds there. Hell, we drove all the way out to New Jersey and paid a toll to get here. We're smart enough to get everything we might possibly need in just one big trip. Besides, if we don't take the item now, we may not be able to find our way back without going through the whole maze again.

Appeals to the Senses

Once the Gruen Transfer has been achieved—once the consumer has been effectively disarmed—retailers are free to attack us with an entirely different set of weapons from an arsenal that they developed concurrently with the theme environment. This second school of environmental design, coercive atmospherics, focuses on the environment as an "affect-creating medium," according to the *Journal of Retailing*. Coercive atmospherics is the study of how floor arrangements, colors, sounds, and even smells stimulate us to buy more stuff. Where theme environments might be considered a derivative of art and archeology, coercive atmospherics comes straight from behavioral psychology. Themes work more like AMREP parties, setting the stage, neutralizing our defenses, and provoking emotional responses. Coercive atmospherics constitute a more precise, scientific attack—like the specific NLP techniques that an AMREP salesman might use on you after you've arrived at the party and had a few drinks.

Where themes appeal to the subconscious, coercive atmospherics target the specific senses. Instead of using thematic and emotional devices, they use almost mechanical ones. Think of a coercive atmospheric working like the violet lights in bug zappers. Scientists studied mosquitoes to see precisely what frequency of light would attract them, then placed bulbs that emit this light within electrified mesh. The mosquitoes' instinctive reactions to particular frequencies of light are exploited to draw them to their deaths.

Coercive atmospherics work the same way. Instead of looking at humans as conscious beings with behaviors that change in different habitats, psychologists use coercive atmospherics to operate on our brains directly through the only portals they have to work with: the five senses.

Through our senses, the designers of coercive environments can access some of the main control knobs for our behaviors. They can speed up or slow down our movements, draw us toward or away from particular areas, make us feel inexplicably anxious or safe, alter our perception of time, and, most important, increase the amount of money we spend.

The easiest and most commonly exploited sense is our sight. Visual stimulation as a marketing device was first used in the 1890s, when early department-store designers like Frank Baum began testing blends of color and light, glass and mirrors, to stimulate positive emotional responses to certain products or areas in the store. Psychological jargon was just beginning to come into vogue, and store managers took pleasure in using words like "stimulus" and "response" to justify their costly displays with hard science.

One of the first principles they discovered was that the eye tends to isolate human forms within any visual field. Designers quickly capitalized on this phenomenon by using mannequins to draw focus where they wanted it. In 1902, the novelist and retail designer Theodore Dreiser was already trying to record his early successes with the strategy in the most scientific-sounding language he could muster: "[Mannequins] create an atmosphere of reality that aroused enthusiasm and acted in an autosuggestive manner."[10]

Other store managers studied the way people moved through retail environments, and found that the exploitation of natural traffic patterns could be as important as a store's thematic environment. In many cases, the "don't touch" display aesthetic that Frank Baum had devised gave way to the idea of unfettered access. Doorsteps were removed, and "saloon architecture" was utilized to generate greater traffic flow. "A step at the entrance is a mistake," offered *The Dry Goods Economist* in 1907. "No hindrance should be offered to people who may drift into a store."[11]

Store owners learned that more entrances, and more activity at those entrances, drew more traffic. The sight of other human forms in motion attracts people. This is why revolving doors, which highlight such motion, became so popular. Meanwhile, analysis of traffic patterns revealed that human beings tend to slow down when an aisle gets wider. Thus, the more expensive goods were placed in the middle of the store, in courtyardlike settings for maximum exposure. The shoppers would slow down as soon as the aisle widened out, and spend more time near the higher-ticket items.

For the next few decades, because psychological research was still limited and expensive, storeowners employed their psychological tricks on a trial-and-error basis. They learned to put sale items near the elevators, so customers would have to walk through the entire store to see the discounted items. They began to use escalators, both for their hi-tech appearance and to create a sense of movement throughout the store.

This use of psychological manipulation finally rose to the level of a science in the early 1970s, with the publication of Professor Kotler's articles on atmospherics in the *Journal of Retailing*. Stressing the impact of sensory stimulus on purchasing decisions, Kotler enumerated the portals of access to the human psyche and proclaimed atmospherics the new "silent language in communication" on which marketers could rely to stimulate unconscious reactions in anyone entering a retail space. He wrote of documented "causal chains," where an object "nested in a space characterized by certain sensory qualities" would elicit behaviors it could not otherwise. "Just as the sound of a bell caused Pavlov's dog to think of food, various components of the atmosphere may trigger sensations in the buyers that create or heighten an appetite for certain goods, services, or experiences."

The rise in popularity of behavioral psychology in the 1970s led to the implementation of coercive atmospherics in almost every retail environment. Above and beyond using themes to court our attention or numb our defenses, atmospherics psychologists engineered our movements and decisions through Pavlovian "cues."

Casino designers had the least reticence to employ these techniques as soon as they were developed. They were already relying on our psychological weaknesses and their own sleight of hand to drain our wallets. Coercive atmospherics was just a means of sweetening the pot.

The atmospherics rules for casinos were published in dozens of hotel- and casino-management journals throughout the seventies and eighties. The strategy was quite orthodox. First, designers would create a completely self-contained environment without windows—no light or sound would enter from the outside world. Air was pumped in at a regulated temperature and oxygen content, eliminating the element of chance. The smell of increased humidity, for example, might cue the brain and body that a thunderstorm was imminent, leading a person to become anxious and perhaps even to think of going home. Eliminating all external stimuli prevented any random psychological reactions.

Further, the exclusion of all real-world sensory stimuli meant that patrons were dependent on manufactured cues for their behaviors. Psychologists in the 1950s had already proven that people who are denied a sense of the passage of time were more easily manipulated. Casino managers also realized that the less aware gamblers were of how late the hour had grown, the longer they would stay at the tables—which is why, apart from being sealed off from daylight, casino patrons will never see a clock on the wall.

Another cardinal rule for casinos was to use the color red whenever possible. According to one industry journal, red could "stir up casino visitors' emotions, making them feel as if they were somewhere hot or stimulating."[12] Carpets, walls, and drapes in most casinos still bear crimson hues.

Slot machines with the brightest lights and loudest sounds were positioned near entrances, according to the law of attraction to motion, to draw the attention of passersby. Cocktail waitresses wore the most revealing costumes possible to distract gamblers from their cards and decision making. In some casinos, they offered players free drinks to further blur the senses and to allow them to believe they had gotten something for free.

Shopping-mall designers picked up where casino designers left off, and developed an even more sophisticated battery of visual cues to direct their shoppers. Because the mall was invented just as coercive atmospherics were gaining acceptance, it became a testing ground for many coercive atmospherics cues.

The walking surfaces of malls were given close attention. Promenades were generally made of marble or hard parquet tiles in contrast to the floors of individual stores, which were covered with carpet or softer vinyl surfaces. Shoppers were thus encouraged to stay within shops if they wanted their feet to feel good. While some malls chose high-gloss marble for its ability to reflect light and create an illusion of motion, more advanced studies demonstrated that housewives felt inadequate walking on any surface shinier than their floors at home.[13] Fashion malls catering to the higher-income clientele, however, often still use the shiniest floor finishes available, presumably because customers in their target demographic do not suffer from gloss anxiety.

Unlike their gaming-industry counterparts, retail environment researchers determined that mall customers tend to show better "shopping endurance" when they have some sense of the passage of time. Accordingly, shopping malls developed much more complex lighting and air-conditioning systems which were capable of re-creating many of the cues normally associated with different times of day. The temperature was cycled to reach highs near noon, and the lighting changed from cooler morning hues to warmer, more incandescent colors in the evening.

Mall-design literature is filled with rules about the positioning of stores and how this positioning affects shopper psychology. Many of these rules work to minimize the perceived distance shoppers have to walk in order to get where they want to go. Because many shoppers plan to visit two or more of the department stores—JCPenney, Macy's, etc.—when they visit a mall, the positioning of these "anchors" is crucial. They must be kept apart from one another so that shoppers who want to visit them are forced to walk through the entire mall. One rule states that an anchor store should never be visible from the entrance of another. Studies have shown that most American shoppers have grown so dependent on cars that they will not voluntarily walk more than 600 feet (about two football fields). For this reason, anchor stores are always placed at the end of 600-foot corridors that are at angles to one another, breaking the line of sight.

Over time, the visual cues employed in shopping malls formed a kind of language. Just as the designers are counting on our predictability of movement, we slowly become dependent on their consistency of design. Fluorescent signs are reserved for the restaurants in the food court. We know to expect to see anchor stores whenever we turn a corner onto a long corridor, and to expect toy and music stores at remote corners of the mall, where their young patrons won't disturb other customers.

The predictability of the mall's organization and standardization of its visual language help us feel comfortable even though we are otherwise absolutely disoriented. By learning and accepting the visual language of the self-contained shopping environment, we voluntarily succumb to the mall's own rules of guided behavior.

The Music Men

While architects and designers were busy developing a visual language capable of steering mall patrons' behaviors, another set of technicians devised psychological attacks for a different portal: the ear. The music piped in through speakers throughout a mall certainly contributes to the creation of a familiar social atmosphere. As long as they're piping it in, however, they might as well use the most behaviorally affective sounds possible.

The Muzak corporation began developing soundtracks for shopping and work environments back in 1928, when an Army general named George Squire, the company's founder, discovered how to transmit compressed music over telephone lines. Although he originally intended to compete with commercial radio, Squire had more luck selling his commercial-free broadcasts to stores and businesses. Today, after more than seventy-five years of research into how music influences our emotions, work habits, shopping behaviors, physical movements, chewing rates, and ability to think for ourselves, Muzak offers sixteen different channels of prerecorded music for a wide variety of applications.

Muzak distributors do not shy away from discussing the impact of their product on the approximately 80 million people who are exposed to it in the United States every day at work, shopping, in elevators, or even "on hold." As its promotional literature explains, the company's driving philosophy is "selling productivity." Department-store customers exposed to Muzak shop eighteen percent longer and make seventeen percent more purchases. Office workers make twenty-five percent fewer typing errors if Muzak is piped into their cubicles.

More extensive research into rhythm, pitch, and style of music has revealed that a careful selection of sounds can have a significant impact on consumption, production, and a variety of other measurable behaviors. Grocery shoppers respond best to Muzak that has a slower tempo, making a whopping thirty-eight percent more purchases when it is employed. Fast-food restaurants use Muzak that has a higher number of beats per minute to increase the rate at which patrons chew their food. Garish clothing sells better where loud club music is played. Cheap accessories sell better in louder environments, too, because customers spend less time examining the quality of the merchandise. Meanwhile, men's-clothing departments employ gentle "covers" of familiar 1970s music. Because fashion is still dangerous emotional territory for most men, the stores use music that keeps men from feeling they have strayed too far into the unknown.

Wherever Muzak is played—during work, shopping, or eating, in elevators or waiting rooms—it follows a precise twenty-four-hour schedule to maximize its effectiveness throughout the day. Grocery stores, for example, benefit from a few slightly more rhythmic selections during the late-afternoon lull.

For its Environmental Channel's "Functional Motivation Program," Muzak programmers plot out an eight-day schedule of music designed to maximize productivity.[14] Using something called "Muzak's Stimulus Progression Formula," computers assign each song a "stimulus value" between 2 and 6 for tempo and instrumentation. The computer then assembles hundreds of fifteen-minute blocks of music. Each block begins with a low stimulus value and then slowly increases. This way, workers are programmed to perform in fifteen-minute energy cycles for maximum efficiency. During the afternoon, one or two entire segments might be composed of relatively high-stimulus-value songs.

Competitors to Muzak are now offering even more customized environments of sound for particular businesses. The Cyber Music and Consumer Experience Company, based in the U.K., offers music by satellite transmitted through computers. Store managers or automatic sensors can input variables into the computer terminal, such as the store traffic, the age of the clientele, or the quality of the clothing. The music then adjusts itself for the target audience.

The study and practice of influence through music has become so advanced, in fact, that today's programmers argue not about how to achieve certain effects but about which effects they wish to create. As one psychologist explained the strategy,

Most people's perception is that time flies when you're having fun . . . [but] if you like the music and concentrate on it,
time passes more slowly. Music you dislike makes time contract. Fast music makes your perception of time increase.
The dilemma for the retailer is, do they want people to like
the place or to feel that time is going quickly?[15]

For traditional Muzak to work, we are not supposed to be
consciously aware that it is playing. As Muzak vice president
Bruce Funkhouser put it, "If your head goes up to the ceiling,
we've blown it."

And yet in spite of Muzak's efforts to the contrary, we are becoming increasingly aware of the sound piped into our environments, which has reduced Muzak's effectiveness. Since Muzak is
nearly everywhere, no one who uses it enjoys a competitive advantage anymore. This situation has led to a new theory of
sound atmospherics that postulates that background music
ought to become foreground music. "Marketainment," a word
coined by AEI Music Network vice president Mike Malone, is
the idea that the music itself, along with giant video screens,
should become an overt component of atmospheric styling—
even if certain elements within the music are a bit more discreet.

Malone's company provides state-of-the-art custom walls of
sound for The Limited, Starbucks, Banana Republic, Marriot,
Gap, and more than 100,000 more of the most cleverly coercive
environments in the world. The strategy is to make music that
people listen to consciously, so that they associate a particular
soundtrack with a particular store. Red Lobster's custom-made
soundtrack combines rock, tropical contemporary, and reggae
island music for a "signature sound" all their own. As Malone
explains, "The more focused you are, the more you want everything—including the music—to support your merchandising direction."[16]

But where there is a foreground, a background can't be far behind. For Niketown, AEI has augmented a selection of motivational musical tracks with the sounds of basketballs bouncing and tennis balls being hit. AEI does not refer to these sounds as subliminal but, rather, as "stimuli." Just the same, the customers are not supposed to be able to consciously discern the individual sounds, but instead are to be drawn subtly into an aural ambiance of sports.

Stores and businesses are certainly welcome to play whatever music they believe will help them reach their goals. But as long as covert aural cues continue to turn over merchandise, we'll likely be subjected to a constant barrage of sound calculated to affect our moods and behaviors without our knowledge. As the director of one U.K. satellite-music service explains, "The sound of silence is a missed selling opportunity."

Scents and Sensibility

The olfactory sense is another crucial aspect of atmospheric design. While only a handful of shopping malls employ scents through the entire mall to influence customer behavior, several of the cookie and pastry chains have taken to pumping their oven exhaust through vents over the entrances to their stores. Several studies have proven that cookie sales go up in direct proportion to the customers' ability to perceive the location of a cookie store from greater distances. Moreover, the mere smell of baking pastries has a marked effect on human behavior. One study showed that people are more than twice as likely to provide change for a dollar to a stranger when within the scent range of a Cinnabon store.[17] The right smells make us more cooperative.

The effect of particular scents on shopping and productivity is still being actively researched. Marketers have spent millions of dollars on "aromacology," the study of how smell affects behavior. As a result, Victoria's Secret now uses potpourri scents to augment their customers' feelings of femininity, Publix supermarkets make sure the smell of roasting chickens hits patrons as they enter the store, and some car dealers augment the "new car" smell in the interiors of both new and used cars.

By today's standards, such efforts are considered primitive. According to a new class of scent analysts, who presented their findings to the Thirteenth Annual Meeting of the Association of Chemoreception Sciences, the above odors can be dismissed as mere "ambient scents."[18] Because these scents are already associated with the products they are meant to sell (even potpourri is associated with a woman's lingerie drawer), they depend on simple olfactory association. True scent coercion involves changing human behavior through pure olfactory stimulation using scents that work directly on the synaptic structures of the brain, not on the conscious mind. Studies by these chemoreception scientists have demonstrated that casinos purposefully scented with new, receptor-specific chemicals derived from plant extracts, insect venoms, and animal hormones boast a forty-five percent increase in slot-machine use. Other studies have shown that a person believes less time has passed when he waits for service in a chemically scented environment than if he waits in an unscented one. The molecular compositions and exact neural functions of these scents are well-guarded industry secrets.

In Japan, the Kajima Corporation employs a Total Environment Perfume Control System in the air-conditioning system of its "intelligent" office building.[19] The system uses microprocessors to release different fragrances at different times of the day to promote productivity. Citrus scents are used in the morning and after lunch, for their proven rousing effects. Floral scents, which encourage concentration, are used in midmorning and midafternoon. Woodland scents help employees relax immediately before lunch and at the end of the day.

In Britain, a company called Atmospherics produces what they call "corporate scents." The firm developed a fragrance for shirt maker Thomas Pink's retail outlets called "line-dried linen," which evokes memories of freshly laundered shirts. The company relies on a series of research studies conducted at Toho University in Japan, where scientists measured the brainwaves of human subjects before and after exposure to a wide range of primary scent categories. The brainwaves corresponded to certain moods and behaviors considered more or less desirable for different applications. One department store in Japan has gone so far as to utilize smells proven to induce a sense of dread—in their complaints department, of course. Intimidated through scent, an irate customer is more likely to accept the complaint officer's explanations and leave the store without a refund.

Passive Coercion

This interplay between visual, olfactory, and aural cues and customer expectation amounts to a kind of ongoing dialogue between patrons and their coercers. Although marketers may seem to be communicating to us via a one-way broadcast into our brains, they have very precise methods of gauging our moment-to-moment reaction to each of their thematic and atmospheric inducements. Thanks to video technology, they now have the ability to monitor our every move.

Armed with the rationalization that they are actually the customers' advocates, today's store and mall designers base their decisions on our ever-changing shopping behaviors. By paying attention to patrons' actions, these marketing experts are capitalizing on patterns that already exist rather than working to stimulate new ones. Their technique amounts to leaving a glue trap where you know a mouse is going to walk instead of baiting a trap that is intended to draw him in. This sort of passive coercion is more discreet and doesn't seem as cruel or manipulative.

The leading practitioner of passive coercion is Paco Underhill, proprietor of Envirosell. I spent several hours with Mr. Underhill at his New York headquarters, located inconspicuously on the second floor of a rather plain office building in midtown Manhattan. He is a large, balding, and unassuming baby boomer with a disarmingly endearing stammer. His own disheveled desk is propped up on plywood crates. Paco Underhill genuinely believes he is making the shopping experience more efficient for customers and merchants alike.

When I questioned him about coercive atmospherics, he dismissed such efforts as obsolete and ultimately annoying. "Clever seventies logic," he said with a wave of his hand. "It is a short-term solution and a long-term headache." According to Underhill, customers subjected to such heavy-handed influence techniques may not understand exactly what is being done to them, but they will remember feeling the uncomfortable squeeze from an indistinct but undeniable "they," and choose not to return.

Underhill sees himself as conducting something much closer to what he calls "public advocacy work." Indeed, his own background inspires comparisons to Victor Gruen's. As an undergraduate at Columbia University in the 1970s, Underhill attended a lecture on the subject of urban anthropologist William Whyte, who had founded an advocacy group called Project for Public Spaces. Whyte's project aimed to improve the function and efficiency of public spaces by setting up cameras and recording how these squares and town centers were actually being used. After analyzing the data, the committed urban anthropologist could make meaningful suggestions about reconfiguring city parks or post offices to better serve the people inhabiting them.

Eventually, the inexorable pull of the marketplace absorbed these innovations just as they did Gruen's. After a few years at his mentor's side, Underhill realized that these same techniques of recorded observation, analysis, and redesign could be applied to commercial environments, helping retailers to better serve their customers' needs. In some cases, Underhill's method was as simple as showing a drive-through fast-food chain that patrons couldn't easily read the menu from their car windows. "You have to look back over your shoulder," Underhill told me. "That's a real problem, particularly when you are set up to deal with seniors." His work has thus spared countless aged necks from strain.

But Underhill's main product is pure research, and it's up to his clients to decide how to apply it. "Our job is to recognize and articulate opportunity," he said. "What our clients do with that opportunity can range from being benignly clever to demonically clever." To gather data, his assistants plant video cameras throughout a store or mall, and then painstakingly analyze the footage back in New York. Such research has provided a new set of ground rules for store designers who hope to capitalize on the ways we look at things, move through spaces, touch objects, and, most important, buy stuff.

His massive collection of eight-millimeter videotapes, stored in ceiling-high stacks of shoe boxes and Tupperware containers throughout his office, has formed the basis of a series of environmental axioms that his clients—ranging from Radio Shack and Burger King to Exxon and Citibank—apply with religious fervor. For example, the "Decompression Zone" at the entrance to a store must never be used to showcase products of value. The average customer needs at least twelve feet to slow down from walking speed to a browsing pace, and any products displayed before the downshift has occurred will be ignored. Underhill's law of the "Invariant Right" stipulates that a vast majority of customers will automatically turn right on entering a store. For this reason, the most important products should be placed on the right-hand side of the store.

Underhill's hidden cameras have also led to his postulation of the "Butt-Brush" phenomenon. Apparently, no matter what product a woman is examining, she will immediately stop if another customer inadvertently brushes her behind. Though it may seem silly, hundreds, perhaps thousands, of retailers have expanded the widths of their aisles and moved important merchandise based on this single observation.

In some cases, Underhill's studies have convinced storeowners to do less, not more. For example, by tracking eye movements of individual customers, cameras have revealed that a consumer can absorb only so much marketing information at the checkout line. In fact, if there are too many displays near the cash register, the customer will perceive less room on the counter for his or her own purchases, and therefore may buy less merchandise. The bigger the checkout counter looks, the more products we will feel comfortable putting on it. (Take a look at the cash register area the next time you visit the Gap for an example of this philosophy taken to the extreme.)

On touring the Envirosell offices, I came upon a young woman sitting in a tiny cubicle, her eyes glued to a television monitor as she fastidiously marked a clipboard with mysterious glyphs. She told me she was analyzing videotapes recorded at a Blockbuster Video location. She was counting how many times customers would approach the counter and look through the return slot. They were checking to see which tapes had come in but hadn't yet been shelved. The customers repeated the same motions again and again: They went to the wall of "new releases," only to find their favorite selection out of stock; they

brought the empty cardboard package to the counter and peeked
through the opening to see if the plastic case holding their chosen videotape had been returned. Customers might repeat this
action three or four times before finding one of their selections in
the return bin or settling for something else.

The young assistant dutifully registered each occurrence of the
"slot-peek" effect; how many times each customer performed it;
and whether the customers found their tapes in the just-returned
bin, chose something different from the shelf, or found something new in the bin itself. These tallies would be totaled and
presented to Blockbuster as part of Envirosell's complete study
of the chain's effectiveness in "articulating opportunities" for
sales.

When they receive the results of the study, said Underhill,
Blockbuster will have to choose what changes to implement. According to Underhill, they should make the just-returned-but-
still-unshelved videotapes more accessible to customers, perhaps
even identifying the recently returned stock with a sign.

"But couldn't this be taken a step further?" I asked. "If people
go to the return bin this often, Blockbuster might do better to re-
stock their shelves *less* often, leaving tapes in the high-status 'just
returned' area for longer periods."

The assistant paused the videotape to hear her mentor's response.

Underhill seemed reluctant to answer, so I gave him my best
conspiratorial smile and added, "Hypothetically, of course."

"Blockbuster makes its money on its older library rather than
its current hits," he said finally. "So if I spiked that rack with a
few from the library . . . the customers will think, 'Somebody
just rented that.'" Another opportunity articulated. And his
choice of words well encapsulates the heart of his work: Don't
lead the horse to water, simply spike the stuff that he's already
drinking.

Underhill's field of study may have developed innocently enough. But as with so much of behavioral science, the better it predicts the way we think and act, the more easily it can be used to manipulate our behaviors. Like his peers in the atmospherics industry, Underhill believes he is rendering retail environments *less* coercive by making their very architecture more responsive to consumers' own natural tendencies. He is simply narrowing the gap between our desires and the people who aim to fulfill them.

But when the desires themselves are left to the realm of the subconscious, understood only by retail anthropologists armed with video cameras, the effect is to automate processes of which we are not fully aware.

In the hands of casino managers, for example, the result is that gamblers lose more of their money in less time. Armed with thousands of video cameras hidden behind mirrored panels, casinos not only keep tabs on card counters at the blackjack tables but also record their patrons' traffic and consumption patterns for later analysis by passive-coercion technicians. Using Underhill's methodology, these technicians learned that casino patrons tire of the closed, controlled atmosphere after a few hours, and then wander outside for air. By letting gamblers get a view of the boardwalk, the managers of one Atlantic City casino increased the average number of hours their gamblers remained at slot machines. Contrary to what researchers previously believed, Underhill's techniques demonstrated that the most effectively controlled environments are those that seem to be part of the greater world outside.

Make no mistake about it: Casino designers are not letting up on their coercive atmospherics because they feel sorry for us. They simply have learned that today's patrons will gamble longer and harder if they are granted a few subtle cues from the natural world.

By honing in on the particular behaviors they want to acceler-
ate and ignoring all others, the designers of the worlds we in-
habit on a regular basis succeed in skewing our reality toward its
most compulsive possibilities, be they gambling or consuming.
Like short-sighted farmers reducing the varieties of crop and de-
pleting their own soil, reality designers promote and amplify
only the behaviors that serve their clients. However lifelike, such
environments are not organic but are crafted simulations with
specific coercive agendas that necessarily subvert unwanted behaviors.

The trick is to create the sense that there is no alternative—
and no need for one. The ultimate coercive atmosphere is one
that doesn't seem like an atmosphere at all but an entire world—
the real world.

Mickey Mouse Eats Times Square

A walk through the newly renovated Times Square offers a great
view of just such a "real" world.

Disney's Broadway spectacle *The Lion King* has just let out its
matinee audience. I watch a family of tourists emerge from the
Disney-restored New Amsterdam Theater into early evening air
as well lit as the most lumen-rich stretch of Las Vegas's main
drag. The overwhelming neon signs bathe the street, the cars,
and the people in the same rich tones of red, blue, and green.

The mother's jaw drops as she beholds the storefronts before
her: Three stories high in Day-Glo hues, they dwarf Forty-
second Street, creating a new sense of scale for this former porn
district. It's as if the intricacies of cracked pavement and tiny
magazine stands have been replaced by a child's building blocks.

The family stands frozen as the Gruen Transfer sets in. The el-
dest daughter seems transfixed by a giant video display across

the street. The mother turns back and forth, first toward the theater exit, as if she has forgotten something, then away again, as if she has forgotten what she had forgotten. The father checks the night sky, as if to make sure he's not enclosed in an enormous dome like the one covering the stage-set town in the movie *The Truman Show*. It is the youngest child who breaks free of this trance—or maybe he's the first to fully surrender to its effects. He yanks his mother's wrist, leading her into the fluorescent Disney store, ever so conveniently located right next to the theater, and the rest of the family follows them in.

Not that the store's interior is any different from the street outside. For Times Square has been reclaimed from the grimy urban culture that dominated it for so many decades. In a cooperative effort between The Walt Disney Company, New York City agencies, and now dozens of other businesses, the entire district has been transformed into a simulation of itself. It is still the real world—yellow taxicabs still glide through, and the subway still rumbles underfoot—but one painstakingly tuned to promote the agendas of the media companies who funded this urban renewal.

To be sure, Disney, Virgin, MTV, Conde Nast, and the other companies who paid to transform a seedy porn district into a flourishing theme park have done the city a great service. Though they received tremendous tax incentives for agreeing to take up residence in Times Square, they also took a great risk. Thanks to the renovations these companies undertook, visitors and locals alike can now stroll through this area without fear of being mugged or harassed. The adjacent Broadway Theater district also stands to benefit from the increase in pedestrian traffic as well as the emergence of clean, tourist-friendly establishments like Madame Tussaud's Wax Museum and the All Star Café. It's hard to criticize this successful effort to reclaim the splendor of

Forty-second Street's past, especially when every plan proposed by the city itself over the past three decades failed so miserably.

But relegating urban planning to a private consortium of media companies has its drawbacks, too. The local, living culture of New York and the unpredictability of the real world has been sacrificed to a planned environment where the designers exercise absolute control. Unlike Disneyland, a gated theme park that we enter consciously and willfully, or Las Vegas, which was designed to be an entertainment center, Times Square is a public space. Or was. The street itself has been transformed into a self-contained coercive environment. There may as well be a dome over it.

Merchants lucky enough to be able to afford to rent or buy one of Forty-second Street's giant locations are subjected to zoning regulations as strict as those in a shopping mall. One regulation requires buildings to feature at least one prominent illuminated sign. The thirty-four-foot-wide Panasonic-NBC video screen, the mammoth MTV scoreboardlike display, a Virgin Megastore neon monstrosity, and dozens of other electronic advertisements combine to create a uniform wash of brilliant color. It is at once breathtaking and overwhelming—and precisely the means for inducing the Gruen Transfer.

Although it creates the illusion of tremendous consumer choice, urban renewal of this kind merely forces us to make our choices *as* consumers. Our roles as citizens, creators, or even activists with independent will and a sense of direction are under the influence of a meticulously executed carnival of entrancing simulations. And our media, through their fictional representations on TV and movie screens, only heighten the very same perception of reality they are peddling on the street. This is our real world.

I finally caught up with the family of tourists as they were hailing a cab back to their hotel. I asked the father if he felt over-whelmed by the scale of this spectacular environment.

"We don't live here," he snapped. "Leave us alone."

I tried to be as nonthreatening as I could. "I only wanted to ask you—"

"We don't want to answer any questions," he said firmly. "Thank you."

Though they had bags filled with Disney merchandise, per-haps these tourists were more resistant to the numbing effects of the Gruen Transfer than I thought. Or maybe they were simply afraid of the possibility that I was about to wreck the illusion they had traveled so far to find. If I forced them to think, even for a moment, I would destroy the spectacle.

CHAPTER THREE

Spectacle

We need to work with whatever voice speaks unity.
—Monsignor James Wall
Promise Keepers counselor

Thanks to a rather generous employee benefits program at the hospital where my father used to work, starting in the mid-seventies and for many years afterward, our family was given a set of four season tickets to the New York Jets. Year after year, winter after cold winter, we would pack up the station wagon and head out to Shea Stadium to watch Joe Namath and his successors defend our city's honor against all comers.

The stadium cheer was simple but heartfelt: "J, E, T, S. Jets! Jets! JETS!" Easy enough even for New Yorkers, we used to joke. I never was sure if the name of our team referred to the fictional New York street gang in the musical *West Side Story* or to the real aircraft that flew noisily over the stadium as they departed from nearby LaGuardia Airport, or maybe it stood for the jet-setting cosmopolitan atmosphere of the Big Apple itself. In any case, to me the team represented everything great about my home city: Broadway Joe, the Van Wyck Expressway, the 1964 World's Fair. When you're a Jet, you stay a Jet.

I wonder if the eleven-year-old boy who sits in front of me at the games today—let's call him Peter—feels the same way. Jets still fly over his head, but they are the 747s of Newark Airport, not Queens. Citing poor field conditions and parking problems, in 1984 the Jets organization followed the New York Giants to the Meadowlands sports complex in New Jersey. Sacrificing hometown pride for profit margins, the Jets now play on a polyester rug in Giants Stadium.

We've sat in a section with Peter's grandparents, Daryl and Joseph, since as long as I can remember. Joseph was a Jets fan before they were even known as the Jets. "The Titans wore blue and gold," he still likes to remind anyone who will listen. "Now *those* colors say 'New York.'" In that sense, Joe is our connection to the history of our team. After any play, he'll be ready with his analysis—comparing a stunning off-tackle to one performed by John Riggins in 1975, or a well-timed fake kick to one conceived by Hall of Fame coach Weeb Ewbank thirty years ago.

On the whole, though, Joe is far less enchanted with the New Jersey incarnation of his favorite sports team. He and his family used to take a subway to the games at Shea, just four stops from their home in Queens. Now they take a subway to the Port Authority in Manhattan, and then a bus from there to New Jersey. All in all, a two-hour, twenty-dollar ordeal. These expenses, plus the inflated price of tickets, forced Joe to surrender two of his four seats by the late 1980s. Now, Joe must choose between bringing his wife or his grandson to each game.

On a frigid Sunday in December, he sits with young Peter—but the two hardly talk. Joe wears his radio headphones, not so much to hear the play-by-play analysis as to block out the shrill, overamplified advertisements that blare incessantly from the stadium's public address system. Peter, meanwhile, tends to his

Tamagotchi "virtual pet" and looks up only to view the promotional pitches and product giveaways that are broadcast between plays on the colossal video screen mounted beneath the scoreboard. Both Joe and Peter are enjoying valid and fully designed aspects of the modern sports spectacle. Joe struggles to enjoy the football game of a bygone era, while his grandson intentionally ignores the cues designed to get him involved in the game and instead dedicates himself to the many promotions that form their own kind of entertainment.

Meanwhile, my date and I long to see more evidence of the spirit that is supposed to underlie such sporting events, and we wonder whether there's a minor league team playing on natural turf in a small town where the game itself is still the thing that matters most. We are hopeful that recent plans to bring back the original Jets team logo or to build an old-fashioned stadium back in Queens may restore some of the game's former splendor.

Like so many other venues for mass communication, today's sports spectacles are desperately looking for new ways to appeal to all of their potential audiences. A well-designed spectacle has the power to unify tens of thousands of different people into a single, cheering mass. However the energy of the mob may have been directed in the past—toward particular political, religious, or cultural ideologies—today an afternoon at the Meadowlands has been fine-tuned to elicit our allegiance to the corporations sponsoring the game. The emotionally aroused spectators are exposed to commercial messages nonstop. Corporate logos adorn every available surface—the walls, a blimp overhead, the water coolers, the turnstiles, even the tickets. Every time we look up to check the stats, we are reminded who really keeps score: the half-dozen corporations whose logos alternately loom over the scoreboard.

The timing of commercial interruptions is meant to capitalize on the cresting emotional states of the crowd. At the conclusion of particularly exciting or narrowly decided plays, an announcer with an amplified, God-like voice calls our attention to huge state-of-the-art video screens. After watching a two-second commercial message ("This instant replay is brought to you by . . ."), we are treated to video recap framed within a corporate logo. It is with desperate and rapt attention that the crowd beholds the video image. Our critical faculties are suspended during these moments of heightened passion. That's why they cost the most for a company to sponsor.

After dutifully singing the National Anthem (and forcing Peter to stand and put a hand on his heart), Joseph replaces the headphones over his ears and watches sadly out of the corner of one eye as his grandson reflexively responds to each marketing appeal made during the game.

For young Peter, these are the only moments of the game to be watched. The boy welcomes the video recaps as a consumer service, isolating for him the only moments of the game he needs to pay attention to while letting him spend the rest of his time filling out contest applications from the program, watching for special promotions, and, of course, minding his computer pet. By coming to recognize the cues from the loudspeaker, Peter can keep himself from being fooled into watching the whole boring game like his grandpa.

To capture Joe's attention, marketers need to take a different approach: They must insinuate themselves into the action of the game itself. No matter how much he hates the commercialization of his sport, Joe and older fans like him can be counted on to cheer for their team—whoever might be instructing him to do so. Today, everyone in the stands has been handed a colorful cardboard sign with the words "Sack Attack!" printed on one side. A voice on the public address system before the game instructs us all to hold up our signs whenever our defense squad successfully "sacks" the opposing quarterback.

Who has paid for these colorful signs? A restaurant called Outback Steakhouse, who was sure to put its own name and logo on the back of the placard. So whenever Joe thrusts his "Sack Attack" sign into the air, he is faced with an ad for a steak house. At the same moment, the announcer makes the association explicit: "Outback Sack Attack!" he cheers, before launching into an ad for the sponsor.

The brilliance of the promotion is its perfect isolation of the moments during the game when the crowd is experiencing its greatest rush of collective aggression. One can assume that the sponsor intends for the two forms of carnage—the sack and the steak—to be linked in the spectators' minds with the wild Australian outback and its namesake restaurant. When Joe tells me he feels like eating a thick sirloin for dinner after the game, I can't help but sarcastically suggest he head over to Outback. He doesn't seem to get the joke.

Another sponsor has purchased the touchdowns. After a wide receiver sprints to the end zone, the triumph is honored through an instant replay, sponsored by an airline. As the young man dances jubilantly, we hear the name of the corporation to which his sweat pays tribute. Immediately after the extra point, one of the referees calls for an official time out.

"Someone must be hurt," Joe explains, turning up the volume on his headset.

No one is hurt. The network broadcasting the event has suspended the game to make room for an extra television commercial break. They are the ones paying the bills, after all. To entertain us in the interim, a local sporting goods store sponsors a short contest in which three members of the crowd attempt to catch as many footballs as they can in the hope of winning a huge sum of cash.

During shorter lulls in the action, we are asked to look at the scoreboard—sometimes to watch a commercial, other times to find out if our ticket number entitles us to a prize. Since any of us could be the next lucky winner, we are conditioned to pay equal attention to all of the announcements.

Peter tells me that he thinks he's "hacked" the format of these commercial breaks, enabling him to distinguish between the ads and the prize giveaways at the earliest possible moment.

"They all start with 'Please direct your attention to the scoreboard,'" Peter confides. "But if they're giving away something they always say 'for today's game' or something else only about this one game."

At the very next pause, however, the announcer reads from a script containing Peter's requisite cue for a contest. The boy's eyes stay glued to the scoreboard as we learn that "in today's game" a local appliance store will donate one hundred dollars to a charity for every touchdown the Jets score. Apparently, the sponsors are one step ahead of this eleven-year-old in their marketing tactics.

"They're still giving something away," Peter says, defending his theory through an embarrassed blush at nearly having been fooled.

Finally, at halftime, Joe removes his headphones and looks around the half-filled stadium.

"It's pretty cold today," I say, attempting to rationalize the poor attendance.

"Real fans would've shown," Joe grumbles. "The seats all belong to corporations now, not fans. We're going to be in the play-offs and no one will be here who cares. Just a lot of clients."

Meanwhile, some activity on the field has captured Peter's attention. It appears that a representative of McDonald's is attempting to get the crowd to perform the "wave"—another case of a spontaneous moment of jubilation seized by marketers. The wave, a stadium-wide cheerleading phenomenon, first emerged quite unexpectedly at a University of Washington homecoming game in 1981. Fans stood and raised their arms in sequence as the "wave" passed around the entire arena again and again. The wave quickly caught on elsewhere. Throughout the next decade, stadium crowds would revel in displays of coordinated enthusiasm, less as a team-supporting cheer than as an experiment in group dynamics. The wave spread to rock concerts and other stadium events. It felt great to be part of a colossal, 40,000-person organism. Soon, team owners and their sponsors attempted to direct the energy of the wave toward officially sanctioned demonstrations of team spirit as well as paid promotions. But fans became suspicious when they were asked to perform the wave on demand. As spontaneity was sacrificed to marketability, the wave died, and now it exists only in its methodically provoked, spiritless incarnation.

Today's attempt to generate a wave turns out to be just an introduction to McDonald's main program: a game of Simon Says in which a hundred or so fans from the crowd have been brought down to the field to compete. The winner will get a cash prize; the losers a gift certificate to McDonald's. The fans in the stands are encouraged to play along, although no prize awaits them for successfully following the caller's commands.

Even promotion-savvy Peter stands and participates in the game. He shushes his grandfather as the old man asks him what he'd like from the concessions booth, and dutifully places his hands on his shoulders, nose, or hips as instructed by the man with the microphone.

Meanwhile, down on the field, a young man who has been called "out" by the McDonald's officials protests his rejection. The crowd, resentful of this corporate usurpation of the halftime show, seizes on the controversy as an opportunity to voice its collective dissatisfaction. Before long, much of the stadium is shouting "Simon sucks! Simon sucks!" The promotion ends in disarray with no clear winner, and the McDonald's representatives pack up their banners and retreat from the field in golf carts.

"This is what we get instead of marching bands?" Joe asks me and anyone else within earshot as he takes Peter's hand and drags him to the rest rooms.

As the McDonald's marketers painfully realized, a crowd's energy is easier to stimulate than it is to control. There are many risks to transforming sports spectacles into a series of commercial promotions. The crowd has come to root for the home team, and the spectacle unites them in their resolve to combat the enemy. As a result, the traditional sports event tends to promote ethnic, regional, or ideological solidarity. This is why a crowd of New Yorkers who are already hostile to the opposing team can so easily unite against the half-time incursion by McDonald's. Anyone is fair game for the crowd's anger.

When we are part of a crowd, we are free to experience heightened levels of emotion that just aren't possible for smaller groups. Relieved of our responsibility to make considered judgments, we can allow ourselves to be swept away by the enthusiasm of the greater body. Whatever everyone in the crowd has in common—yet may not be free to express in daily life—is amplified by the intensity of the spectacle and the protection that the anonymity of a mob affords.

The sports spectacle provides one of the last public forums for the expression of politically incorrect sexual and racial biases. Young girls clad in as little as law allows are paid to gyrate in appreciation of the brute force of their male counterparts, and fans are free to discuss why Samoans make the best front line, "scrappy" young blacks become wide receivers, and white boys remain the decision-making quarterbacks. The crowd's newfound freedom to enjoy and express such feelings gives voltage to the spectacle and unifies the spectators.

Throughout history, nations and their leaders have used this

sense of mass complicity and celebration to unite their constituencies, especially against foreign threats. In ancient Rome,
sports spectacles won support for costly wars in far-off lands as
citizens were given the vicarious, ritualized thrill of the conquests for which their tax dollars were paying. As class conflicts
and civil unrest grew, a Roman ruler could also demonstrate his
absolute privilege of mercy or wrath by deciding whether to
grant a fallen fighter new life or savage death with the mere direction of his thumb. In the most emotionally charged moment,
all eyes turned to the emperor or local governor for his decree—
unifying the assembled mass in their obeisance. The coercive
power of these spectacles was so well understood that gladiator-
ial contests were forbidden in election years.

Battlefield games like football and soccer served a similar purpose through much of the past century, stirring up national, ethnic, or local loyalties—especially when the mass in attendance
already shared a sense of common identity. Without proper
channels for its expression, however, the unresolved rage stoked
in soccer contests has led to rampant rioting and even deaths in
many of Europe's arenas. Their reasoning suspended, the fans
give voice, and fist, to the frustration of waning nation states
and the anxiety accompanying European union.

In the United States, most of this violence has been avoided,
not because American audiences are less prone to such outbursts
but because the energy of these spectacles has been channeled
toward corporate agendas. It's a trickier proposition than unit-
ing a crowd of Belfast soccer fans against the visiting team from
London, and—as McDonald's no doubt learned—has achieved
only mixed results.

Hometown teams today have little pull on the citizens of their
namesake cities, with players being drawn from around the
world. And the people assembled at a modern sports spectacle
have less in common with one another, too. The same methods

cannot be used to appeal to a traditionalist like Joe, his Cool Kid grandson, and New Simpletons like my girlfriend and me. What little we three groups do have in common—that we have come to root for the home team or that we share the same racial and sexual biases—must be converted into a desire to buy products.

Marketing, for the most part, is a targeted effort where knowledge of the individual prospect is crucial. You wouldn't ask a car salesman to close a deal without conducting his assessment phase, yet corporate sponsors are hoping to do exactly that through sports spectacle: to take advantage of a massive crowd's heightened emotional state to unify it toward the common goal of buying goods.

The National Basketball Association has weathered the transition to commercial interests better than football has. With commissioner David Stern at the helm, in fact, the NBA has retooled a sport originally designed to promote cooperation among Catholic boys into a celebration of individual achievement. Stern's three-prong strategy has been to push a kind of "star system," to infuse the sport with a unifying racial identity, and to systematically reduce local influences.

The rules of the game themselves have been altered to discourage passing and to promote the hot-dogging style of aggressive young shooters. Shot clocks, no-blocking zones, and other recent innovations encourage individuals to penetrate the defense without regard to their fellows. Advertisements for games pit the star players of each team against each other, as if the game were a boxing match. Basketball today is meant to be a clash of individual egos and styles—not teams or cities.

To this end, Stern has also mandated uniformity from arena to arena. No matter where it may be, an NBA game will begin with a high-tech light show and a computer-generated video presentation showing a few landmarks of the host city before tracking dramatically through the streets and into the arena, as if to demonstrate how energy from the street will be brought into play. Changing the arena soundtrack from heavy metal to hip-hop, and the graphics from stencil to graffiti were the first steps toward introducing the strident individualism of young urban black culture. The players' uniforms were also changed to look more like hip-hop fashion, with lower waistlines and baggy pants. But the style retains a measure of decorum: A player's pant legs must not drape closer than one inch to the knee or he will be penalized and fined.

The uniforms themselves are altered every year or so. Thus fans are required to buy new jerseys at regular intervals if they want to remain current. Because individual players are highlighted instead of entire teams, the pressure for a young fan to be dressed just like his hero is magnified. In a game emphasizing team spirit, a traditional or antique uniform might demonstrate a fan's long-held loyalty to the team. When the emphasis shifts toward individual players as consumption role models for fans, then the object of the game, for the spectator, is to match brands with the hero. Make no mistake—Nike and Champion don't make their money selling uniforms to the teams. They profit from selling "official" team merchandise to *us*.

Most powerful, by incorporating the strengths of urban black youth culture—individualism, improvisationary play, hip-hop, and fashion—into a formerly white-person's sport, Stern has created a cooler and more progressive-feeling spectacle through which younger, modern audiences can be unified along unspoken but strongly racial sentiments. No matter how many millions of dollars they make, these street-smart young African-Americans represent the underdogs in our society, and it is easy for us all to rally behind them.

The Voice of the People

When unspoken racial tensions are stoked for purely commercial enterprises, only cultural anthropologists and raging killjoys tend to be concerned. Our kids might buy a few more jerseys than they need, but the entertainment value of the sport itself remains at least partially intact, and the foundations of civil society are not fundamentally threatened.

The modern sports spectacle is cousin to a much more pointedly political sort of rally, however, in which the same basic set of crowd-unifying techniques are used to promote something much more potentially dangerous than simple consumerism: ideology. It is a tradition that finds its most extreme expression in the political rallies of dictators like Adolf Hitler, who depended on pageants and spectacles to keep their followers committed to a collective mission and free from taking individual responsibility for what they were doing.

In 1998, a debate raged in New York City about whether or not to allow the Million Youth March to take place in Harlem on Labor Day. City officials and local papers put forth a very reasonable rationale for why such a spectacle shouldn't. The rally was more of a stationary event than a march, and it presented tremendous traffic and safety problems at the proposed location, a busy thoroughfare of upper Manhattan.

Underlying this reluctance, however, was the very real fear of the power of spectacle—and, in this case, a highly volatile, racially charged one, organized by Nation of Islam renegade Khalid Abdul Muhammad, who made a name for himself by calling Jews bloodsuckers in the early 1990s. Mayor Giuliani fought against the rally in court, while black organizations less extreme than Muhammad's proposed alternative events in other locations to try to siphon away potential demonstrators. City officials and moderate African-American leaders alike were frightened of just how provocative a man like Muhammad could be, and of how a crowd of black youth might choose to vent its collective rage once it was effectively stoked by racist rhetoric.

As defense lawyers after the violent Los Angeles riots argued, when we are caught up in the madness of a crowd, we no longer feel individually responsible for our emotions or actions. We can allow ourselves to shout, sing, cry, or strike without the temperance imposed by personal accountability.

The more repressed a culture, the more pent-up its passion becomes. In those rare opportunities when we are permitted to vent this energy, we are brought into unfamiliar emotional territory. We feel alive as never before, and strangely honest—as if in our daily lives we have been living a lie. We may shed tears of joy or sadness, but underlying these tears is a sense of rage at not having been allowed to express these feelings all along, which magnifies the rage even more.

A person who is able to name this sensation at just the right moment can direct the raw emotional energy at such a gathering to almost any end he chooses. In a rally about race, that end is more than the selection of a postgame steak house. Because spectacle is capable of inspiring dormant rage, it is a powerful medium for delivering rhetoric, even in the service of racist ideologies.

Political and religious leaders who understand this dynamic have produced spectacular rallies in order to consolidate their constituencies and spur them into action. Adolf Hitler and his propaganda chief Paul Joseph Goebbels were masters of the political pageant. Like the ancient Romans, they used mass gatherings both to celebrate their distant victories and, when the war was not going so well, to rationalize their defeats. It was a simple, if faulty, logic: When the Nazis were winning, then victories were a sign of divine providence and grace; when they were losing, the losses were evidence of the global Jewish conspiracy against them. Hitler's spectacular Nuremberg rallies were concocted to emotionally convince his followers of this irrational syllogism.

The first job of any spectacle planner is to create a spectacular environment. Hitler chose to conduct his annual rallies at a Zeppelin field, itself a tribute to "superior" German aviation technology. But by 1934, as he began to gear up his supporters for global conquest, he enlisted the genius of architect Albert Speer to build a correspondingly more inspirational stage set.

For emotional, religious, and even political effect, Speer commandeered 130 antiaircraft searchlights and spaced them at 40-foot intervals around a giant field. As Speer later joked, "Goering made a fuss at first, since these hundred and thirty searchlights represented the greater part of the strategic reserve. But Hitler won him over: 'If we use them in such large numbers for a thing like this, other countries will think we're swimming in searchlights.'"[1] The immense rays of light rose more than 20,000 feet before diffusing into the heavens. According to Speer, "The feeling was of a vast room, with the beams serving as mighty pillars of infinitely high outer walls . . . a cathedral of light."

Speer's intentions were to overwhelm rationality with grandeur and to mask naked rhetoric with emotion. His theatrics worked so well that the architect found himself drawn into the spell. He reported in his autobiography that he remembered attending the rallies and admiring Hitler's speeches. But on rereading them years later, Speer claims he had no idea what it was he had admired: "I found it incomprehensible that these tirades should once have impressed me so profoundly. What had done it?"

It is no mystery. Speer was the victim of his own efforts as well as the way Hitler's rhetoric capitalized on the emotional impact of the spectacle they had created together. Though bolstered by stage sets and special effects, the technique is fairly simple. Think of any great spectacle as having three main acts: First, unify the crowd; second, stoke their passion; and third, speak as God or Nature.

Each of the three stages of spectacle can be achieved in a variety of ways, addressing a multiplicity of agendas simultaneously. Elements of religion, history, oppression, conspiracy theory, numerology, metaphor, and racism all figure into the three-act coercive drama. No matter how many disparate ideas are addressed, however, unification is required at the outset. At a sporting event, this premise generally is built in to the event. We know to root for our "home" team even though its players may have been drawn from around the world. At ideological spectacles, however, the crowd's unity must be earned. This is why nearly every key speech performed at a spectacle begins with the speaker addressing what everyone in attendance has in common.

The Nuremberg rallies began with unifying rituals before Hitler ever took the stage. Men representing various local and competing groups entered separately holding flags, then marched together with Rockette-like precision into huge revolving swastikas. The shining silver eagles atop each flag united them all in a sea of shimmering light. It's the same technique used today in the videos that precede every NBA basketball game: We gathered from many places around the city to be here together, tonight.

In the first speech of the 1934 rallies, Hitler began with the simplest of commonalities: They all were men. He told them how the "man's world is the State" and the "woman's world is her husband, her family, her children, and her house."* These

*Hitler's speeches translated in Raoul de Roussy de Sales, *Adolf Hitler: My New Order* (New York: Octagon Books, 1973).

values, Hitler explained, were being threatened. "We would protect ourselves against a corrupted intellectualism which would put asunder that which God hath joined." Those intellectuals were eventually singled out as "Jewish forces" bent on compromising the purity of the German race. Hitler committed to developing "a tradition in the art of leading a people which will not permit that men of alien spirit should ever again confuse the brain and the heart of the Germans."

During a spectacle, refering to symbolic attacks provokes a greater emotional response than recounting the details of any actual oppression, which appeals more to the intellect. The less specific the details, the more iconic and universal the reference. It is easier to unite—and incite—a mass of people under a symbol. While individual tales often are told during spectacle gatherings, the speaker always raises his rhetoric to more totemic and universal themes near the climax. As he does so, he becomes a lightning rod for the entire group's righteous indignation.

In Leni Riefenstahl's 1935 documentary about the Nuremberg rallies, *Triumph of the Will,* Hitler walks a tremendous gauntlet, apparently mourning the deaths of some soldiers in coffins. The camera moves in tight on Hitler's face as he stares sadly, but determinedly, ahead. Then Riefenstahl cuts to where Hitler is looking—not at the wreath or the funeral pyre at all, but at the giant stone swastika above it. An attack against a symbol is more spectacular than one against human beings. It is universal.

At precisely the moment that the crowd makes the leap from personal to universal rage, the speaker can embark on his third and most difficult task: presenting himself as the voice of God (or whatever higher authority he decides to emulate, be it the divine spirit of a nation or the father of a particular race). Usually, this is done with a subtle tongue. In 1936, Hitler used religious phraseology to cast himself in a messianic role: "How could we not feel once again at this hour the miracle that brought us together! You once heard the voice of a man, and it struck your hearts. It awakened you and you followed this voice . . . Not every one of you sees me, and I do not see every one of you. But I feel you, and you feel me! . . . It is a wonderful thing to be your Führer."

At the end of nearly every inspirational rally, the audience is entreated to take a collective oath. In the midst of a crowd of thousands of brethren, we are to pledge our support. Unfortunately, we are not in a position to rationally consider what we are doing. Hitler went so far as to threaten his followers with punishment for noncompliance, warning that "he who breaks his vow of loyalty . . . must not be surprised if one day he also finds himself lonely, betrayed, abandoned. . . . For us the mere proclamation of faith does not suffice. Only the oath 'I fight!'"

Although Hitler might be considered an extreme example, the arc of coercive rhetoric at ideological spectacles has remained very similar to this day. Louis Farrakhan followed a nearly identical formula for his famous Million Man March in Washington, D.C. He unified his crowd with a long speech about the buses they rode from distant cities. He stoked their passion with references to a symbolic defeat: "White supremacy caused Napoleon to blow the nose off the Sphinx because it reminded you too much of the Black man's majesty." He referred to himself as continuing the lineage of Moses, Jesus, and Muhammad, then entreated his assembly to take a collective, solemn oath.

Spectacles such as these are just as powerful, and just as potentially dangerous, as those from past eras on which their coercive styles are based. Worse, by applying their rhetoric to religion instead of politics, these people have proved much harder for others to criticize without being accused of bigotry. Only those groups specifically targeted by the rhetorical attacks feel justified in speaking out.

Feminists were the first people to openly criticize the 50,000-

person extravaganzas organized by the Promise Keepers, a revival movement that uses the coercive power of spectacle to rally its all-male initiates toward a common spiritual calling that includes "taking back authority" in the home.

Conceived in 1990 by the head football coach at the University of Colorado, the Promise Keepers owe their success to the same principles that win football games: a unified team, a sense of rage, and commitment to a "higher" goal. After several years of exponential growth, the Promise Keepers held a nationally televised rally in 1997 called "Stand in the Gap" on the same plot of turf where Farrakhan had held his Million Man March: the National Mall in Washington, D.C. Dozens more have followed each year in stadiums around the country.

A former member of the organization, who I'll call Hank, traveled several hundred miles from his home in upstate New York to attend a Promise Keepers rally held in Philadelphia in July 1998. The home video he shot of the event amounted to an instructional tape in the art of coercive spectacle. The two-day "wake-up call" included prayer, confession, "Jesus cheers," stirring speeches, participatory songs, responsive readings, beach balls, a version of the wave, public confessions, a candlelighting ceremony, and a sacred oath. Predictably, it ended with the assembled men, many in tears, vowing their commitment to seven promises about loving Jesus, living a moral life, and spreading the doctrine to others.

Apparently, feminists are not the only ones who see more than the Holy Spirit at work here. The Center for Democratic Studies has dedicated an entire newsletter, called *PK Watch,* to tracking the movement's activities. According to a book published by the center, *Promise Keepers: The Third Wave of the American Religious Right,* the movement has more political aspirations than it admits: "In its conception and execution, Promise Keepers is one of the most sophisticated political movements the right wing has yet conjured up." The National Organization for Women has likewise declared Promise Keepers "the greatest danger to women's rights."[2]

The rhetoric of the Promise Keepers is no more frightening or extreme than that of many other radical religious groups. But the methods they use to spread their doctrine evoke terror in their opponents, who recognize the awesome power of these spectacles to suspend logic and to foment rage. Those who have attended such rallies in an attempt to analyze them find themselves swept up by the enthusiasm of the crowd. Newton Maloney, a specialist in psychology and religion at Fuller Theological Seminary in Pasadena, attended a 75,000-strong gathering of Promise Keepers in Los Angeles. Although he went to chronicle their methodology, he soon forgot all about his original purpose and began having a "wonderful time." He later told a skeptical reporter who was covering the rally, "I knew all the crowd techniques . . . [but] it was amazing, spontaneous, like a religious revival."[3]

Hank, too, found himself inexplicably drawn in during his first Promise Keepers experience. "I felt they were talking right to me," he said. "I had some problems with my marriage, and the speaker sounded like he knew it. Just when I was thinking about it, he mentioned it. I cried, and other guys cried, too."

As he learned later by reading "anti–Promise Keepers" materials that his wife had downloaded off the World Wide Web, Hank was not subjected to divine intervention but a simple market study. Promise Keepers' demographic researchers determined that sixty-two percent of their members struggle with infidelity and the allure of pornography. As this was the single largest concern of the men polled, the Promise Keepers planners capitalized on it as an appeal to confess.

At the rally, in the heat of the moment as his sins were discovered, Hank turned off his video camera and walked toward the field to join in a mass confession.

Hank was a victim of well-honed psychological techniques: Through play, song, confession, and confusion, participants are quite nearly hypnotized and made to regress to a childlike state of mind, where they are hungry for direction from above. The speakers then indoctrinate their vulnerable assembly to the arts of "spiritual warfare" and "soldiering for God." Like young college-football players looking up to their coach for an inspirational locker-room speech after a difficult half, or young Nazi soldiers looking to their führer for guidance, the Promise Keepers are rendered psychologically and intellectually defenseless, however much testosterone might be coursing through their veins.

In fact, as in any deliberately coercive spectacle, the programming occurs precisely during these heightened moments of rage or fear. Just as the Outback Steakhouse chooses the brutal "sack" for its point of attack, the Promise Keepers make their final call to confess when hearts are pounding hardest. At such moments we are not familiar with the emotions we are feeling, and we gladly accept any outlet for the primal energy summoned through the mass ritual. We need to believe we have found the natural expression of our fervor, even if it is ill-defined.

When Hank returned home from Philadelphia, he found his wife and children resistant to his newfound determination to exercise his supreme, God-given authority over them. Their insubordination sent him into a rage. On one occasion, Hank's wife became so frightened of the measures he might choose for demonstrating his "resolve" that she took her children to a neighbor's home for the night.

Promise Keepers leaders contend that the emotional fallout a family experiences after a member's awakening results from the man's inability to assert himself skillfully, from the decadent propaganda of liberal women's groups, and from years of sinful living that simply cannot be healed overnight. But after several weeks of arguing with his family and a few sessions of counseling with his minister, Hank decided that the Promise Keepers "said good things but were not for me." The rally succeeded only in making him more aware of his dissatisfaction with his personal relationships, his unsatisfying job, and his inability to find a place for God in his life. It did not provide him with an appropriate set of tools to make any changes.

Because of the many unresolved emotions it leaves in its wake, spectacle is a dangerous way to generate enthusiasm for one's cause—which is why New York's custodians were so fearful of a Million Youth March occurring within city limits, especially when it was aimed at one of its most oppressed demographic groups: young black men.

Mayor Giuliani was so afraid of this spectacle's coercive power that he took every possible measure to prevent it from attaining critical mass. Police divided the crowd area into isolated segments, each no bigger than half a city block, to prevent mass contagion. The event was given a strict time limit—so strict, in fact, that Giuliani sent police onto the stage to pull the plug on Muhammad two minutes after his deadline had passed. Ironically, it was just such a show of force that Muhammad was waiting for. He easily convinced the assembled young men that they were under attack by their enemies, and he provoked a small riot. "Take their guns in self-defense," he shouted. Still, it was policymakers' fear of the power of spectacle that had precipitated the eventual violence.

The young participants of the Million Youth March were left no better off than Hank and his fellow Promise Keepers. Their blood was brought to a righteous boil, but they weren't given any tools to exercise their passion. Their rage had been artfully stoked, but what did they receive for their trouble except the crack of a billy club?

Sex, Drugs, and Rock 'n' Roll

Do spectacles ever give their participants the tools they need to work out their heightened emotions in a constructive way? Is it even possible for mass spectacles to be used toward positive ends, or are all spontaneous gatherings doomed to be co-opted? Spectacles such as the March on Washington and Woodstock in the 1960s seemed to hold the promise for broad positive change for their participants, but the current incarnations of these events—Woodstock II, Lollapalooza, and the Million Man March—seem contrived, commercial, or downright destructive. Perhaps the emotional energy of spectacle can no longer be channeled in a healthy manner. Maybe it never could. Still, that doesn't keep people from trying.

When my good friend Aaron Naparstek called me in June 1998 to tell me he had just signed on to help devise a new kind of concert gathering, I knew that whatever it was he had gotten himself involved in would not suffer from a lack of good intentions. A mature twenty-eight, Aaron has been working since he was a teenager to develop youth programs that help participants explore alternative methods of conflict resolution. At an international camp called Seeds of Peace, Aaron brings Palestinian, Arab, and Israeli children together each summer for workshops and role-playing games, where they are forced to find ways to work together. In one such program, all the children are divided into separate tribes, each missing one essential resource. By the afternoon's end, only the tribes who have learned to negotiate and trade with the others will survive.

Although the games are programmed to teach a particular lesson (the decks are stacked, so to speak), that lesson is usually a positive one—or at least one that relies on problem solving instead of holy war. Aaron's programs have been so successful that he has received funding to continue his international workshops on the Internet.

Youth programming and community building might be Aaron's passions, but they don't always pay the bills. For that reason, he took a job last year in "virtual community" planning for Microsoft's online service Sidewalk.com. There he was responsible for helping to organize marketing spectacles, like a rally in New York's Bryant Park in which the assembled crowd stood in line to receive discount coupons to local restaurants featured on Microsoft's Web site. As he applied his well-honed skills toward helping people network according to the corporate agenda of the software giant, he found himself slipping into a malaise. Luckily, just as Microsoft was restructuring its online service to become more commercial—and handing community makers like Aaron pink slips—he partnered with an old friend who had the resources to make a progressive spectacle into a reality.

Thomas Hoegh is best known as the theater director who choreographed the opening ceremony for the Lillehammer Olympics in 1994. Pageantry is his forte, and the native-born Hoegh had no compunction about using every tool at his disposal to celebrate Nordic culture. Though CBS opted to broadcast an interview with knee-bashing conspirator Tonya Harding instead of the ceremony, the 34,000 in attendance at Lillehammer were treated to classic over-the-top spectacle. A characteristically Norwegian reindeer-drawn sled driven by one of the region's indigenous Lapps gathered participants and speakers from around the world. Eight parachutists dropped down from the heavens, holding a 400-foot Norwegian flag. Speakers inspired the assembled masses with talk of international peace and brotherhood. Norway's royal family entered with the pomp of Michael Jordan stepping onto the basketball court, and for the climax, a ski jumper holding a flame performed a death-defying jump across the stadium before lighting the main Olympic torch.

Hoegh left theater behind after inheriting his family's fortune and starting a venture-capital firm called Arts Alliance, which specializes in online projects, marketing, and software. He took a job at a Massachusetts company called Firefly in order to learn about the "intelligent agents"—small programs that search cyberspace for an Internet user's requests and presumed desires— they were developing for big business. There he met Naparstek, and the pair quickly realized they should be working together on something more culturally relevant and more fun than marketing software.

While most of his previous Arts Alliance projects had involved investing in and advising online companies, Hoegh had an idea that appealed to Naparstek: to design a massive youth culture event that revived some of the positive energy of spectacle. Something had divorced the modern rock concert from its ritualistic roots, Hoegh and Naparstek thought, and the two were determined to restore this connection through a traveling, global road show, fittingly entitled the "Ritual."

Because I had experience researching and writing about youth culture, the two well-meaning conspirators decided to bring me in on the action. After a few preliminary meetings, I realized their task was Sisyphean. Since the 1960s, almost every effort to ignite a genuinely free-spirited expression of mass energy in the form of a musical event had been quickly snuffed—either by a music industry determined to capitalize on the phenomenon or by well-meaning progressives who weighed it down with political "causes." How could these two hope to accomplish anything better?

As envisioned by Hoegh, the Ritual would be a traveling spectacle designed to provide a spiritual, communal awakening for a global youth culture in quest of just such an outlet. With little more than this basic goal, the two gathered about a dozen experienced rave promoters, online community makers, musicians, DJ's, and youth culture advocates to "brainstorm" a spectacle worthy of the mission.

Those of us who assembled for the one-day meeting in a funky studio in New York's Greenwich Village were treated to something of a program ourselves. Naparstek had outlined the day's proceedings on a large flip chart. We played "show and tell," broke into smaller focus groups, made presentations to one another, and strove to pay attention. Still, most everyone was suspicious, and our cynicism was palpable.

We sat at tables arranged in a polygon, and listened to Hoegh as he described his vision. "The artist has gone from presenter to facilitator," he explained. His intention, he told us, was to facilitate a ritual that would be actualized by its participants, or, in his words, to "create a space for a story to take place." The space would consist of dozens of giant shipping containers connected to form a tremendous circle. At the center, a stage fitted with projectors would cast images directly up onto an "organ of mirrors" that would, in turn, reflect the images onto the surfaces of the containers. Using 3D sound technology, musicians on the stage would be able to direct the sounds of their instruments to different locations in the circle.

Most important, the musicians and visual artists would merely set up "frameworks" for the participants to make their own content using devices situated throughout the arena. The ticket for the event would be a CD-ROM disk, distributed far in advance. The CD would contain software allowing ticket holders to create music and videos that could be broadcast throughout the event. A World Wide Web site would offer participants the chance to communicate with one another during the months before the show came to their hometown, and perhaps even form separate "tribes" that would come together at the Ritual, as a sort of conclave. Those who participated the most online or with local organizers would be entitled to work most directly with the professional artists on the tour.

Though we could all sense Hoegh's earnestness as he told us his ideas, we couldn't help but attack him with our questions. Is this a concert, or what? Who gets the money? Who decides which audience contributions are actually used? What's this Ritual supposed to convey?

Maybe we were right to question Hoegh's vision. Or maybe we simply had gotten so used to the coercive use of spectacle that we saw a hidden motive behind every one of his ideas.

Toward the end of the day, Genesis P-Orridge, an expert in occult practices and the notorious founder of British "industrial" band Throbbing Gristle, was asked to give us some background about the tribal roots of ritual. He spoke of mystics and rain dances, the unpredictability of nature, and the technologies of survival. The mystics of a tribe were responsible for identifying patterns that others couldn't, he explained. And the rituals they created were designed to bring back the conditions—be it rain, harvest, or prosperity—that had arisen spontaneously and without effort before but that seemed to evade them now. "Rituals are based in a people's need to build something in order to make something happen that had happened before," the tattooed and scarified counterculture legend insisted.

An unmistakable chill swept through the steamy, un-air-conditioned loft. Were we to assume the role of our society's mystics, re-creating the conditions that allowed for a spontaneous spectacle to emerge? Most of us had been active participants in one countercultural movement or another, and knew all too well what happens when someone tries to corral that natural energy. Besides, how is "making something happen that happened before" progressive? The Ritual was beginning to sound more like a rally to restore the Promise Keepers' once-assumed role of authority in the family.

A young black Harvard intellectual-turned-musician, DJ Spooky, finally broke the ice, giving voice to our shared paranoia: "So we're talking about starting a cult?"

The Ritual retains a line on the Arts Alliance balance sheet, but—as of this writing, anyway—has not yet gathered the necessary momentum to come to fruition. Perhaps Hoegh realizes he's fighting a losing battle and that self-consciously concocted spectacle, no matter how well-intentioned, is bound to fail.

For in light of their tendency to draw on old traditions, spectacles aren't the most hospitable forums for promoting new ideas or alternative agendas. Spectacles bring their followers into the future only by lauding achievements and values of the distant and sometimes mythical past. They are a call to arms, where confessed sinners and the newly virtuous vow to wage war against the alien forces of change that have compromised their common, God-ordained mission.

It's hard for a spectacle to be much more than that. By encouraging emotional or nostalgic reactions and demanding conformity, spectacles tend to discourage the kind of mindset that leads to progressive change. Occasionally and usually spontaneously, a legitimately novel form of spectacle arises, where individuality is preserved and open-minded tolerance prevails. They don't usually last for long. Spontaneous expressions such as these are either co-opted by the very forces and industries they hoped to change or surrendered to the intrinsically coercive structure of spectacle itself. Either a new tribe or a new demographic is formed.

The sudden countercultural surges provoked by movements like rock and roll, punk, and rave are no exception. For all their lip service to progressive agendas and psychedelic illumination, most stadium concerts today are merely desperate attempts to rehabilitate the former "platinum" status of waning supergroups or the faded glory of the rock and roll era. As a result, the vast majority of music festivals are bound by traditional values and are nearly as coercive as a Promise Keepers rally. Whether in support of God's masculine image or U2 singer Bono's latest chart-buster, any stadium filled with people pumping their fists in the air or slamming against one another in mosh pits is more under the influence of hormones than common sense.

By the time a rock group reaches the status necessary to perform at a full-fledged spectacle, its managers are usually more concerned with maintaining sales than pushing any creative envelope. Newer groups, who serve as warm-up bands for monster acts, gain audience and legitimacy through their association with the established headliner. Meanwhile, anything truly novel about them will forever be associated with the veteran rock and roll institution. Their voluntary alliance with the number one band is a not-so-tacit acknowledgment of a direct and devotional lineage.

Stadium concerts today are not so much about the bands or their music. They are increasingly about spectacle, and they are designed to artificially re-create the sensations of tribal loyalty. Employing the same sorts of techniques used by the Promise Keepers, concert promoters reverse-engineer the allegiance of their audiences. Rather than amplify a rock group's genuineness, the spectacle manufactures the physical and emotional conditions associated with loyalty in order to consolidate a stable and continuing source of financial revenue.

Rock concerts, of course, have long served as vehicles for the political and spiritual agendas of their stars. The Grateful Dead used their concerts to share Eastern and psychedelic philosophies, while The Who began to address unemployment and other social fallout from the downward trend in the British economy. Woodstock, however earnestly conceived, was really just a rally for the antiwar movement. The event itself was more important than the music. Musicians and promoters with political agendas were capitalizing on the energy of mass spectacle to unite young people in their opposition to continuing militarism in Vietnam. Though earnest and well-meaning, they were also manipulating.

Today, rock concerts in support of specific agendas are common and overt. Live Aid, Band Aid, Rain Forest, and Free Tibet concerts make no pretense of the fact that they are directing the energy they generate toward social or political causes. Still, many of the performers are aware of an inherent incongruity. As Beastie Boy Adam Yauch admitted to Gen-X *Swing* magazine of his Tibet concerts, "We're trying to create something that as closely as possible represents Tibet, which is obviously ludicrous because we're doing it in the middle of a stadium with a bunch of kids running around, playing Western music."

The promoters of these events have our best interests at heart. Although there is something odd about a rock star having more political influence over young people than, say, a working environmentalist, legislator, or social activist, it's hard to feel too terrible about concerts that generate awareness about global threats. But the same persuasive techniques used to direct rock audiences toward social issues are being used much more often and more perniciously by businessmen hoping to make a buck for themselves.

By the mid-1990s, the popularity of relatively anonymous electronic dance music and the failure of supergroups to maintain customer loyalty had pushed platinum album sales to dangerous lows. Although young people are buying more recorded music than ever before, they can no longer be counted on to purchase albums by the same artists, year after year. Some experts blame the Internet and channel surfing for breaking the predictable, linear purchasing habits of young people. With the ability to sample music online from countless new bands, digital kids drift from genre to genre. Where once they could have been counted on to buy four or five albums from the same supergroup, now they buy just one and move on to another. The rise of electronic music, usually recorded and performed by unseen musicians and with no lead vocalist, has further eroded the support base for traditional high-profile concert bands. To fans of electronic music, the cults of personality associated with famous rock groups seem contrived and superfluous.

The music industry's dependence on formulaic marketing, coupled with a growing disillusionment about role models and pop icons, has left the music business desperate for the huge moneymakers of the classic rock era. So they turn to the tactics of spectacle to revive the aging heart of rock and roll.

Concert promoters now strive to make their shows bigger, louder, and more extravagant than their predecessors'. Fireworks and explosions, not passionate musical refrains, are what bring the crowd to its feet on cue.

In its best light, the self-consciously re-created rock concert can be seen as a kind of second-order ritual—a ritual of a ritual. But rock promoters have a much less postmodern attitude toward all this. To them, it's about business.

Consider U2's 1997 PopMart tour, perhaps the most expensive and self-consciously devised rock and roll extravaganza ever to travel around the globe. The show's title revealed its true purpose: PopMart. With an ironic wink, the tour sought to stake U2's claim to the throne of "world's greatest supergroup" by launching a ritualized invasion.

"There are times in rock and roll when military language becomes inescapable," explained band manager Paul McGuinness. "You talk about things like invasions and battle plans in various countries because you want people to buy your records and come see your shows."[4]

The East Bay *Express* was not amused. "When you've got The Most Audacious Stage Show in Rock History in front of you, it's easier simply to let your jaw drop at the setup: a 170-by-56-foot video screen (sort of like Times Square), an enormous toothpick spiked with an olive (sort of like Times Square), and a huge golden arch (sort of like McDonald's) blasting floodlights directly into the night sky (sort of like a 1930s Nazi rally)."[5]

In spite of a $2.4-million-per-week budget and countless more spent on hype and publicity, most of U2's shows failed to sell out or even come close. Not that the tour wasn't profitable—ticket receipts easily exceeded expenditures. Still, the overwhelming reaction of audience members I interviewed was negative. They saw through the hoopla to the hollow marketing at the spectacle's empty core. Lead singer Bono responded defensively to his critics: "I don't buy the notion that you are somehow committing an offense to the spirit of rock and roll by becoming popular." But popularity was not his crime; manipulative spectacle was.

The so-called "alternative" rock scene offers the most grotesque contortions of spectacle gone awry. Lollapalooza, a touring festival started in 1991 to bring attention to lesser-known bands, quickly became a victim of its own success. As alternative bands like Nirvana became supergroups in their own right, the festival got more contrived. Ironically, it also got less popular, less profitable, and entirely predictable. As *New York Times* reviewer Jon Pareles put it in a review of the festival, "Most bands simply filled their niches. The thrill is fading; fewer than 12,500 were sold out of 27,500."[6]

In an attempt to restore some of its former street credibility and cash flow, Lollapalooza engaged Perry Farrel, the concert's original organizer who had since moved on. Faced with the dilemma of how to make this festival different from a run-of-the-mill testosterone party, Farrel strove to associate the road show with legitimate social causes. The theme he chose was "toxic waste," but more than one reviewer noticed the many incongruities between the concert's stated agenda and the actual event.

At the show I attended, the smell of cooking hamburgers wafted over an earnest anti-beef display. As a *Spin* reporter explained,

> After reading about the evils of dioxin-producing PVC plastic at the Greenpeace table, you could visit "the Temple" and watch one of the official Lollapalooza dancing girls hang from a crotch harness in what looked suspiciously like a PVC bondage thong. More than one fan made the mistake of offering up dollar bills to Miss Thang in her sling, suggesting the difference between postfeminist performance art and alterna-porn is in the groin of the beholder.[7]

Lollapalooza enacted the "social-issue strategy" in reverse. Instead of the rock show being used to rally people behind a social cause, a social cause was being used to rally people behind a rock show—which, perhaps, is why neither was effectively promoted. True to the overbearing nature of such spectacles, the only female performers at Lollapalooza were backup singers. It was such a blatant omission that a collection of popular "girl bands" decided to tour on their own that same summer, to much better receptions and reviews.

The closest young people got to liberating themselves from the agendas of marketers and social activists alike was when they abandoned the festivals devised for them and took to devising their own. By the late 1980s, many young people in Europe and the United States were already tiring of the traditional rock concert, but they still had the urge to gather together in massive numbers and dance.

Luckily, some vacationing British revelers on an island called Ibiza off the coast of Spain stumbled upon what turned out to be at least a temporary answer: raves. These spontaneous festivals, which quickly spread to the British countryside and America's West Coast, consisted of little more than electronic dance music mixed on turntables, and thousands of people willing to move to it. Although mild versions of psychedelic drugs were very often a component of the scene and its psychology, the unannounced and usually illegal gatherings succeeding in bonding literally thousands of people together through a leaderless mass spectacle. Most of the participants didn't know quite what to do the next morning with the emotional states they had achieved the night before, but they felt certain they had experienced group cohesion on a level more profound than they previously thought possible.

Raves were transformational experiences on the order of a Promise Keepers rally, except they appeared to have no overriding or imposed agenda. Young people attending and organizing raves were so wary of social or commercial causes co-opting their experience that they generally shunned even the worthiest of affiliations. Much to the chagrin of 1960s radicals and record executives alike, for a long time raves remained amateur events in the best sense of the word, and their organizers strenuously resisted efforts to turn them into anything else.

The most commonly reported effect of the rave experience was "loss of self." Rave participants said the parties made them feel "liberated" or "free from ego." Unlike Promise Keepers, who found liberation through confession of their sins and then quickly took an oath, the ravers claimed to find liberation through little more than dancing with others. Instead of wanting to take an oath or subscribe to a new set of tenets, ravers felt an urge only to accept themselves and one another unconditionally. In contrast to most other mass spectacles, sexually aggressive or predatory behavior was minimized, not amplified. In fact, more young women attended raves than young men. "It's not a pickup scene, like at a club," one San Franciscan girl explained to me. "You're just free to dance and feel the group energy."

The other distinguishing feature of the rave was that in spite of its intense group dynamic, individual thinking and behavior were not intentionally impaired. Dancers tended to move freely about the crowd, dispensing with the convention of partners or standard motions. Since there was no real performer—only a DJ—there was no stage to face, which lent an amorphous character to the entire event. Raves allowed for group cohesion and at the same time permitted individuals to relate to the phenomenon as they chose. The gatherings were exercises in tolerance and coordination and, according to their organizers, miniature models of civilization.

Unfortunately, not even raves could resist the forces of the market. By removing themselves from the commercial club and stadium environment, rave promoters unintentionally created an alternative, underground economy. Rampant drug dealing also contributed to an eventual stand-off with law enforcement and community leaders. The British government passed a law called the Criminal Justice Act, which made public gatherings illegal and forced these parties into commercial, established venues.

It was a recipe for disaster. Commercial bars, which depend on liquor sales to turn a profit, had no way of generating income from young people who used Ecstasy and herbs to get their highs. Since people on Ecstasy tend to dehydrate, unscrupulous barkeeps began the practice of turning off bathroom faucets and charging exorbitant rates for bottled water. After a few well-publicized "Ecstasy-related" dehydration fatalities, the rave movement was effectively squashed.

In the States, the rave spectacle slowly gave way to hero worship and the star system as promoters and record labels looked for ways to make money by establishing brand recognition. DJ's took center stage, and a new category called "electronica" was born. Massive promotional efforts behind performances by supergroups like Prodigy and The Chemical Brothers restored a traditional order to these formerly free-form events. They also robbed what had been an essentially amateur movement of its unrehearsed vitality.

Another effort at co-option, led by an ex-priest, attempted to commandeer the energy of the rave spectacle for religious conversion. The basic formula and aesthetic of the gatherings remained the same, but immediately following the "peak" of the party, the revelers were treated to spiritual lectures and hip, updated versions of Christian rituals. The proliferation of these "rave masses" made many young people suspicious of raves altogether, and the original movement deteriorated further.

Like a corporate sponsor attempting to exploit the joy of a spontaneous wave at a Jets game, the people hoping to capitalize on the rave for commercial and spiritual purposes simply sucked the life out of it. Perhaps that's the only fate possible for a spontaneously occurring group event once it is discovered by those who hope to make use of its coercive potential. Unfortunately, influence professionals are getting better at recognizing such opportunities all the time.

I don't mean to imply that every spectacle is necessarily coercive in its intent or its effect. But spectacles do function to suspend rational processes in favor of emotional ones. The intellect is neutralized, along with its ability to protect us from hateful or illogical rhetoric. We are made vulnerable. Maybe our only choice is to understand the intentions of a spectacle's organizers before we attend.

Like dreams, spiritual explorations, or even lovemaking, spectacle can offer us rare access to the subconscious as well as the mythic sides of our individual and collective experience. But it grants this same access to whoever might be hoping to engineer our sentiments toward his own ends. Revel at your own risk.

CHAPTER FOUR

Public Relations

The truth never hurts you, unless the truth hurts,
and then you don't use it.

—*Howard Rubenstein*

The scandal had made the headlines by the time Howard Rubenstein got the call from Kathie Lee Gifford's attorneys.

"Everyone had seen the story break," Rubenstein explained to me from his office overlooking midtown Manhattan. "It got tremendous play. They had portrayed her as a knowing participant in sweatshop manufacturing for clothing, and it was awful."

In April 1996, the *Daily News, New York Post,* and just about every other newspaper in town reported that clothing being sold nationally under Kathie Lee's name had actually been made by people working under atrocious conditions in Honduras. America's sweetheart turned out to be a character straight out of the pages of Upton Sinclair. Worse, as far as Rubenstein was concerned, a labor union that had long been looking for a media hook to publicize its underreported cause had finally found one in the famous television star. "They had what they thought was a pigeon." And without Rubenstein to guide her, Kathie Lee was fluttering out of control.

"She went on the air, and she attacked the critics. She attacked the union that was in back of it. She was stunned very badly and lashed out at her critics." That's when Kathie Lee and her lawyers called for help.

Howard Rubenstein, founder of Rubenstein and Associates Public Relations, is a man to have on your side in a crisis. He'll make you apologize, he'll make you work, and he'll make you pay for your mistakes—but you'll end up smelling like roses.

In Kathie Lee's case, Rubenstein used his time-tested technique of putting the embattled client on the offensive. In terms of storytelling, his job was to change her from a villainous antagonist into an active protagonist. He knew that this fiasco would probably associate Kathie Lee with sweatshops for the rest of her life. So why not turn this situation to her advantage? What Jerry Lewis is to muscular dystrophy, Kathie Lee would be to sweatshops.

"The first thing I wanted to know was if it was true," Rubenstein says. "She was adamant in saying she didn't know about it. So I said, 'You have a clear path on what you have to do: you have to lead the fight against sweatshops. And be serious about it.'"

Within hours, Rubenstein was on the phone with the angry union, offering them something they wanted even more than a pigeon: a celebrity-fronted publicity campaign. With Kathie Lee's face and Rubenstein's contacts, it was easy.

"We made several moves," Rubenstein told me. "We had dinner with [Labor] Secretary [Robert] Reich, and came to an understanding of her position. We met with the governor of New York State, George Pataki, and also said we'd help him in getting through anti-sweatshop legislation, which happened. I called

Cardinal O'Connor and asked if he would help, and he said 'Absolutely.'"

By the time Rubenstein had finished working the phones, Kathie Lee Gifford was standing next to Bill Clinton in the White House Rose Garden, unveiling a program to help manufacturers certify that their garments had not been produced in sweatshops. Eventually, the Smithsonian Institution included Kathie Lee in its display on sweatshops as a leader in the fight against them. The original story—Kathie Lee revealed as an exploiter—had been spun into a different narrative entirely. The villain became the ingenue, as Kathie Lee—a symbol of American naïveté—learned the hard lesson that the Third World is a dark and dangerous place for its oft-victimized inhabitants. Drawn into battle, she would adopt their plight as her own and forever carry the torch of freedom and dignity for these oppressed people.

"It started with her inaccurately being portrayed as the sponsor of sweatshop clothing, and at the end of the line being praised as leading the fight against them. . . . What I tried to do was first tell the story that she was not a bad person and that she did not encourage sweatshops. The second thing, we tried to galvanize government and the private sector to a real fight against sweatshops. We took charge of the story."

Howard Rubenstein is not a devious man. Quite to the contrary, the sixty-something Harvard Law dropout ("I got bored") prides himself on the integrity of his campaigns, as evidenced by the fact that journalists rarely feel the need to double-check the assertions he makes in press releases. Although he is famous for taking on "crisis" clients like Marv Albert and George Michael, he spends most of his time managing the long-term images of corporate icons such as Rupert Murdoch and George Steinbrenner. He has become the most respected public-relations man in the business not because he knows how to fool the public into believing lies but because he understands how to use the media to change the truth.

Rubenstein has survived in a fast-changing business because his storytelling strategy is always based in reality. "I try to find out what happened, I try to get somebody to say 'I did wrong— here are the reasons I did,' maybe, and 'I shouldn't have done it, and I apologize to you, now.' And then I try to correct the thing that has been wronged. Visibly correct the error."

Like the many public-relations specialists who preceded him, Rubenstein crafts his campaigns to fit the requirements of his audience. For today's sophisticated television public, this means admitting one's mistakes and then taking charge of the story by leading the media in its quest for retribution. Even though Kathie Lee had indirectly violated our sense of morality, she seemed to more than make up for it with her highly visible campaign to end improper labor practices around the world.

Rubenstein admits to focusing on visibility. When the Department of Labor busted a sweatshop manufacturing clothes for Kathie Lee in midtown Manhattan, Rubenstein made sure her husband, Frank Gifford, was photographed by a multitude of journalists as he handed envelopes of cash to the confused laborers as compensation. For Rubenstein's clients, such photo-ops are always backed by a genuine commitment to help solve the problem with which they have become associated. As far as the clients are concerned, this may or may not be because they wish to do the right thing. More often than not it's because paying lip service to an issue is no longer sufficient to restore one's public image in a crisis.

At the core of Rubenstein's strategy is a technique that public-relations artists have been using for centuries: figuring out what the target audience believes, finding the inconsistencies in those beliefs, and then leveraging those inconsistencies into a new story. For Rubenstein, the new story will always more accurately depict the reality of the situation. He feels he is correcting public misperception, and he knows he wouldn't get away with a fallacious cover story for very long. In the age of the Internet and twenty-four-hour news, Rubenstein's style of follow-through is costly and time-consuming, but mandatory for getting the job done. It wasn't always this way.

For many of Rubenstein's predecessors, the new and improved stories created for the target audience bore no more relationship to the truth than the story the public already believed. Still, the essential methodology involved—pacing the audience in order to gain control of the narrative, and then rewriting the story to lead the audience to a new conclusion—remains the same.

Like salesmen, public-relations specialists seek to mirror the conscious and unconscious concerns of their targets in order to change their perception of reality. Just as a car dealer sizes up his walk-in clientele, researchers working for governments, public-relations firms, and corporations expend a great deal of effort sizing up their constituencies on a regular basis. Once they understand our belief system and, more important, where the irrationality and emotional triggers lie in those beliefs, they can work to move us in a different direction. "Closing the sale" in these cases might mean gaining public support for a war, changing an industry's reputation as a polluter, or simply restoring voters' trust in a president who has lied to them.

Instead of focusing on one prospect at a time, however, the PR man must work on a target that consists of thousands or even millions of people. In order to pace and lead such a large group, the practitioners of mass communications must reduce their entire target population to a single, malleable mass—much in the way the promoters of spectacle aspire to transform a stadium filled with thousands of individual, thinking adults into a single, surging body.

Alien Nations

Mass communications find their historical foundations in centuries of imperialist cultural coercion. Funded mostly by their governments, well-meaning (and a few not-so-well-meaning) anthropologists developed methods for analysis and redirection while studying "primitive" peoples from foreign cultures. Whether or not they were aware of their sponsors' intentions, these anthropologists laid the groundwork for subsequent military invasions.

The early Christian missions of the fifteenth and sixteenth centuries, for example, served as the first outposts for the European troops that would eventually invade South America. These missions were not generally sponsored by the church but by the monarchy. As a result, the visiting missionary served the dual role of converter and intelligence gatherer. Ultimately, both functions simply prepared the target population to be taken by force.

The procedure for cultural domination invariably followed the same three steps used by public-relations specialists today: First, learn the dominant myths of the target people and, in the process, gain their trust; second, find the gaps or superstitions in their beliefs; and third, either replace the superstitions or augment them with facts that redirect the target group's perceptions and allegiance.

Christian missionaries to the New World first studied the indigenous people in order to appraise their pantheistic belief system and to gain their trust. They observed local rituals to learn about particular beliefs associated with each god. Then they

converted people by associating local gods with the closest corresponding Catholic saints or deities. The native god for animals, the people were taught, is really just Saint Francis. The
drinking of chicken's blood is really just a version of the commu-
nion. And so on, until a local, hybridized version of Christianity
evolved.

In the 1500s, Franciscan brothers studied the language and religion of the people of Tenochtitlán before choosing to build the
hilltop basilica of the Virgin of Guadalupe on the site of an
Aztec temple dedicated to the earth goddess Tonatzin. In its new
incarnation, the mountaintop church became an homage to
Mary, who is pictured stepping on the stars and moon, the symbols of her pagan predecessor. She overlooks what is now called
Mexico City. Just as Mort Spivas used the old woman's revela-
tion about her husband's irrational self-deprivation to sell her a
bed, the missionaries used their target audiences' devotion to
local gods to sell them the saints.

This is the two-millennium-old process by which Christianity
absorbed the rituals and beliefs of the peoples it converted. The
Christmas tree began as part of a solstice ritual practiced by Germans to light the darkest night of the year. Smart missionaries of
the time realized that this ritual had developed in connection to
people's fear of the darkness of winter. The tannenbaum exposed
the Germans' deepest fear—and the missionaries understood
that it thus represented the most fertile ground for conversion.
By identifying the tree with the holy cross and the birth of
Christ, the Christians augmented the pagan ritual and redirected
its sense of hope toward their own messiah.

Although business interests eventually replaced the church as
the dominant force behind imperialist expansion, the techniques
of population analysis and coercion—pacing and leading the target audience—remained the same. The British East India Company, for example, was formed in 1600 and given a "perpetual

charter" from the British monarchy for trade in the East Indies and, later, China. In a series of well-funded wars spanning centuries, the company used a private army to effectively annex India for the British Monarchy, and Queen Victoria eventually became empress of India in 1876. Instead of using pure military might, the imperialists exploited researched tensions between the Indian Moghul emperors and their constituencies. After successfully breaking down Moghul rule, the smaller factions were easily conquered.

What remains a little less known about these efforts is that they involved active intelligence-gathering and social-influence techniques. After learning of the Indian people's respect for architecture, the British built a tremendous train station in Bombay dedicated to the new empress, Victoria Terminus, with vaulted Gothic ceilings and other construction techniques that demonstrated British technological superiority. The structure, an imported version of London's own cultural icon, Victoria Station, was not-so-coincidentally erected on the site of a former shrine to Indian goddess Mumba Devi. The motif included both Western and Indian imagery, to imply that Indian society had been incorporated into the culturally dominant West.

In the early twentieth century, science replaced economic liberty as the cloak for governments seeking to extend their territorial reach. The United States funded dozens of research expeditions to the Far East and the South Pacific, all in the name of anthropology. While the young anthropologists of the 1920s may have had scientific inquiry in their hearts, military strategists looking for insights into the indigenous peoples of these territories often exploited the intelligence they gathered. The work of Margaret Mead, in particular, with its focus on the traditions and values of the natives of the South Pacific islands of New Guinea and Bali, came in handy when the regions were contested by the Japanese in World War II.

How was anthropological data used in war? For one, it offered insights into winning local support for the establishment of military bases and for convincing townspeople to inform on neighbors who might be working for the enemy. During the Vietnam war, the United States printed comic books and other propaganda that displayed a sensitivity for native customs, while they attempted to sway native loyalty.

In military decision making, it was also crucial to have a handle on the local or national psyche. For example, although Franklin Roosevelt had considered assassinating the emperor of Japan to force the nation's surrender, his advisors learned through anthropological research that such a move would surely backfire. With no emperor, there would be no one with the authority to surrender. Moreover, the attack on the emperor would so infuriate the people that they would likely fight until the last man was standing. Only a tremendous humiliation—such as that endured at Hiroshima—was deemed sufficient to force the Japanese emperor to admit defeat.

After World War II, Air Force Brigadier General Edward G. Lansdale emerged as the preeminent "counterinsurgency" strategist for the CIA. Over a period of three decades, he developed a wide range of intelligence and propaganda theories that were employed and refined in the field.[1] For example, in the 1950s, as part of his counterinsurgency campaign against the Huk rebels of the Philippines, Lansdale conducted research into local superstitions. He learned that the Huk battleground was believed to be inhabited by an *asuang,* or vampire figure. To capitalize on this mythology, his "psywar" units would follow Huk patrols and then quietly ambush the last man on the trail. They would kill the soldier by means of two punctures on the neck, drain him of his blood, and then leave him to be found the next morning. On encountering the victim, the Huks in the area would retreat for fear of further vampire attacks.

By the 1980s, such psywar techniques had been catalogued by the CIA in a volume called *Counter Intelligence Study Manual*,[2] which was used mainly in Central American conflicts. The psyops book provides as clear a depiction of the kinds of demographic research and influence techniques used by public-relations experts as you're likely to find.

To gather information on the target population, agents mix in among the population at "pastoral activities, parties, birthdays, and even wakes and burials" to learn of their beliefs and aspirations. Psyops officers also organize "discussion groups" to gauge local support of planned actions.

Once influence is to be exerted, the agents identify and recruit "established citizens" to serve as role models for cooperation by giving them jobs in "innocuous" but highly visible areas. Their next task is to smooth over difficult or irrational concepts with simple slogans. As a rationale for carrying guns, for example, the guerillas are instructed to say "Our weapons are, in truth, the weapons of the people, yours." Whatever the guerilla group actually intends, they are required to "make the people feel that we are thinking of them." In cases where CIA interests are irreconcilably opposed to those of the people, the manual suggests creating a "front organization" with a set of stated goals very different from what will be the movement's real agenda. Finally, all efforts at conversion are fine-tuned to the preexisting propensities of the target group: "We should inculcate this in the people in a subtle manner so that these feelings seem to be born of themselves, spontaneously."

For a culture as "alien" as that of the Huk rebels, the mythologies and superstitions fueling their emotional triggers are easy to locate. The more foreign the belief system is from that of the anthropologist, the more easily it can be observed with some measure of distance and objectivity. Besides, the trick only needs to work long enough to win (or avoid) a war. Even if the "truth" emerges sometime later, at least the primary objective has already been achieved. At the very worst, the enemy won't be fooled as readily in the future.

It is much harder for anthropologists to identify and exploit the emotional inconsistencies in their own cultures. That's why when American corporate and governmental interests adopted these techniques for use against the American people, they needed to cloak their assault in a seemingly benign manifestation: the focus group. About ten "average" members of a target population are brought into a room and asked to discuss an issue while a team of researchers, clients, and a camera record their responses from behind a one-way mirror. A researcher stays in the room with the subjects, asking them questions and pushing them in new directions. The focus group offers a laboratory in which interactions and discussions between real human beings are dissected and analyzed for their inconsistencies and leverage points.

Bob Deutsch, an anthropologist who worked for the Department of Defense before offering his services to the private sector, has conducted at least a thousand focus groups during his career. He is well known in the advertising and public-relations industries for his ability to extract material from his subjects that no one else seems to be able to get. His secret, as he tells it, is to let the subjects speak freely until they stumble on their own faulty logic.

I first encountered Deutsch when he was giving a lecture to advertising researchers on how to lead and analyze focus groups. He showed a videotape of himself on ABC's "Nightline," in which he led focus groups revealing Americans' irrational beliefs about Japan. "You want to uncover in your audience what I call a 'spasm of sentiment,'" he explained. "It's their illogic—their emotional logic." He told us how in focus groups with average American citizens, he learned that most people still associate the

Japanese with Pearl Harbor: "People say, for example, 'Japan took our lives in 1941, and they took our livelihoods in 1991.'" Because Japan disrupted America's self-mythology of being invincible, the nation would never be forgiven in the irrational American sentiment.

A few months later, I found myself consulting to the same advertising agency as Deutsch—and, although I was initially wary of his self-consciously gurulike manner, I came to realize the brilliance of his work, as well the innocent sense of inquiry with which he performs it. To prepare me for a study on cult branding, the agency let me review videotapes of focus groups Deutsch had conducted with the Hells Angels about their extreme affinity for Harley-Davidson motorcycles.

On the tapes, he walks into a room filled with scary tattooed and leather-jacketed motorcycle thugs, sits down arrogantly, and says, "Tell me something: Why can't you buy a simple fucking Jap bike and live happily ever after?"

The bikers are immediately charged up, and the biggest one challenges him: "Who the hell are you to ask that?"

"I'm just a guy that asked you to come and you came," he replies. "For a lousy hundred dollars. So don't fuck around!"

"I don't want this videotaped," another burly biker protests.

"Why not?" Deutsch asks.

"Well, I just escaped from Rikers Island," the biker answers.

Again, Deutsch stands his ground, telling the ex-con to live with the camera or leave.

Instead of becoming violent with Deutsch, the bikers delivered one of the most revealing focus groups he had ever conducted. Deutsch's provocative tactics not only earned him the Hells Angels' trust but also engaged them in a genuine emotional conflict. What he learned, he later told me from his temporary office at another agency—the plush, pop-art filled DDB Needham headquarters on Madison Avenue—was that "they are protecting themselves. That's what their core story is about. Images are created to defend loss, not maximize gain."

Deutsch discusses his subjects with an air of detachment, a scientist's objectivity that he derived from his upbringing. As a child, Deutsch always felt out of place in America, where "ninety-nine percent of the linguistic universe was stereotypes." He was attracted to primitive cultures and became an anthropologist precisely so he could live and work among them. "These people live in the same world I do. They live in a world of emotion, nature, storytelling, and mythology."

On returning to the United States, he had the "magnificent insight" that the farther away our modern experience takes us from our mythological routes, the more we long for media, ideas, and images that help us to reconnect to them. "We're living at the subterranean level, anyway." While he adamantly opposes the putative goals of public relations, calling it a "charlatan profession," he is absolutely dedicated to focus groups for what they can reveal about a given population's connection to metaphor and archetype. "The mind is an organism that will make patterns. It doesn't care if there are no real patterns to be had. We make conclusions to stories all by ourselves."

In identifying these patterns, however, whether Deutsch likes it or not, he is revealing trigger points in our reasoning that can be exploited. During a focus group about Ronald Reagan, one of Deutsch's participants confessed, "I like the way President Reagan handled that conflict. I've forgotten which one." While many researchers would discard such a statement for its irrelevance to any real data, Deutsch sees such illogical statements as the goal of his inquiry: "It's not a stupid statement!" he told me, banging his hand on his borrowed designer desk. "It is literally

prelinguistic. Noncontingent on any attributes—it cannot be justified even by the person who holds the opinion. Everything else
just falls away. What I'm trying to do is understand the subjec-
tivity of the audience in its full complexity and contradiction and
illogic."

Once Deutsch has discovered the emotional core of his audience's mythology, he can begin to construct what he calls the
"grand narrative," the overriding story of the group in relation
to the subject being studied. It is the framework they use to organize their perception of the world. Because such mythologies are
emotionally based and devoid of rationality, they are particularly vulnerable to reengineering from the outside.

While Deutsch limits such engineering to clever advertising
campaigns (he came up with the "Q" campaign for Compaq
based on his insight that computer users value good questions
more than the "solutions" offered by IBM's marketers), others
hope to capitalize on our irrational beliefs for much bolder efforts. Take the following anecdote as an example: "I volunteered
at the al-Addan hospital. . . . I saw the Iraqi soldiers come into
the hospital with guns, and go into the room where fifteen babies were in incubators. They took the babies out of the incubators, took the incubators, and left the babies on the cold floor
to die."

Does that story sound familiar? It was offered as testimony to
the House Human Rights Caucus by a fifteen-year-old Kuwaiti
girl, first known only as Nayirah. Presented in late 1990, the
story helped the United States muster domestic support for its
entrance into the Gulf War. The incubator tale made the headlines and evening-news shows across the nation. The never-
photographed image of Kuwaiti babies being hauled from their
incubators has stayed with us to this day.

Less known, of course, is that the anonymous fifteen-year-old

Kuwaiti girl presenting the American people with this arresting image was the daughter of Sheikh Saud Nasir al-Sabah, Kuwait's ambassador to the United States. The girl's story, which has subsequently proven impossible to corroborate, was prepared by a public-relations firm called Hill & Knowlton as part of an $11 million campaign financed by the Kuwaiti government.[3] (Though the firm has since apologized for and distanced itself from the campaign, it still demonstrates their mastery of the coercive story.)

What better image to select for the American public than babies being ripped from their incubators? In the early 1990s, abortion was even more of a hot-button issue than it is today. Further, television news surveys have shown that the abuse or death of first-world babies is the most compelling story one can broadcast. If the fifteen-year-old had told us that babies had been taken from their homes, they still might have seemed foreign to the American public. Kuwait is an Arab country whose customs are unknown to us. We might have imagined the babies living in primitive stone huts or tents. By depicting them in incubators, Hill & Knowlton made the babies seem not only more helpless but more like members of the technologically advanced West. The image also resonated with an American public who feared that its own technological superiority—largely a product of a free-flowing supply of oil from the Middle East—was threatened by Arab barbarians.

Once we were fully engaged in the Gulf War, the Bush administration adopted slogans and symbols designed to stifle reasoned debate. As if following the CIA manual's suggestions for smoothing over dissonance with easy slogans, Bush's public-relations people created meaningless mottoes specifically crafted to replace thought with emotion. The response to any question about the appropriateness of our military action was reduced to

"Support our troops." Do we support our troops? Well, of course we do. They are our sons and daughters—but that's not the point. As Noam Chomsky explained:

> Support our troops. Who can be against that? Or yellow ribbons. Who can be against that? The issue was, Do you support our policy? But you don't want people to think about that issue. That's the whole point of good propaganda. You want to create a slogan that nobody's going to be against, and everybody's going to be for. Nobody knows what it means because it doesn't mean anything. Its crucial value is that it diverts your attention from a question that *does* mean something: Do you support our policy? That's the one you're not allowed to talk about. So you have people arguing about support for the troops? "Of course I don't *not* support them." Then you've won.[4]

Public-relations efforts of this kind amount to a systematic assault on our ability to make rational decisions. The idea is to blur any real policies in emotional platitudes or in evocative storytelling, based on research into the target group's mostly unconscious triggers. This is a delicate science, and it can easily backfire.

"PR is bullshit," Deutsch told me when I pressed him for information about how his own work might be applied by governments. "It's a very short-term deal and it's superficial. I don't know how to do public relations. I'm not that smart." Perhaps no one is.

Hill & Knowlton's efforts at promoting the Gulf War worked in the short run but ultimately served only to confuse Americans when George Bush refused to "finish" the war and kill Saddam Hussein. When the press revealed Nariyah to be an ambassador's daughter and the majority of domestic coverage as having been spun by Hill & Knowlton, America's relationship to the Gulf War and its propaganda abruptly changed. The public-relations firm's reputation was irreparably compromised.

Stung by the bitter lessons of tinkering with a public's mythologies, public-relations experts have found a new cloak for their emotional arguments: facts and figures. By appearing to remove themselves from the influence equation, they create the illusion that they are simply telling us how it is. In this way, they can make the irrational seem rational.

Figuring in the Facts

Although America was founded on the principle that public opinion should dictate public policy, the polling of citizens' responses to proposed policies has become a way of manipulating rather than acting on the collective will.

Beginning in the late 1930s, several companies dedicated to monitoring public opinion were formed in America, bringing about a kind of merger of the fields of psychology, business, and politics. Since then, these companies have provided research to political candidates, corporations, and special interests. Although they appear to be conducting research and analysis of our opinions in order to shape policies according to our beliefs, the true policies and economic goals of these interests remain unchanged by what they learn about us. The results of these studies merely serve to alter the way corporate or government policy is packaged.

For example, most corporations understand by now that Americans are concerned about their environment. While chemical and waste-management industries would like to see legislation allowing them to dump toxic materials with fewer costly regulations, it is not in their interest to disclose this desire to a

public that, when polled, clearly opposes such practices. By renaming their trade and lobby groups, or creating CIA-style
"front organizations," environmentally unfriendly industries
take the first step to changing public perception.

The sewage industry's main public-relations organization, for
one, formerly called Federation of Sewage Works Associations,
went through several "greenings" of its name until it emerged in
1960 as the Water Pollution Control Federation. Today, it is
called the Water Environment Federation.

Likewise, when public-relations firms realize that we are absolutely opposed to their clients' policies, they simply rename the
policies to reflect the opposite intention or effect. Dozens of
Clean Water acts sent to voters in referendums around the
United States in the 1990s were actually sponsored by chemical
companies and industries looking to *loosen* the regulations on
their toxic-waste dumping and land use.

The book *Toxic Sludge Is Good for You!*, by public-relations
watchdogs John Stauber and Sheldon Rampton, chronicles the
process by which the Water Environment Federation worked to
quell growing criticism about its practice of spreading potentially toxic sludge on farmland.[5] The Federation conducted a
contest among its members to come up with a friendlier name
for sludge. In 1991, the Federation's "Name Change Task
Force" adopted the term "biosolids," which it defines as the
"nutrient-rich organic byproduct of the nation's wastewater
treatment process." This wordplay paved the way for a revision
of the standards by which sludge could be applied to farmlands.
What had been known previously as toxic sludge and deemed
too dangerous to be disposed of even in a regulated sanitary
landfill could now be dumped freely on farmland, without a
whimper of public outcry. Deceptive renaming is not limited to
environmental referendums. The infamous California Civil
Rights Initiative was a proposition designed to end affirmative

action and special programs for recruiting women and minorities in that state.

Policymakers and their public-relations firms also use polling and demographic research to fight laws that threaten their interests. Through telephone surveys and focus groups, they identify lingering and perhaps unexpressed anxiety about proposed bills. Then they find facts and data that amplify these objections, which can be used to attack a policy just as easily as support one.

The battle against the Clinton health-care-reform package, waged by the pharmaceutical and insurance industries, was an example of this kind of campaign. Borrowing a technique from the CIA manual on guerilla warfare, the firms fighting the bill recruited spokespeople who normally would be considered the chief beneficiaries and allies of health-care reformers, including the homeless and Vietnam veterans. Meanwhile, focus groups conducted by an insurance-industry front group revealed that the main vulnerability in Clinton's proposition was its use of the phrase "mandatory health alliances." The group promptly named itself The Coalition for Health Insurance Choices and launched a series of television ads called "Harry and Louise," in which a middle-aged couple lamented the impending loss of choice that such a "mandatory" set of alliances would cost them.

To create the illusion of a public outcry against the plan, the coalition sponsored advertisements on Rush Limbaugh's radio show, where listeners were told they could call a toll-free 800 number for more information about the dangers of the plan. As Stauber and Rampton explain,

> Calling the number would connect them to a telemarketer, who would talk to them briefly and then patch them through directly to their congressperson's office. The con-

gressional staffers fielding the calls typically had no idea that the constituents had been primed, loaded, aimed, and fired at them by radio ads on the Limbaugh show, paid [for] by the insurance industry, with the goal of orchestrating the appearance of overwhelming grassroots opposition to health reform.

Members of Congress are not the only people subjected to slanted presentations of public opinion. Many of the polls we read about in the daily papers are sponsored by special interests with the express purpose of leading, not reflecting, public opinion. Just like spectacles, opinion polls work to stimulate a crowd mentality. When we learn what other people are thinking—or are led to believe what other people are thinking—we tend to follow along.

Pollsters have a vested interest in generating survey results that support the people who pay them. While most reputable polling organizations do not fabricate results, they have instead developed sophisticated methods of gathering information so that they don't have to. If a survey doesn't come out quite the way they wanted it to, they'll adjust their questions slightly and take another poll. Once they've got the answers they want, they send the results to a public-relations firm for dissemination.

When the United States Treasury considered eliminating the penny from the monetary system in the 1970s, for example, a poll mysteriously showed up in local newspapers across the country announcing that Americans wanted to keep the penny. Of course, the Gallup survey showing sixty-two percent of respondents in favor of the penny was sponsored by the zinc industry, and then distributed as a press release to papers looking for quirky, human-interest stories—especially those backed by "hard" research that can masquerade as news.

Further aiding the pollsters and their clients, newspapers often allow survey results to shape their perspective on a story. Confronted with a press release announcing popular support for the penny, no papers wrote headlines denouncing the fact that their own readers were clinging to inefficient and costly coinage. Most didn't even report how the same poll revealed that, without even being informed of the penny's expensive legacy, more than one-third of Americans were already willing to get rid of it for good. Instead, falling prey to the influence techniques of the pollster, the people who are paid to be our first line of defense against misinformation wrote heartwarming pieces about America's curious love affair with the copper-colored darling.

Pollsters have many methods for generating the results they want—the most common and obvious technique being to stack the group sampled. The White House, for example, often determines the popularity of a presidential decision on the basis of calls to the switchboard. As Cynthia Crossen explains in her book, *Tainted Truth,* Richard Nixon announced to the press in 1972 that calls to the White House were five to one in favor of his orders to mine North Vietnamese ports.[6] To earn these favorable numbers, however, White House operators registered favorable calls immediately but put those opposed to the policy on hold for up to twenty minutes, making them wait for someone to record their opinion.

Pollsters have also conducted extensive research into the ways wording can affect their results. In a classic 1950s experiment studying survey methodology, subjects were asked two questions: "Do you think the United States should let Russian newspaper reporters come here and send back whatever they want?" and "Do you think Russia should let American newspaper reporters come in and send back whatever they want?" If only the first question were asked, only thirty-six percent answered that they thought the United States should allow Russian reporters into the country. If they were asked about U.S. reporters being let into Russia first, a sense of fairness seeped into their second answers. The number of people responding that Russian reporters should be allowed into the U.S. doubled to seventy-three percent.

As a result of such studies, today's pollsters are quite proficient at producing leading questions and then ordering them for maximum results. For example, as Crossen reveals, a mail-in questionnaire in *TV Guide* asked the question "Should the president have the Line Item Veto to eliminate waste?" Ninety-seven percent of respondents answered yes. When the response group was selected randomly instead of being limited to mail-in volunteers, the percentage in favor reduced to seventy-one percent. When the question was changed to the less leading "Should the president have the Line Item Veto, or not?" only fifty-seven percent of the respondents said yes. The language of the original survey gave the subject a reason to respond favorably to the question.

No matter how aware we think we are of these tactics, most of us trust polls more than we do any other source of information. According to Professor Benjamin Ginsberg of Cornell, when polling data conflicts with other news sources, we tend to question the credibility of the other sources. A good poll is worth more than an eyewitness account.

Most destructively, polls change the ways we think about our own considered opinions. When news agencies conduct polls during and immediately after important speeches and debates, they are subtly suggesting to us that we should be capable of forming opinions that quickly. In many polls, "undecided" is not a possible response. Often, pollsters for political candidates are told to pressure undecided respondents to say how they lean. We are supposed to have opinions about everything, all the time.

Ultimately, public opinion becomes more malleable. Instead of taking the time to make reasoned responses based on the issues, we are encouraged to make snap decisions on an emotional level. Who *won* the debate is certainly less important than who, based on his or her policies and capabilities, we think is a better candidate for office. As so many people in and out of the media have complained, incessant polling reduces the election process to a horse race. Worse, it pulls our attention away from the issues underlying our decisions, and trains us to make choices based on no real information at all. The preponderance of negative advertising, smear campaigns, and emotional appeals with little substantive content all work because we have been conditioned to believe our instinctual reactions are what matter most.

Often, only weeks or months after a poll is taken does anything close to what we can call genuine "public opinion" emerge. During the Clarence Thomas confirmation hearings, for instance, polls indicated that the American public thought Anita Hill was lying about her allegations against the judge. Senator Arlen Specter and others trusted these results enough to berate her during her testimony and to remark to the press that they thought she was lying. A year later, polls indicated that most Americans thought she was telling the truth all along. And the senators who had based their conduct during the hearings on misleading surveys were left to face their own withering poll results.

Although the public tends to trust polls of its own opinions more than the opinions of the pundits, firms that simply cannot find polling data to support their claims sometimes do better to buy their facts from respected institutions. In a controversial move, the American Medical Association, in dire need of funds for its antismoking campaigns, sold Sunbeam Corporation the exclusive right to put the AMA seal on its medical equipment in 1997. With the AMA anticipating royalties in the millions of dollars, their endorsement marks a departure from their long-standing refusal to lend its name to specific products. Similarly, the American Cancer Society accepts an annual fee of a million dollars from the Florida Orange Growers Association for its exclusive certification of orange juice. When questioned by *Time* magazine about the controversial endorsement, a Cancer Society spokesman explained that the exclusive certification was meant to serve only as "an example of the kinds of foods [found] in a healthy diet."[7] While both Sunbeam and the Florida Orange Growers Association might truly offer healthy products, their ability to garner the exclusive official support of these respected organizations has more to do with boosting sales than with medical reality.

Corporations also pay respected institutions to underwrite research claims about their products. "Oat bran reduces cholesterol levels" is such an accepted fact that Quaker Oats has earned the right to publicize it on oatmeal boxes. It should come as little surprise that much of the research "proving" the benefits of oat consumption has been sponsored by Quaker Oats. Still, the names on these studies—paid for with research dollars— were enough to lend Quaker Oats's press releases the credibility it needed: "Landmark Study Published in *Journal of the American Medical Association* Confirms Cholesterol Reduction Benefit of Oat Products in Diet." Or, as *USA Today* translated it: "Oat Bran Does Cut Cholesterol."

Today, even schools are looking for support from corporations, in spite of the sponsors' often dubious agendas. Television is piped into the classroom, complete with commercials for sport shoes and other products. The energy, chemical, and pharmaceutical industries donate "curriculums" to public schools desperate for materials. These free textbooks and lesson plans invariably take the form of thinly veiled public-relations efforts. As concerned parents and teachers successfully deconstruct these corporate schemes, industry publications suggest more sophisticated methods of camouflage. Editors at *Plastics News* warned their industry in 1995 that when a company chooses to develop an education package, management should "read it with a critical eye, exactly the way your competition, cynical parents, and some teachers will study it. If you don't, and your program ends up as an example of naked corporate promotionalism on the 6 o'clock news, then your effort will have caused more damage than it sought to correct."[8]

As today's public-relations experts understand, the preponderance of investigative journalism, as well as the emergence of interactive media on the Internet, has made it hard to base a campaign on assertions that aren't true or on motives that aren't earnest. Just as misleading polls work only until a genuine public opinion coalesces, unfounded scientific claims stand only until our insight, or the evidence, refutes them. Good information has a way of floating to the surface, sooner or later.

The Truth Wins Out

My first ever public-relations consultation involved just such a futile effort to fight the facts. I had been hired to give a talk at a conference in Europe, where major corporations hoped to learn about the effect of new media on their businesses. It was early in my speaking career, and I was so shocked when I saw the price of the first-class ticket they'd sent me that I decided to cash it in and fly coach.

After my talk, I was approached by a stern, middle-aged European man. He handed me his card: He was a vice president of the airline on which I had flown. I was sure I had been discovered and began to apologize profusely for greedily exchanging my ticket for cash. He stopped me, saying that he had no idea what I was talking about. He wanted to know if I could stay over in Europe just one more day, to do a brief consultation for

his airline, which was on the brink of an "Internet crisis." He
would be happy to pay me for my trouble and upgrade my return ticket to business class—"a nonrefundable upgrade," he
added.

He wouldn't give me any details about the consultation, so I
spent the night brushing up on my "new media will revolution-
ize the world" sound bites. The next morning I reported, as instructed, to a conference room at the airport hotel. I was
promptly handed a three-page nondisclosure agreement, which I
signed before anyone said a word. This job was beginning to feel
spooky. I got the sense that my optimistic platitudes about Internet culture were not what these folks were after.

A young woman in a business suit spoke first.

"As you may know, we are currently in contract negotiations
with our pilots."

I explained to her and the seven other executives that I didn't.
She went on.

"As a point of leverage," she said in oddly constructed English, "the pilots are threatening to use the World Wide Web."

"Can you tell us what that is?" a thick-accented older man
asked.

I proceeded to explain what the Internet and the Web are. As I
spoke, the young woman translated what I was saying for the
non-English speakers. I slowed down to give her time to translate after each sentence.

"You may speak naturally," she said. Amazingly, she could
translate in real time. I began to feel that I was more interested
in hearing my own words being instantaneously converted into
another language than the assembled suits were in listening to
my diatribe about the tremendous promise of an interactive
global mediaspace. When I was through, one of the non-English
speakers nodded for the woman to say something.

"The pilots claim that through the World Wide Web," she

continued, "they can publish stories and statistics intended to scare our customers about flight safety."

I remained silent as all eyes turned toward me.

"We want to know, can they do this?" she asked.

"Well," I stumbled, "the Web is a publishing medium. It wouldn't take much to put that kind of information, if they have it, onto a Web site."

"But how many people see this World Wide Web?" the vice president who invited me asked.

"A lot," I answered. "A couple of million, maybe." This was back in the early nineties. "But that's not the issue," I continued. "Once it's on the Web, that's a big enough story for other media to cover. The TV news would definitely cover a story like that. More people would see it on TV in a single night than would ever find the Web site."

They weren't happy with my response. I looked down.

"Isn't there a way to use the Internet to stop them?" the young woman asked me.

"The Internet's better at spreading information than censoring it," I admitted. I wondered if I was going to earn my free upgrade after all.

"Well, then," another of the businessmen began, "how do you handle this sort of situation on your Internet?"

"These things these pilots plan to say," I posed gently, "are they true?"

No one said anything.

"Maybe you better think about why your pilots feel so strongly about the way they are being treated that they'd be willing to wage such an attack."

"But can't you tell us anything as a media consultant?" the vice president asked. "You seem to understand the way the Internet works."

"I would if I could," I said, unsure if that were really true.

"You might try to find the figures on other airlines and show that your airline isn't any worse. But that wouldn't make you any friends. Or you could anonymously post false accusations about your own airline that you later prove are incorrect, so that people assume the other charges are false, too. But that would probably backfire. You'd better just find out what it is the pilots want and give it to them."

As I flew back to New York, I wasn't sure whether I should be happy that I was unable and unwilling to help a huge corporation thwart its workers' efforts at media terrorism, or embarrassed that I took their money for doing nothing. Still, I didn't think the old crisis pro himself, Howard Rubenstein, would have handled the situation much differently.

"I've advised a lot of clients to settle right away," Rubenstein reassured me after I recounted the airline incident. "We've had maybe twenty sexual-harassment cases. Big ones. And I ask the same questions: Did you do it? What kind of policy does your organization have? Do you adhere to it? Do you educate people on it? And usually it's no. And then they make all kinds of excuses. But if the women who are accusing these big companies went out to the Internet and searched for others, or used it to publicize? God help some of those companies! [Especially] if they had a pattern of abuse!"

As Rubenstein is well aware, the Internet and cable television networks have emerged as the media's great equalizer. "Maybe twenty years ago the intensity of the media coverage was far less," he says of his early days in PR. "In a few days the scandal would pass. They (the people or companies in trouble) usually went underground and didn't say anything. There were no worldwide networks . . . You didn't get the pickup the way you do today. Today, your strategy has to understand that if you are in a prominent, difficult, or important situation, almost everyone in the world will have an opportunity to hear or see or read about it. And anything anyone says is questioned."

Rubenstein insists he never changed his fundamental strategy of telling the painful truth and moving on: "I've always found that telling the truth, even if it harms you to some extent, even if it dents you, is the right thing to do." But he has had to increase the sophistication with which he enacts his truth campaigns to match the sophistication of the modern, new-media audience.

The Rubenstein technique has become such a prevalent defense in crises from political sex scandals to airplane crashes that today most of the public is more fascinated by the way these stories are spun than by the stories themselves. Movies like *Wag the Dog*, in which a film producer stages a war to distract the American public from a president's sexual indiscretion, have turned the spin doctor's art into entertainment. Like sports fans, we watch to see if the spin doctor can successfully reinvent his disgraced client.

The Marv Albert sex scandal typified this extremely self-conscious reaction to spin control. After pleading guilty to unsolicited sexual biting, the sportscaster held a penitent press conference. Over the next week, he appeared on a wide range of television shows, each with a slightly different purpose. "Albert's tour of Sweeps Week talk and morning shows was, in fact, a revealing cross-section of the state of TV talk, circa 1997," noted the *Buffalo News* in just one of the many articles taking America's awareness of spin tactics for granted.[9] Albert chose the obsequious Barbara Walters for his coming out (although co-anchor Hugh Downs, protesting the machinations of Marv's spin, refused to appear on the show). Marv went on Larry King and David Letterman and finally worked his way up to the "Today" show with Katie Couric, who, by refusing to accept his pat answers, proved the most difficult of his interviewers.

Such appearances matter to the shows that book them. Hugh Grant's post-arrest appearance with Jay Leno was responsible for pushing the NBC talk-show host ahead of his rival, David Letterman. Marv Albert raised Larry King's ratings thirty percent above normal.

But nowhere, except in the courtroom, did Albert admit his guilt. On TV he denied almost everything, and sought to diminish the incident's significance. He did not make himself part of a new story—he merely attempted to extricate himself from the story in which he had already been cast. He sought to make up for his lack of remorse with a string of appearances, and it didn't work. Newspapers complained that Albert hadn't waited long enough to create the illusion of penitence. Others attacked Albert's frequency and selection of appearances. Even his hired gun, Howard Rubenstein, attempted to distance himself from the rehabilitation tour. When asked about Albert's "volume" strategy, Rubenstein told *The New York Times,* "He wanted to tell his story fully and quickly. He's overexposing himself for a week, then you won't hear him talk about this again."[10] Asked if he had counseled Albert to use this approach, Rubenstein simply replied, "No comment."

So Marv Albert had cast himself in a new story after all: the story of his own efforts at spin control. He created a story even more compelling than that of a sports announcer wearing women's panties and biting his lover's back—that of a sports announcer fighting to correct this impression through spin control—and in a way created a new strategy for our PR-saturated times. Marv Albert, already more a media personality than a real one, was attempting to return home, and the strategy finally paid off. A year later, he earned himself an anchor spot on a new sports show.

President Clinton employed a similar strategy in his television

campaign to depict himself as a victim of Republican conspirators and the diminished privacy that all Americans face today. It
was a smart defense, as far as traditional public relations was
concerned, exploiting a festering grand narrative about our own
loss of privacy in a seemingly totalitarian age of new media. But
however insightful Clinton and his advisors were about using
television, they were utterly unprepared for the corrosive impact
of the Internet on traditional spin-doctoring.

Clinton's presidency marked the high point and, arguably, the
end of TV's dominance over the political process. Indeed, the
moment that secured Bill Clinton's first bid for the presidency
against incumbent George Bush was a perfectly executed TV
talk-show maneuver. During the famous "Oprah-style" debate,
a black woman from the audience questioned Bush about his
personal relationship to the experiences of the impoverished. He
didn't understand the question.

Clinton seized on the opportunity to demonstrate his comfort
with real Americans and their chosen media forum. He spoke directly with the woman, sharing her pain and crossing so far into
the audience that the TV cameras had to shoot him from behind.
He broke the invisible "fourth wall" of the TV set and walked
into our homes. By contrast, Bush nervously checked his wrist-
watch, as if wishing for the show to end.

Similarly, Clinton's media handiwork when reacting to scandal has always been aimed at the sensibility of the television audience. His "60 Minutes" appearance with wife Hillary, for
example, in which he took charge of the explosive tabloid story
about his affair with Gennifer Flowers, returned him to the active protagonist's role in a narrative that could have otherwise
unraveled his campaign. According to Bob Deutsch, it was this
commanding appearance alone that set Clinton apart from the
pack of contenders for the Democratic nomination. The strategy

was so successful, in fact, that it became the default spin procedure for sex offenders from Michael Jackson to Frank Gifford: Go on TV with your better half.

But Clinton's campaigns both before and during his presidency were specifically pre-Internet in design and character. While Ross Perot campaigned for "teledemocracy" and "virtual town halls," Clinton played the sax on late-night TV, jogged for the camera, and swapped press secretaries based on their telegenics. His interactive-media policies, on the other hand, were characterized by embargoes on encryption technology, the V-chip, and federal "back doors" on privacy programs. Clearly, he thought of the Internet and its culture as something that could be contained.

Neither Clinton nor his once cooperative cohorts in the mainstream entertainment industry's "news" magazines had any inkling that the Internet would upstage their own coverage and ultimately thwart their ability to regulate what news content was fit to print. Matt Drudge's Web scandal sheet broke the Monica Lewinsky story while editors at *Time* and *Newsweek* were sorting out the ramifications of revealing the president's escapades. (Just a few weeks earlier, Clinton had graced *Time* magazine's star-studded Seventy-fifth Anniversary Gala in New York, garnering the glossy some much-needed prestige and TV exposure. How dare they bite the hand that fed them?)

As more sordid details surfaced, only the Drudge Report, *Salon,* and other Web sites saw fit to publish them—that is, until Gingrich and the Republicans released the entire Starr report, also on the Internet. The text itself, depicting the graphic realities of this perverse presidential performance, would have been outlawed by the administration-supported Computer Decency Act, and may never have worked its way onto television uncensored were it not for the Internet leading the way.

Throughout these revelations, Clinton sought to stave off disaster by tinkering with public perception rather than following the Rubenstein credo of apologizing completely, visibly correcting the error, and then moving on. Using a tactic that seemed to work so effectively for so long, Clinton simply prevented the story of his own demise from gaining momentum. After a single denial ("I did not have sex with that woman, Monica Lewinsky"), he refused all comment on the allegations, preventing a media chess game from taking place and depriving the many news shows covering the scandal of food for analysis. It was the antinarrative technique.

Meanwhile, television helped to humanize Clinton as it always had. When Congress released the tape of Clinton's Grand Jury testimony, media pundits incorrectly predicted that the broadcast would destroy what was left of the president's public image. On the contrary, the portrait of a fatigued president fighting for his political life against an off-screen interrogator evoked grand narrative archetypes of inquisitorial priests and police interrogators. The audience only identified further with the struggling victim.

Dedicated to TV-style crisis management, Clinton ordered frequent polls to help him decide whether or not to tell the truth about Lewinsky and his cover-up, as if adjusting his ongoing performance to an ever-present Nielsen meter. But where TV promoted the theatrical humanity of our lawmakers, the Internet injects politics with a dose of truth serum. Clinton might have avoided impeachment had he listened to what Howard Rubenstein has been saying all along: "In a crisis, you have to focus on the true grit of the situation."

If Rubenstein is correct, the evasive and distorting tactics of traditional public-relations campaigns have been rendered obsolete by the preponderance of nonaffiliated media outlets and communications technologies. Those who ignore the new-media terrain do so at their own risk.

"I think Hill and Knowlton learned a lesson from what they did," Rubenstein explains candidly. "The lesson is not to do it. Sure, people come to you and say, 'Let's set up a committee and we'll call it so-and-so, and we'll hire someone to run it,' and my attitude is: What's known is known. Simple. What is known gets published. So it's foolhardy to set up a fig-leaf committee and hope nobody will look under the fig leaf and see what's there."

Similarly, according to Rubenstein, the exploitation of story and narrative will have diminishing or even destructive returns once the truth inevitably surfaces: "When a story is in motion, you can't think for a minute that the elements won't be picked up on by the media, analyzed, and disclosures made. No guru can come in and say, 'Here's a silver bullet and you'll get through this.' It doesn't work that way anymore."

Clinton and others who depend too heavily on traditional public-relations tactics have vastly underestimated the impact of new media on our access to information. More perilous, they have ignored the way the Internet encourages us to think for ourselves. New media undermines our naïve acceptance of the television image, diminishes our dependence on stories and pat answers, and leads us to value raw data over expert opinions and their skewed interpretations.

Good public-relations specialists have voluntarily abandoned their most coercive styles in this environment, opting to work as best they can with the truth as it exists or as it can be altered. Advertising agencies, on the other hand, whose work hasn't had anything to do with real-world facts for half a century, have proved much more eager to retool their techniques for the interactive age and its interactive audience.

CHAPTER FIVE

Advertising

Customers need a rational excuse to justify
their emotional decisions. So always include one.

—*David Ogilvy*

The new headquarters of Wells BDDP still smelled like paint, glaze, and putty. The advertising agency, formerly known as Wells, Rich, Greene, had just moved in the fall of 1997 to the twelfth floor of a landmark building at the base of Madison Avenue, and no expense was being spared to bring the firm's image into the highly competitive twenty-first century.

The walls were adorned with the latest high-concept art. Frosted-glass doors discreetly hid rows of conference rooms outfitted with racks of high-end video gear and flat-screen displays. Long corridors opened into huge atriums furnished with bright leather couches, hefty wooden end tables, and boldly upholstered chairs—no two the same.

At the same time, this manic obsession with detail and design struck me as just one clue that the agency, and perhaps the entire industry, was in trouble. Caught between a desire to look hip and a need to appear authoritative, advertising seemed in the midst of an identity crisis.

"We call this 'The Well,'" explained Douglas Atkin, the agency's debonair head of planning as he escorted me through a colossal, loftlike gallery overlooking downtown. This part of the office space was the architect's accommodation to the firm's creative function and image. A grand piano and a butcher-block coffee bar served as bookends to an area where Wells executives hoped that young copywriters and graphic designers could brainstorm their latest campaigns in a social, freeform atmosphere. Flexible spaces like these came into vogue in the eighties as firms used kindergarten-style floor plans to lead their employees (and their clients) to believe in the playful, spontaneous intellectual process this untraditional architecture was supposed to engender. Now they were an expected feature of an agency's floor plan. If you didn't have at least one such open space, it meant you were behind the times. BDDP's plans also called for a curved wall to be built around one side of The Well to separate the greater space from the agency's main conference room. Originally, this wall was to be transparent, but management decided that a more opaque surface would allow for greater discretion.

On this early autumn afternoon, no one could have imagined that by the time that wall's construction would be finished, the firm would be, too. Who would believe that such a fate would befall what had once been New York's vanguard agency? With Mary Wells at the agency's helm through the 1960s and 1970s, Wells, Rich, Greene had been responsible for some of the most innovative advertising that Madison Avenue had ever seen. The agency once enlisted surrealist Salvador Dali for a daring Alka-Seltzer television commercial in which the artist painted the effervescent medicine's passage through the human body directly onto the skin of a female model.

Although Wells had retired long ago to an island chateau in

Europe, and the agency had subsequently suffered an embarrassing bout of setbacks, by the late nineties Wells BDDP—the added letters signifying a merger with a respected European network—was back on the fast track to an altogether new run of glory days. And their newest partner, Douglas Atkin, was widely held to be a man who could not only revitalize this agency but whose techniques could help stimulate the creative energy of an entire industry.

He had his work cut out for him. For two decades, cable television had been drawing viewers away from broadcast programs and the commercials that sponsored them. Network television ratings were down, even though the cost of advertising minutes had gone up. As a result, big business had started to sour on advertising in general. Many companies were turning instead to direct marketing, special promotions, in-store displays, sports sponsorships, and tie-ins with other products. To make matters worse, budget cuts and heavy competition had led many companies to bring their advertising in-house. They could no longer justify the huge sums Madison Avenue charged to conduct esoteric research and devise sophisticated ad campaigns. Besides, what could an advertising agency possibly tell Nike it didn't already know about sport shoes and their wearers?

Atkin, a tall, bald British man in his early forties with a regal countenance, was imported by Wells to the United States in the hope that his new discipline of account planning would systematize the process by which market and consumer research is converted into an actual campaign. In traditional advertising, the account executives deal with clients, while the creatives develop the copy. Account planners arose to serve as an interface between the two disciplines, translating the clients' needs into specific propositions for the agency's creatives, and then backing the agency's resulting proposals with research from the field. Although copywriters and graphic designers execute the creative work, the account planners are responsible for igniting the initial spark and, of course, convincing clients that their agency's insights will translate into market leadership.

To Atkin, account planning means coming up with a set of reusable tools that can be applied to any number of different campaigns. By developing a language to codify the creative process in a series of off-the-shelf advertising strategies, Atkin hoped to arm Wells BDDP with the resources it needed to compete effectively in a shrinking marketplace and, perhaps, even restore the role of the advertising agency as the preeminent source of consumer research and media know-how. His success would be an affirmation of the effectiveness of advertising above all other kinds of marketing.

To this end, Atkin brought in high-priced experts from fields normally considered tangential to the advertising arts. Young account planners flocked to the agency, both to work with Atkin and to take part in the graduate-school-like atmosphere he created. He hired anthropologist Bob Deutsch to conduct focus groups and share new methods of analysis, a systems theorist named Sally Goerner to teach his staff about the wonders of chaos math, and, in the fall of 1997, me, to reverse-engineer the concept of the media virus (as I'd outlined it in a book by the same name) into a step-by-step procedure for disseminating ideas through the mediaspace.

As I strolled through the unfinished offices of Wells BDDP with Atkin, advertising no longer seemed to me like a coercive attack on an unsuspecting public, but more like an art form struggling for its life. Atkin didn't appear to me to have a coercive bone in his body. By joining his ranks, I felt I would be participating in the evolution of an ongoing dialogue between brands and consumers.

What I didn't realize was that Atkin had been shielding those of us who worked with him from the harsh realities of his industry. The research we were having so much fun conducting—how people get into a cult, or the psychology of ordering a beer—also needed to yield results. In the short term, this meant convincing clients that the millions of dollars being spent on their behalfs would result in breakthrough campaigns capable of reaching consumers on an entirely new level. In the long term, it meant either generating noticeably higher sales or losing accounts to other agencies.

On my first real consulting day at Wells, I attended a crisis meeting for the Amstel Beers account. The campaign that Atkin had conceived for the company's new line of non-"light" products wasn't working. Atkin's Garrison Boyd campaign was the result of months of research. Costly focus groups had revealed that most Americans associate Amsterdam, the city where Amstel is produced, with open-mindedness. The problem with marketing a brand on the open-mindedness platform, however, was that everyone has a different idea of what it means. About ninety percent of those polled like to think of themselves as open-minded, but each respondent saw his own open-mindedness as reflecting a different set of social values. One man's open-mindedness was another's conservatism, and vice-versa.

Atkin's challenge was to help the Amstel brand claim the concept of open-mindedness—the way Nike had claimed individual achievement or Levi's had taken authenticity—without ever defining precisely what open-mindedness is. Research had determined that the beer's target market is college-educated adults between the ages of twenty-one and thirty-four, with incomes of more than $40,000, who enjoy active lifestyles. According to the agency's original written proposal to Amstel, the target was "the kind of person who would say, 'I don't necessarily want to cross-dress, but if someone else does, it's fine with me.' They are somewhat rebellious and dislike being told what to do. They like to do the opposite of what authority figures tell them to do."

How to communicate open-mindedness to such a group? They don't want to be lectured to—they are too sophisticated for that. Besides, they are a rebellious bunch. There lay the account planner's creative spark: Convince by contrast. Use reverse psychology.

Atkin's staff came up with the curmudgeonly character of Garrison Boyd—a bespectacled old man in a plain gray suit who despises open-mindedness as well as everything else from Amsterdam. As founder of the fictitious organization Americans for Disciplined Behavior, Boyd took it on himself to combat Amstel's recent "attacks" on American decency by placing bumper stickers and posters on top of regular Amstel billboards, with slogans like: "Resist the Amstels from Amsterdam" and "Shield your eyes!"

Meanwhile, this campaign would exploit the new, mutant media of which Atkin was such a fan. Familiar with the rules I had set out in *Media Virus,* Atkin understood that advertising that has the seeds of a media story within it will generate interest and, in turn, more media. Who was Garrison Boyd? Why was he attacking Amstel's billboards? About thirty percent of the people who saw the advertisements thought they were real and that Garrison Boyd represented a legitimate but misguided group of ultra-conservatives attacking an imported beer. But the ads generated even more excitement among those who "got" it. Who paid to advertise *against* one's own brand? *The New York Times* and MSNBC ran stories about the bizarre campaign, which in turn led to more media coverage, and so on.

What Wells BDDP counted on was that creating a story "with legs," as public-relations people like to say, would be the most efficient way to spread its message. The news media can carry your campaign along for you if it's novel enough, and the Amstel campaign would cost only about a fifth of what most competitors were spending on new-product launches. But although TV awareness of the brand had quadrupled, and radio awareness grew by a factor of eighteen, all this awareness hadn't yet translated into sales—which is why the Amstel campaign was now in a crisis.

The account executive who had worked with Amstel parent Heineken's brand manager for years claimed he never liked the Garrison Boyd strategy to begin with. The adman was a relic from an earlier age and saw in Atkin everything that was destroying his business: research and creativity at the expense of schmoozing and salesmanship.

I was invited to the meeting to help refine the Garrison Boyd campaign. I made a lengthy presentation to the agency that morning about media viruses and chaotic systems. How would I put this idea into practice more effectively with Boyd? I was asked. I was intrigued that a real campaign had made use of my abstract theories, and I strove to explain why it hadn't yet sold more beer.

"Boyd is a great viral shell," I explained, "but there's no content inside him." Wrapped around any great media virus, there is a provocative outer casing or "shell" of media. For the Rodney King media virus, it was the camcorder tape of the man being beaten. The story spread because the camcorder had been used in a brand new way. The videocassette *was* the initial story. The Boyd campaign's mock-guerilla style certainly satisfied the shell requirement. By breaking the rules of media, they had caused a sensation. But unlike the Rodney King virus, Boyd had no ideas—no ideological "code" within his shell. The Rodney King tape, once disseminated, released potent images of police brutality and provoked discussions and rage. By avoiding the specific kinds of open-mindedness that Boyd was protesting—marijuana use? free sex? cross-dressing?—the Garrison Boyd virus had no ability to stir people up once they had taken notice. I suggested the agency take a gamble and instill its virus with some real content.

Atkin seemed interested in my proposal, but before we could even discuss it, the surly account executive stopped the conversation dead.

"We have to kill Boyd," he insisted. "I agreed to him before," he admitted as if he had been convinced against his better judgment, "but we have to kill him now or we'll lose this account."

Atkin was incensed. This was not a problem of advertising but of distribution. His senior vice president presented an extensively researched flip chart that showed how successfully the Garrison Boyd campaign had increased consumer awareness of the new Amstel brands. The only obstacle to increasing sales was the fact that the beer was still unavailable in most bars and grocery stores. Although advertising could create demand, it couldn't stock the shelves.

These were the kinds of excuses that old-timers had come to expect from vanguard creatives, who they believed were more interested in developing their craft than in serving the client's bottom line. Sure, they had done the research to back up their claims, but ultimately they just passed the buck to one of the client's other departments. The account executive cited his relationship with the brand manager at Heineken to suggest that he had the power to break rank. He was the only one who understood how this man thought and how far he could be pushed. They had reached their limit with Garrison Boyd, and he wasn't about to report back to the client without something more traditional, something that promised a real increase in sales.

Unable to agree on a single strategy, Wells BDDP eventually lost the account, along with the rest of Heineken's business. Atkin soon decided to seek a position elsewhere, and shortly after his own and other key departures, Procter & Gamble, a company known for its slow and methodical decisions, suddenly pulled all of its business from the agency in a dramatic and unprecedented move. Taking away about seventy percent of

Wells's revenues, the defection made the headlines and sank the agency.

The forces leading to the collapse of Wells BDDP are the same ones threatening the rest of the advertising industry. Traditional advertising executives depend on the nontraditional ingenuity of people like Atkin to reach increasingly rebellious target markets. The vanguard young creatives, however, refuse to develop campaigns that don't break new conceptual or artistic ground. They don't want to create advertising merely to sell things; they want to have fun. Firms like Wells struggle to straddle the divide, simultaneously peddling their campaigns to both disgruntled clients and cynical target audiences. Fueling this crisis most of all are the media-savvy consumers who, like bacteria treated with antibiotics, grow ever more resistant to the machinations of this fractious industry.

Most of us know by now that they don't call the stuff on TV "programming" for nothing. The people making television are programming not just their fall lineups; they're programming *us.* Or at least they're trying to. Over the past few decades, however, the sophistication with which advertisers package and deliver their messages has been matched only by the sophistication with which we, their audience, deconstruct them.

Currently, marketers appear to be in a race with their customers. New media and the youth culture raised within it have demystified most of the traditional methods of marketing. Many members of today's television audience are armchair media theorists, confident in the language of programming and capable of decoding the messages coming into their homes. Advertisers are scrambling to understand the postmodern mediascape as thoroughly as their audiences do, and to develop new sorts of programming tricks that work in the new environment.

But advertisers are in a bind. While some viewers are busy deconstructing every image and evaluating its semiotic components, others are simply watching the TV and trying to figure out what's going on. Marketers whose advertising depends on inside jokes and discreet winks may elicit a chuckle out of a college kid but at the same time alienate his mom. Advertisers who over-compensate for the cynicism of one group find that their adjusted tactics then fail to speak to a different segment of the population. As a result, major corporations reevaluate their marketing plans weekly, and change advertising agencies almost as frequently as the agencies fire (or lose) their creative directors. In this age of new media, the programmers are the visitors, and we, for once, have the home-field advantage.

Branding Products, Branding People

It wasn't always this way. Not so long ago, before marketing became a branch of psychology, branding and advertising were simply ways to publicize and identify one's products.

The brand began, quite literally, as a method for ranchers to identify their cattle. By burning a distinct symbol into the hide of a baby calf, the owner could insure that if it one day wandered off his property or was stolen by a competitor, he'd be able to point to that logo and claim the animal as his rightful property.

When the manufacturers of products adopted the brand as a way of guaranteeing the quality of their goods, its function remained pretty much the same. Buying a package of oats with the Quaker label meant the customer could trace back these otherwise generic oats to their source. If there was a problem, he knew where he could turn. More important, if the oats were of satisfactory or superior quality, he knew where he could get them again. Trademarking a brand meant that no one else could call his oats Quaker.

Advertising in this innocent age simply meant publicizing the existence of one's brand. The sole objective was to increase consumers' awareness of the product or company that made it. Those who even thought to employ specialists for the exclusive purpose of writing ad copy hired newspaper reporters and traveling salesmen, who knew how to explain the attributes of an item in words that people tended to remember.

It wasn't until 1922 that a preacher and traveling "medicine show" salesman-turned-copywriter named Claude Hopkins decided that advertising should be systematized into a science. His short but groundbreaking book *Scientific Advertising* proposed that the advertisement is merely a printed extension of the salesman's pitch and should follow the same rules. Hopkins believed in using hard descriptions over hype, and text over image: "The more you tell, the more you sell" and "White space is wasted space" were his mantras. Hopkins believed that any illustrations used in an ad should be directly relevant to the product itself—not just a loose or emotional association. He insisted on avoiding "frivolity" at all costs, arguing that "no one ever bought from a clown."

Although some images did appear in advertisements and on packaging as early as the 1800s—the Quaker Oats man showed up in 1877—these weren't consciously crafted to induce psychological states in customers. They were meant just to help people remember one brand over another. How better to recall the brand Quaker than to see a picture of one?

It wasn't until the 1930s, 1940s, and 1950s, as Americans turned toward movies and television and away from newspapers and radio, that advertisers' focus shifted away from describing their brands and to creating images for them. During these decades, Midwestern adman Leo Burnett concocted what is often called the Chicago school of advertising, in which lovable characters are used to represent products.

Green Giant, which was originally just the Minnesota Valley

Canning Company's code name for an experimental pea, became the Jolly Green Giant in young Burnett's world of animated characters. He understood that the figure would make a perfect and enticing brand image for an otherwise boring product and could also serve as a mnemonic device for consumers. As he watched his character grow in popularity, Burnett discovered that the mythical figure of a green giant had resonance in many different cultures around the world. It became a kind of archetype and managed to penetrate the psyche in more ways than one.

Burnett was responsible for dozens of character-based brand images, including Tony the Tiger, Charlie the Tuna, Morris the Cat, and the Marlboro Man. In each case, the character creates a sense of drama, which engages the audience in the pitch. This was Burnett's great insight. He still wanted to sell a product based on its attributes, but he knew he had to draw in his audience using characters.

Brand images were also based on places, like Hidden Valley Ranch salad dressing, or on recognizable situations, such as the significant childhood memories labeled "Kodak moments," or a mother nurturing her son on a cold day, a defining image for Campbell's soup.

In all these cases, however, the moment, location, or character went only so far as to draw the audience into the ad, after which they would be subjected to a standard pitch: "Soup is good food," or "Sorry, Charlie, only the best tuna get to be Starkist." Burnett saw himself as a homespun Midwesterner who was contributing to American folklore while speaking in the plain language of the people. He took pride in the fact that his ads used words like "ain't"—not because they had some calculated psychological effect on the audience, but because they communicated in a natural, plainspoken style.

As these methods found their way to Madison Avenue and came to be practiced much more self-consciously, Burnett's love for American values and his focus on brand attributes were left behind. Branding became much more ethereal and image-based, and ads only occasionally nodded to a product's attributes.

In the 1960s, advertising gurus like David Ogilvy came up with rules about television advertising that would have made Claude Hopkins shudder. "Food in motion" dictated that food should always be shot by a moving camera. "Open with fire" meant that ads should start in a very exciting and captivating way. Ogilvy told his creatives to "use supers"—text superimposed on the screen to emphasize important phrases and taglines.

All these techniques were devised to promote brand image, not the product. Ogilvy didn't believe consumers could distinguish between products were it not for their images. In *Ogilvy on Advertising,* he explains that most people cannot tell the difference between their own "favorite" whiskey and the closest two competitors': "Have they tried all three and compared the taste? Don't make me laugh. The reality is that these three brands have different *images* which appeal to different kinds of people. It isn't the whiskey they choose, it's the image. The brand image is ninety percent of what the distiller has to sell."[1]

Thus, we learned to "trust our car to the man who wears the star" not because Texaco had better gasoline than Shell, but because the company's advertisers had created a better brand image.

While Burnett and his disciples were building brand myths, another school of advertisers was busy learning about its audience. Back in the 1920s, Raymond Rubicam, who eventually founded the agency Young and Rubicam, thought it might be interesting to hire a pollster named Dr. Gallup from Northwestern University to see what could be gleaned about consumers from a little market research. The advertising industry's version of cultural anthropology, or demographics, was born.

Like the public-relations experts who study their target populations in order to manipulate them later, marketers began conducting polls, market surveys, and focus groups on the segments of the population they hoped to influence. And to draw clear, clean lines between demographic groups, researchers must almost always base distinctions on four factors: race, age, sex, and wages. Demographic research is reductionist by design. I once consulted to an FM radio station whose station manager wanted to know, "Who is our listener?" Asking such a question reduces an entire listenership down to one fictional person. It's possible that no single individual will ever match the "customer profile" meant to apply to all customers, which is why so much targeted marketing often borders on classist, racist, and sexist pandering.

Billboards for most menthol cigarettes, for example, picture African-Americans because, according to demographic research, black people prefer them to regular cigarettes. Microsoft chose Rolling Stones songs to launch Windows 95, a product targeted at wealthy baby boomers. "The Women's Global Challenge" was an advertising-industry-created Olympics for women, with no purpose other than to market to active females.

By the 1970s, the two strands of advertising theory—demographic research and brand image—were combined to develop campaigns that work on both levels. To this day, we know to associate Volvos with safety, Dr. Pepper with individuality, and Harley-Davidson with American heritage. Each of these brand images is crafted to appeal to the target consumer's underlying psychological needs: Volvo ads are aimed at upper-middle-class white parents who fear for their children's health and security, Dr. Pepper is directed to young nonconformists, and the Harley-Davidson image supports its riders' self-perception as renegades.

Today's modern (or perhaps postmodern) brands don't invent a corporate image on their own; they appropriate one from the media itself, such as MetLife did with Snoopy, Butterfinger did with Bart Simpson, or Kmart did by hiring Penny Marshall and Rosie O'Donnell. These mascots were selected because their perceived characteristics match the values of their target consumers—not the products themselves. In the language of today's marketers, brand images do not reflect on products but on advertisers' perceptions of their audiences' psychology.

This focus on audience composition and values has become the standard operating procedure in all of broadcasting. When Fox TV executives learned that their animated series "King of the Hill," about a Texan propane distributor, was not faring well with certain demographics, for example, they took a targeted approach to their character's rehabilitation. The *Brandweek* piece on Fox's ethnic campaign uncomfortably dances around the issue.

> Hank Hill is the proverbial everyman, and Fox wants viewers to get comfortable with him; especially viewers in New York, where "King of the Hill"s homespun humor hasn't quite caught on with the young urbanites. So far this season, the show has pulled in a 10.1 rating/15 share in households nationally, while garnering a 7.9 rating/12 share in New York.[2]

As far as Fox was concerned, while regular people could identify with the network's new "everyman" character, New Yorkers weren't buying his middle-American patter. The television show's ratings proved what TV executives had known all along: that New York City's Jewish demographic doesn't see itself as part of the rest of America.

Fox's strategy for "humanizing" the character to those irascible urbanites was to target the group's ethnographic self-image. Fox put ads for the show on the panels of sidewalk coffee wagons throughout Manhattan, with the tagline "Have a bagel with

Hank." In an appeal to the target market's well-developed (and well-researched) cynicism, Hank himself is shown saying, "May I suggest you have that with a schmear."

The disarmingly ethnic humor here is meant to underscore the absurdity of a Texas propane salesman using a Jewish insider's word like "schmear." In another Upper West Side billboard, Hank's son appeals to the passing traffic: "Hey yo! Somebody toss me up a knish!" As far as the New York demographic is concerned, these jokes transform the characters from potentially threatening Southern rednecks into loveable hicks bending over backward to appeal to Jewish sensibilities, and doing so with a comic and, most important, nonthreatening inadequacy.

Today, the most intensely targeted demographic is the baby—the future consumer. Before an average American child is twenty months old, he can recognize the McDonald's logo and many other branded icons. Nearly everything a toddler encounters—from Band-Aids to underpants—features the trademarked characters of Disney or other marketing empires. Although this target market may not be in a position to exercise its preferences for many years, it pays for marketers to imprint their brands early. General Motors bought a two-page ad in *Sports Illustrated for Kids* for its Chevy Venture minivan. Their brand manager rationalized that the eight-to-fourteen-year-old demographic consists of "back-seat consumers."[3]

The real intention of target marketing to children and babies, however, goes deeper. The fresh neurons of young brains are valuable mental real estate to admen. By seeding their products and images early, the marketers can do more than just develop brand recognition; they can literally cultivate a demographic's sensibilities as they are formed. A nine-year-old child who can recognize the Budweiser frogs and recite their slogan (Bud-weis-er) is more likely to start drinking beer than one who can remember only Tony the Tiger yelling, "They're great!" (Currently, more children recognize the frogs than Tony.) This indicates a long-term coercive strategy.

The abstraction of brand images from the products they represent, combined with an increasing assault on our demographically targeted psychological profiles, led to some justifiable consumer paranoia by the 1970s. Advertising was working on us in ways we couldn't fully understand, and people began to look for an explanation.

In 1973, Wilson Bryan Key, a communications researcher, wrote the first of four books about "subliminal advertising," in which he accused advertisers of hiding sexual imagery in ice cubes, and psychoactive words like "sex" onto the airbrushed surfaces of fashion photographs. Having worked on many advertising campaigns from start to finish, in close proximity to everyone from copywriters and art directors to printers, I can comfortably put to rest any rumors that major advertising agencies are engaging in subliminal campaigns. How do images that could be interpreted as "sexual" show up in ice cubes or elbows? The final photographs chosen for ads are selected by committee out of hundreds that are actually shot. After hours or days of consideration, the group eventually feels drawn to one or two photos out of the batch. Not surprising, these photos tend to have more evocative compositions and details, but no penises, breasts, or skulls are ever superimposed onto the images. In fact, the man who claims to have developed subliminal persuasion, James Vicary, admitted to *Advertising Age* in 1984 that he had fabricated his evidence that the technique worked in order to drum up business for his failing research company. But this confession has not assuaged Key and others who relentlessly, perhaps obsessively, continue to pursue those they feel are planting secret visual messages in advertisements.

To be fair to Key, advertisers have left themselves open to suspicion by relegating their work to the abstract world of the image and then targeting consumer psychology so deliberately. According to research by the Roper Organization in 1992, fifty-seven percent of American consumers still believe that subliminal advertising is practiced on a regular basis, and only one in twelve think it "almost never" happens. To protect themselves from the techniques they believe are being used against them, the advertising audience has adopted a stance of cynical suspicion.

To combat our increasing awareness and suspicion of demographic targeting, marketers have developed a more camouflaged form of categorization based on psychological profiles instead of race and age. Jim Schroer, the executive director of new marketing strategy at Ford explains his abandonment of broad-demographic targeting: "It's smarter to think about emotions and attitudes, which all go under the term 'psychographics'—those things that can transcend demographic groups."[4] Instead, he now appeals to what he calls "consumers' images of themselves."

Unlike broad demographics, the psychographic is developed using more narrowly structured qualitative-analysis techniques, like focus groups, in-depth interviews, and even home surveillance. Marketing analysts observe the behaviors of volunteer subjects, ask questions, and try to draw causal links between feelings, self-image, and purchases.

A company called Strategic Directions Group provides just such analysis of the human psyche. In their study of the car-buying habits of the "forty-plus baby boomers and their elders," they sought to define the main psychological predilections that human beings in this age group have regarding car purchases. Although they began with a demographic subset of the overall population, their analysis led them to segment the group into psychographic types.

For example, members of one psychographic segment, called the "Reliables," think of driving as a way to "get from point A to point B." The "Everyday People" campaign for Toyota is aimed at this group and features people depending on their reliable and efficient little Toyotas. A convertible Saab, on the other hand, appeals to the "Stylish Fun" category, who like trendy and fun-to-drive imports. One of the company's commercials shows a woman at a boring party fantasizing herself into an oil painting, where she drives along the canvas in a sporty yellow Saab.

Psychographic targeting is more effective than demographic targeting because it reaches for an individual customer more directly—like a fly fisherman who sets bait and jiggles his rod in a prescribed pattern for a particular kind of fish. It's as if a marketing campaign has singled you out and recognizes your core values and aspirations, without having lumped you into a racial or economic stereotype.

It amounts to a game of cat-and-mouse between advertisers and their target psychographic groups. The more effort we expend to escape categorization, the more ruthlessly the marketers pursue us. In some cases, in fact, our psychographic profiles are based more on the extent to which we try to avoid marketers than on our fundamental goals or values.

The so-called "Generation X" adopted the anti-chic aesthetic of thrift-store grunge in an effort to find a style that could not be so easily identified and exploited. Grunge was so self-consciously lowbrow and nonaspirational that it seemed, at first, impervious to the hype and glamor normally applied swiftly to any emerging trend. But sure enough, grunge anthems found their way onto the soundtracks of television commercials, and Dodge Neons were hawked by kids in flannel shirts saying "Whatever."

The members of Generation X are putting up a good fight. Having already developed an awareness of how marketers attempt to target their hearts and wallets, they use their insight into programming to resist these attacks. Unlike the adult marketers pursuing them, young people have grown up immersed in the language of advertising and public relations. They speak it like natives. As a result, they are more than aware when a commercial or billboard is targeting them. In conscious defiance of demographic-based pandering, they adopt a stance of self-protective irony—distancing themselves from the emotional ploys of the advertisers.

Lorraine Ketch, the director of planning in charge of Levi's trendy Silvertab line, explained, "This audience hates marketing that's in your face. It eyeballs it a mile away, chews it up and spits it out."[5] Chiat/Day, one of the world's best-known and experimental advertising agencies, found the answer to the crisis was simply to break up the Gen-X demographic into separate "tribes" or subdemographics—and include subtle visual references to each one of them in the ads they produce for the brand. According to Levi's director of consumer marketing, the campaign meant to communicate, "We really understand them, but we are not trying too hard."

Probably unintentionally, Ms. Ketch has revealed the new, even more highly abstract plane on which advertising is now being communicated. Instead of creating and marketing a brand image, advertisers are creating marketing campaigns about the advertising itself. Silvertab's target market is supposed to feel good about being understood, but even better about understanding *the way they are being marketed to.*

The "drama" invented by Leo Burnett and refined by David Ogilvy and others has become a play within a play. The scene itself has shifted. The dramatic action no longer occurs between the audience and the product, the brand, or the brand image, but between the audience and the brand marketers. As audiences gain even more control over the media in which these interactive stories unfold, advertising evolves ever closer to a theater of the absurd.

Story: The Play's the Thing Wherein
I'll Catch the Conscience of the King

The dramatic story has served for centuries, perhaps millennia, as our civilization's chief method of imprinting and perpetuating value systems on large target audiences. The Bible stories, fairy tales, and moral fables we were told as children stick with us for the rest of our lives. They become the resonant elements, or central myths, on which we base our perception of the world. The stories we are told account for our understanding of creation, existence, and even death.

Television commercials are stories, too, and they are designed to impress brand values upon us with the force of cultural mythology, securing and extending our most deeply held beliefs.

Most stories work by generating tension. The plot moves up an inclined plane of increasing stakes and danger, and the audience experiences the agonizing thrill of going along for the ride. The further into danger the character goes, the higher our own level of tension will become. The good storyteller slowly and consistently builds our anxiety—careful not to push so hard that we run out of the theater. As the level of tension increases, we are drawn deeper into the storyteller's spell. The worse it gets, the more dependent we are on the storyteller for a way out. It's all worth the pain, though, because eventually the conflict will be resolved and the audience will be released into delightful catharsis.

Because the audience is willing to accept any reasonable escape from their own state of unbearable tension, the storyteller has the power to concoct whatever solution he wishes. And embedded in that solution can be an agenda. The more intense an audience's level of anxiety, the more preposterous a release it will accept.

The thirty-second advertisement can use narrative tension to influence through catharsis, too. The story just has to generate its anxiety more quickly. I was disturbed as a child by an ad in which a midlevel executive is seated behind his desk. He looks like a nice enough guy—a lot like us, in fact. But something's wrong. His phone is ringing noisily. His boss is angry. He's lost an account. His wife crashed the car. We see he is in great pain. What's he going to do? He opens the drawer of his desk and smiles. What does he see? A brand of pain reliever, of course. He swallows the pills, and we watch as a psychedelic swirl of colors fills the outline of his body, soothing every painful area. He is happy, and his problems seem diminished. I can remember wishing my problems would manifest themselves as a headache so that they could be cured as easily.

As long as an influence professional can build his idea—be it a product, candidate, or lifestyle—into the fabric of a story, he can successfully program an audience to accept it. The better his story—the more profoundly we identify with his character's dilemma—the more fully and permanently we will accept the underlying agenda.

The word "entertainment" means literally "to hold within." The more entertaining a story, the more captivated we are by its teller and the more vulnerable we are to his influence if he chooses to exercise it. Television, theater, and film had better be entertaining, for only a captive viewer will sit and bear the tension of the rising dramatic action.

That's how my grandfather used to watch TV movies back in the 1970s. He'd lean back in his La-Z-Boy recliner with a bowl of pretzels in his lap. The heroine in one of these movies—I think it was Suzanne Pleshette—walks into an apartment where we know a murderer is hiding. She tries the light switch, but it's broken. She ventures into the apartment anyway, and into danger.

If my grandpa likes Suzanne Pleshette as much as most older men of the period did, he will experience anxiety on her behalf.

He is being put into a state of tension. At this moment, some part of his brain makes a calculation. He could change the channel to avoid the tension, but that would require taking the bowl of pretzels off his lap, pulling up the lever on his recliner, rising, crossing to the TV set, and manually changing the channel to another station. But jumping up like this whenever he felt himself in the grip of the action on the screen would defeat the purpose of the entertainment he has come to expect from television. He's been trained to be a well-behaved, attentive viewer. He has what programmers like to call a "long attention span," and he is used to suffering through moments like these. On the other hand, enduring the tension will mean a heightened level of anxiety until someone rescues poor Suzanne.

In an appeal to the La-Z-Boy viewer, television manufacturers developed the remote control. Little did they realize it would thwart the efforts of the people programming television content. A person armed with a remote control makes a completely different set of internal calculations when confronted with an anxiety-producing narrative. With very little effort, he can push a button and release himself from the rise in tension. Young people today pride themselves more on their channel-surfing capabilities than on the lengths of their attention spans. Watch yourself or your child operate a remote control; the impulse to change channels arises more often out of disgust at being made to feel tense than out of simple boredom.

A person with a remote control doesn't need to be sucked into the aspirin commercial any more than he is into the Suzanne Pleshette movie. The businessman in the commercial is obviously having a bad day. Why watch? *Click.* Easy as that.

The television remote allows for easy escape, fundamentally changing the viewing audience's relationship to television. Young people and remote-control-capable adults no longer sit back and watch a television program; they watch the TV set and put it through its paces. They are literally watching and deconstructing styles of programming. Just as journalists and the public watched Marv Albert work his spin control, viewers now watch television programmers and advertisers attempt to draw them into coercive stories.

Skilled remote-control viewers can keep track of five or six different programs at a time. The most practiced of us—usually the youngsters—flip from channel to channel, catching the most important moments of each show or sporting event with uncanny precision. Watching TV this way has become almost a form of postmodern art unto itself, where the action and values of one program are suddenly juxtaposed against another's. An altogether new kind of entertainment emerges from the formerly passive viewing experience: the joy of recombining images, creating our own edit points, and comparing and contrasting different programs, often thwarting their creators' original purposes in the process.

By marketing the tools of media to its consumers, the electronics industry has unwittingly undermined the efforts of advertisers. For many decades, the television screen was an exclusive territory. Only programmers and sponsors had the magic ability to manipulate the images on the screen. The act of broadcasting television was as mysterious and awe-inspiring as transubstantiation, and it was regarded with equivalent reverence. The information that the networks piped into our homes was accepted as if it were the gospel truth. Back in the 1960s, Walter Cronkite had the privilege of ending his evening broadcast with the tagline "And that's the way it is."

The home video game was the first interactive medium to challenge this authority. Just as the remote control deconstructed television, the joystick demystified it. Think back to the first time you ever played a video game. It was probably the primitive black-and-white arcade game called Pong. You felt excitement not just because you had finally found a way to play table tennis without a real table, but because, for the very first time, you had gained the ability to alter the pixels on the television screen. A space that formerly had been off-limits was now absolutely accessible through a simple knob. The pixels, and the screen they composed, had been demystified.

The video camera took this demystification a step further, as amateur photographers came to understand the language of film editing and the ways to "lie" about time and space by splicing together images that may not have actually been shot in sequence. The computer keyboard and mouse turned the monitor into a communications center. Today, the cathode-ray tube is no longer a receive-only device but, through the Internet and commercial online services, a portal to self-expression. Media has become a two-way street.

The proliferation of all these devices, plus the advent of fax machines, VCRs, modems, and cellular telephones, has fundamentally altered the shape and function of the mass media. It is now an open system—a mediaspace. Anyone can contribute, and no one can be sure how what he throws in there will be deconstructed, repurposed, and distributed. A top-forty song might be sampled and recycled by a rapper. A news report may be deconstructed and exposed as propaganda by a public-access show or Internet newsgroup. A rock video may be mocked by commentators like Beavis and Butt-head. A commercial can be satirized by a late-night comedy show for its clumsy efforts at manipulation—and the audience will get the joke.

The media is a chaotic place. Like an ocean or a weather system, it no longer respects authority. In fact, those who attempt to impose their authority are ridiculed, while brilliant and valuable tidbits emerge from the most remote and seemingly inconsequential sources. Advertisements attempting to associate a brand with a celebrity or lifestyle aren't nearly as effective as they once were. No sooner are they broadcast than they are deconstructed into their component parts. Younger, media-savvy viewers instinctively reject authoritative voices and laugh at commercials in which people try to act "cool."

Advertisers are well aware of our changing viewing habits. Now that an increasingly large proportion of the public has adopted this self-protective stance toward the media, marketers have turned to what might best be called postmodern techniques of persuasion.

Consider the microbrand. As consumers became weary of major beer brands and their relentless over-the-top media campaigns, they turned to local breweries and brands for a sense of authenticity. Like do-it-yourself media, these tiny companies gave their customers a sense of local control and connection. No longer content with supporting a national brand devoid of character, consumers sought the distinction and individuality that came with buying a bottle of beer that may well have been brewed around the corner.

The major breweries were quick to respond to the microbrewery phenomenon. Miller Brewing Company released a fake microbrew beer called Red Dog, whose label advertised that it was brewed at the charmingly remote-sounding Plank Road Brewery. There is no such place as the Plank Road Brewery. Anheuser-Busch bought a quiet interest in Seattle's Redhook Ale Brewery, and Coors launched its own line of imitation microbrews from the Blue Moon Brewing Company, whose marketing campaign touted the beer as "handcrafted once in a blue moon."

Fake microbrands are created for a new population of consumers who have learned to resist the pressures of conformity imposed by well-known brand images. Airwalk sports shoes are worn by millions of young people who resent the overwhelming marketing campaigns and widely criticized labor practices of Nike, and American Spirit cigarettes sell to smokers who want to believe they are circumventing the notoriously manipulative cigarette industry. In the end, they are simply succumbing to the counteroffensives of shrewd marketers who have predicted and capitalized on their rebellion.

Advertisers are learning to stay one step ahead in the chaotic mediaspace. If today's consumer will instantly separate a product from its spokesperson, then the answer is to make advertisements that are more difficult to deconstruct. Many billboards and magazine ads have resorted to showing isolated body parts rather than full-body portraits of models using or wearing products. This style of photography, known in the industry as abstract representation, allows the viewer to see himself in the advertisement, rather than the model. Instead of having to identify with a character, he can watch the commercial as if it were from his own point of view. All of our hands and legs are pretty much the same. Ads for Kool cigarettes show only the hand of the lucky man who holds a pack, and the beautiful girl who has turned in his direction. A hugely successful Dockers trousers campaign showed a group of men from the waist down only, as they spoke in random, disconnected sentences.

The less specific or more iconic a representation, the harder it becomes for an audience to resist identifying with it. As a result, icons have become the new unit of communication in a mediaspace characterized by deconstruction. Wary of stories, slogans, and other emotional traps, young people in particular have been drawn to icons as a way of expressing who they are and what they believe in. Kids paste iconic stickers on their skateboards, attach iconic key chains to their backpacks, and collect trading cards and Pogs with simple iconic representations. Because they seem universal and disconnected, they are perceived as somehow safe from the influence of authority.

Advertisers exploiting this same principle have moved toward more iconic ways of representing their products. The simpler and less descriptive the icon, the more universal its appeal. Ask a group of teenagers what the Nike swoosh icon means, and each one will most likely tell you something different—but all the responses will probably have something to do with challenging authority, excelling in sports, being an individual, or "just doing it." The swoosh is a universal icon, capable of representing any number of youthful ideals. Some young people identify so fully with the Nike symbol that they have tattooed it onto their bodies.

Part of an icon's power comes from its indivisibility. The swoosh cannot be further deconstructed into its component parts. Just as golden arches mean McDonald's, and the little red tab means Levi's, the swoosh *is* Nike. The product is its icon, inseparably and without exception. To buy a pair of Nike shoes is to buy the Nike swoosh. By adopting the postlinguistic currency of an iconic culture, marketers can reposition themselves and their brands in a manner consistent with the operating system of today's point-and-click marketplace.

Nowhere to Hide

Media-savvy television viewers pride themselves on their ability to watch programming from the safe distance of their own ironic detachment. Young people delight in watching "Melrose Place" in groups so they can make fun of the characters and their values by talking back to the screen throughout the show. Others turn to shows like "Beavis and Butt-head," whose characters' constant commentary on the MTV videos they watch serves as a built-in distancing device. The wisecracks keep the audience emotionally removed from the seductive charms of the images on the screen.

In addition to using icons, marketers have come to recognize the way irony makes a wary viewer feel safe, and now they regularly employ irony in the commercials targeted at these more difficult demographic groups. "Wink" advertising acknowledges the cynical stance of resistant viewers: Sprite commercials satirize the values espoused by "cool" brands, sometimes even parodying their competitors' obvious image-based tactics, and then go on to insist, "Image is nothing. Thirst is everything." A brand of shoes called Simple developed a magazine campaign with the copy "Advertisement: blah blah blah . . . name of company."

By letting the audience in on the hollowness of the marketing process, advertisers hope to be rewarded by the appreciative viewer. Energizer batteries launched a television campaign where a fake commercial for another product would be interrupted by the pink bunny marching across the screen. The audience was rescued from the bad commercial by the battery company's tiny mascot. The message: The Energizer bunny can keep on going, even in a world of relentless hype.

Of course marketers haven't really surrendered anything. What's really going on here is a new style of marketing through exclusivity. Advertisers know that their viewership prides itself on being able to deconstruct and understand the coercive tactics of television commercials. By winking at the audience, the advertiser is acknowledging that there's someone special out there— someone smart enough not to be fooled by the traditional tricks of the influence professional. If you're smart enough to get the joke, then you're smart enough to know to buy our product.

Like all advertisements, these self-conscious commercials help the viewer define his own identity. The strategy is not as overt as showing Michael Jordan in a pair of Nikes so that young athletes will identify with their hero. Instead, a person's notion of "self" is defined by how sophisticated he feels in relation to the images on his TV set. If he has grown up deluged by coercive advertising and expended effort to break free, then he will identify himself as a media-savvy individual. Wink advertising gives him a chance to confirm his own intelligence.

In the advertising wars between long-distance carriers, underdog MCI attempted to show how they were friendly and perky, especially compared to industry leader AT&T. A beautiful young operator mischievously whispered to us that AT&T doesn't want their customers to hear about MCI's low rates, or their discount Friends & Family plan. She ridiculed AT&T's ads begging people to "come home," and implied that they revealed Ma Bell's desperation. AT&T fought back with their own ads, highlighting the coercive nature of MCI's marketing: that people were fooled into writing lists of their friends and relatives so that MCI could make annoying phone calls trying to enlist them. The advertisements were no longer about quality or service. They were about the advertising campaigns themselves.

Wink advertisements very often borrow imagery from another company's advertisements as a way of eliciting viewer approval. After Lexus made the ball bearing famous by rolling it seductively over the precision engineered lines of its luxury sedan, Nissan did the same thing in their ad to demonstrate how a much less expensive car could exhibit the same qualities. BMW sought to rise above the whole affair, demonstrating their car's unmatched turning radius by putting the whole vehicle through the same tight turns as the ball bearing went through in the other brands' meaningless test. Finally, in an irreverent spoof of the automobile advertising wars, Roy Rogers rolled a ball bearing around the edge of a roast beef sandwich. Get it? *Wink wink.*

In a similar campaign, Levi's made fun of Calvin Klein's heroin-chic, ultra-skinny supermodels. The company pictured healthy models wearing Levi's under the caption, "Our models can beat up their models."

As the techniques of self-consciousness and parody become more recognizable and, accordingly, less effective, advertisers have been forced to go yet a step further, taking the media reflexivity of advertising into the realm of the nonsensical. It's as if by overwhelming us with irony, they hope to blow out the circuits we use to make critical judgments.

The Diesel jeans company ran a series of billboard and magazine ads designed to critique the whole discipline of advertising. One showed a sexy but downtrodden young couple, dressed in stylish jeans and arguing with each other in what looked like the messy, 1960s-era kitchen of a dysfunctional white-trash family. The ad meant to reveal the illusory quality of the hip retro fashion exploited by other advertisers. Diesel would not try to convince anyone that those were the "good old days." We were meant to identify with the proposition that the enlightened values of the sixties, as represented by the media, are a crock. But the meaning is never made explicit. Another Diesel campaign consisted of advertisements which themselves were photos of garish billboards placed in ridiculous locations. One showed a sexy young couple, dressed in Diesel jeans, in an advertisement for an imported brand of ice cream. The billboard, however, was pictured in a dirty, crowded neighborhood filled with poor Communist Chinese workers.

Benetton and The Body Shop ran similar ads, but at least theirs made some sense. One Benetton campaign pictured Queen Elizabeth as a black woman and Michael Jackson as a caucasian to comment on racial prejudice. A series of Body Shop ads featured giant photos of marijuana leaves, presumably to call attention to drug and agriculture laws. These are appeals to a target market that feels hip for agreeing with the sentiments expressed and for grasping the underlying logic. There is, indeed, something to "get."

We are supposed to believe that Diesel's ads also make sociopolitical statements, but we never know quite what they are. In fact, the ads work in a highly sophisticated disassociative way: They make us feel as tense and uneasy as we do after a good scary story—but we refuse to admit to our anxiety lest we reveal we are not media-savvy enough to get the joke. The campaign is designed to lead the audience to the conclusion that they understand the ironic gesture, while the irony is left intentionally unclear. No one is meant to get the joke. In that moment of confusion—like the car buyer subjected to a disassociative hypnotic technique—the consumer absorbs the image within the image: two sexy kids in Diesel jeans. Thinking of yourself as hip enough to "get" it—no matter what "it" may be—means being susceptible to lying to yourself, and to being programmed as a result.

That's all coercion really is, after all: convincing a person to lie to himself by any means necessary. The stance of ironic detachment, while great for protecting ourselves from straightforward linear stories and associations, nonetheless makes us vulnerable to more sophisticated forms of influence. After a while, even a detached person begins to long for a sense of meaning or some value, any value, to accept completely and genuinely. In spite of their well-publicized cynicism, so-called Generation Xers reveal in numerous studies that they often feel lost and without purpose. Disillusioned with role models, the political process, and media hype, they are nonetheless seeking something to believe in.

As people search for a sense of authenticity in their increasingly disconnected "virtual" experience, advertisers seize on the opportunity to help us delude ourselves into thinking we haven't really lost touch. A shrewd advertisement for an airphone service shows a businessman stuck on a jet flight while his young daughter dances in a recital at her elementary school. He has foregone his family obligations in the name of business. But in the airphone commercial, he calls his daughter from the plane after her recital, and, basked in golden light, she is as delighted to hear his telephonic voice as she would have been to see him in the flesh. The television viewer who is searching for meaning in his life will accept the faulty premise of the advertisement: that the airplane telephone can actually connect him with a life he has left behind.

The back-to-basics authenticity of such advertisements capitalizes on a growing sense that we are no longer in touch with who we really are. In the past, advertisers worked to generate this sense of disconnection. In the 1950s and 1960s, a marketer would present an image, personality, or story with which we were meant to identify, and then stretch that image in order to make us feel unworthy, to give us something to aspire to: The girl in the hair-color advertisement looks just like me—when I was twenty years younger and five shades less gray; the woman in the commercial has a dirty kitchen and noisy children just like me . . . but she is confident enough in her rug cleaner to throw a dinner party for her husband's business partners that night. The viewer identified with the character, only to be made to feel unworthy by comparison.

Today, however, a deep sense of disconnection and unworthiness is just the starting point for the detached viewer. As a result, the opposite effect takes place: We welcome the opportunity to let down our guard, even for a moment. Having grown to resent all the striving toward the ideals represented in commercials, we yearn to get off the treadmill of yearning altogether. We yearn *not* to yearn—to be still and content. To just *be*.

The newest approach to the antiyearning urge capitalizes on these feelings. The Calvin Klein CK Be perfume advertisements offer the media-fatigued sophisticate a chance to relax and literally "just be." Uniquely beautiful and detached-looking young people stare confidently into the lens. Beneath them are captions like "Be hot. Be cool. Just be." The slogans in companion ads all stress that people should have the ability to express their individuality and be who they really are. "CK Be fragrance is about who you are . . . it's about the freedom to express your individuality . . . it's about the freedom to be yourself."

The astonishing supposition of these ads is that the young audience for whom they are intended does not feel they already have permission to just be. Unlike the models in the advertisements, who appear to have earned their cool resolve by draining the life out of themselves through dedicated heroin abuse, the audience must expend effort to maintain a sense of self against the onslaught of commercials and other coercive messages. The CK Be ads suggest that if we just buy one thing—a single bottle of perfume—we can finally be who we really are with no further effort.

Like all of the image-based advertising that went before it, the CK Be campaign once again capitalizes on its audience's undetermined sense of self. A person who is striving not to strive is striving nonetheless—perhaps even more desperately than those who are simply yearning for a better lifestyle. Our aspiration toward a simpler, less taxing way of relating to the world around us makes us no less vulnerable to the suggestions of others on how best to get there. Being "in" is a booby prize, since it depends on a false and further self-defeating claim to exclusivity. The emergence of a protective, ironic stance, though temporarily immunizing, only contributes to our longing for ways to feel genuine and connected—and will likely turn out to be just one more chapter in the greater narrative of the history of advertising.

CHAPTER SIX

Pyramids

**I knew if I could get six more people to join,
I'd have enough money to quit.**
—A multilevel marketing dropout

Stephanie didn't know she wanted to be "in." Like many Americans, she only wanted a better, safer, and more prosperous life for her family. Thus she was a prime target.

After two years at state college studying to be an English teacher, Stephanie (not her real name) got pregnant and dropped out to get married. She moved to Houston, Texas, in 1991 with her new husband, who landed a job on the assembly line of a local computer plant. With an income of just under $40,000 per year, life with the three daughters they had over the next five years was modest but manageable.

By the time her youngest had started kindergarten, Stephanie became a bit restless with suburban living. After reading a series of articles in a fashion magazine about women with challenging careers, she decided that her life would be more rewarding if she could generate her own income. She also believed the additional cash would make it possible for her family to move to a well-publicized new neighborhood across town, which had strict residential zoning rules and a private security force. She had been reading the developer's glossy brochures for months. Houston wasn't an extremely dangerous city, but their neighborhood was suffering from an increase in robberies and assaults. With three daughters, Stephanie wanted some of the peace of mind that the private community's literature guaranteed.

Stephanie met with a career counselor, but the pickings were slim. She would need additional training just to qualify to be a temp office worker, a job she didn't even want to do. She hoped to work from her home so she could spend time with her daughters.

Later that week, she noticed a handwritten flyer on the community bulletin board at her local supermarket: "Earn upwards of $8,000 per week in your spare time." Although it sounded too good to be true, Stephanie tore off one of the small tabs at the bottom of the flyer, which had a phone number typed onto it. When she got home she called the number, and that very evening, an impeccably dressed middle-aged woman we'll call Barbara arrived at Stephanie's home in a shiny new sedan.

While Stephanie's husband and daughters watched TV in the family room, Barbara made her pitch to Stephanie in the kitchen. By becoming a distributor of high-quality, all-natural health products, Stephanie could soon be earning more than her husband. After an initial investment of just $600 for a sales kit, Stephanie would be an official distributor. By selling just $200 worth of supplements per week for four weeks, she would become a regional distributor, with the right to recruit distributors of her own. She would then collect a portion of commissions earned by all the distributors under her, as well as the distributors under them once they, too, became regional distributors. And once she had six distributors beneath her, each selling a minimum of $200 worth of health products a week, Stephanie would become a regional director and receive a $500 bonus every week directly from the company, in addition to her regular commissions.

Stephanie was unsure. It sounded like a lot of work, and she was suspicious of marketing schemes. Barbara assured her this wasn't traditional multilevel marketing, but rather a new form of distribution called "network marketing." The difference with this system, according to Barbara, was that "everybody comes out a winner, no matter how much they end up selling."

Stephanie still refused to make the initial investment without a few days to think it over. Barbara said she understood completely and gave Stephanie some samples as free gifts, to use while she made up her mind. Barbara also left her with a videotape that described the great benefits of the products as well as the way they were marketed.

Stephanie and her husband watched the slickly-produced videotapes. A TV actress narrated, and housewives were shown selling health products to one another, earning money and prizes, driving shiny new cars, and even moving into mansions. After watching the tape, Stephanie thought this might be a good idea after all. Her husband insisted it was a scam, however, and convinced Stephanie to try something more conventional.

The next morning, Barbara called with "great news." She had an invitation for Stephanie to attend an event at a nearby motor lodge, sponsored by the health products company. There would be free gifts for everyone who came, and Stephanie would have a chance to clear up any of her misgivings about the company. Before Stephanie had the chance to explain that she had decided not to become a distributor, Barbara had convinced her to come to the party.

The gathering turned out to be more like a rally. As Stephanie sat next to Barbara in a folding chair, she watched women rise to announce how many products they had sold that week, how many new distributors they had signed up, and how their lives had changed since becoming network marketers. After each speech, the other women cheered and applauded. A charismatic woman in front of the room, the vice president to whom all the regional directors reported, showed slides of upcoming products, congratulated the group on breaking a company sales record, and led the women in a short, nondenominational prayer.

Eventually, Barbara rose and announced that she had brought a newcomer, Stephanie. Everyone cheered. Barbara told the crowd what details she knew of Stephanie's life—how she had left college after getting pregnant, and how she wanted to move to a better neighborhood. Stephanie squirmed and wished she hadn't come. She felt self-conscious about being exposed to the others, and uncomfortable being stared at—especially by such well-dressed women when she was wearing jeans and an old sweater.

But after the main event was over, she found herself surrounded by a group of supportive women who seemed truly interested in her life and aspirations. They understood how hard it was to find a good job, especially if you wanted to be home by the time school let out. They understood why Stephanie would hope to raise her daughters in a safer neighborhood. They all had been there. And they all had made something better out of their lives.

Convinced that she had found the answer to her lifelong financial and esteem problems, Stephanie signed a check for $600 and went home with her new sales kit.

Using the forms in her package, Stephanie made lists of everyone to whom she possibly might sell the supplements, putting stars next to the names of friends who might someday want to become distributors themselves. Then she started making calls and reading the prepared sales scripts to the people on her list.

The first week, Stephanie sold more than $300 worth of merchandise. The second week, she sold $220 worth—still above the amount necessary to become a regional distributor. The third week, her daughter got the flu, which is why, Stephanie rationalized, she sold only about $180 worth of products. To keep her total over $200, she bought $20 worth of vitamins for herself. By the fourth week, Stephanie had exhausted her list. She managed to sell an additional $80 worth of health products to her aunt, and a little less than that to her neighbors by going door-to-door. Although she feared she might be getting in over her head, she spent $50 more of her own money buying additional samples of new products to get over the $200 hurdle.

Now Stephanie was free to earn the big bucks by getting her friends to sell the products themselves. She called the people on her list who had bought from her, and (as instructed by her sales manual) encouraged them to share with her the benefits they had already noticed. To her amazement, in that first week as a regional distributor, she managed to get three of them to agree to become distributors. She still needed three more to become a regional director and start receiving that $500 bonus every week.

Stephanie's fourth prospect, the mother of one of her daughter's schoolmates, seemed genuinely interested in making money, but was embarrassed to sell to her own friends. Luckily, the company was throwing its next monthly rally at the motor lodge. Stephanie brought her friend and felt genuine surprise as she found herself standing up to share with the group just how great she felt about the company, and how much money she had made. In reality, because of the products she had bought herself to stay at the $200 level, Stephanie had only broken even, but she preferred to share only her weekly totals—and even inflated those just a bit, in order to impress and encourage her new prospect. Cheered on by close to a hundred other distributors, Stephanie vowed to become a regional director before the end of the month. Her friend signed on that very evening.

With renewed vigor, Stephanie easily sold her $200 quota for the week. In fact, she sold more than $800 worth of health products herself. But failing to find any new distributor prospects, Stephanie decided to sign up her children as the last two members of the team, and then simply sell the additional $400 worth herself. Even if she failed, she figured she would still net $100 profit after she began receiving the $500 checks.

Barbara noticed that two of Stephanie's new salespeople had the same last name, and she called to inquire if everything was okay. Barbara had seen other new salespeople become overextended, and she wanted to make sure Stephanie was working at an appropriate pace. Stephanie considered telling Barbara the truth, but then she thought better of it and explained that she had signed on her sister and aunt. She didn't want to reveal her sorry state to her superior, for fear of losing the opportunity to move up.

What Stephanie hadn't taken into account was that her four distributors wouldn't necessarily be able to sell their $200 quotas. They didn't, so Stephanie never did get her $500 bonus. Within eight weeks, two of her salespeople quit, and none of the four had remained Stephanie's friend. No one was able to sell $200 worth of health products in a week, and everyone wanted out. Meanwhile, struggling to maintain three distributors' worth of quotas herself, Stephanie had accumulated hundreds of dollars' worth of unsold stock in her basement. She called Barbara, who gently told Stephanie that there was no way to return the unused products to the company. Stephanie would have to pay for them herself on her credit card. She was demoted back down to the distributor level, at which point she quit to find another job.

What Stephanie realized too late in her quest to raise her station was that she had fallen victim to a version of one of the most dependable and self-sustaining coercive systems in practice today: the pyramid. Used by cults, businesses, get-rich lecturers, multilevel marketers, and unprincipled stock market gurus, the pyramid combines the techniques of hand-to-hand marketing, the weight of authority, and the positive feedback of social networking to thwart its victims' rational decision-making processes.

Just the idea of a pyramid is enough to evoke an emotional response from most of us. The pyramid pictured on the back of the dollar bill has provided an endless source of speculation for conspiracy theorists. And although that image has long been mistakenly attributed to the Masons, it contains an element essential to pyramid schemes, which is that they depend on the creation of an obscure but highly desirable goal—the glowing eye of enlightenment at the top of the pyramid. Like a McGuffin—the ironically worthless object in a Hitchcock film that everyone gets murdered over—the goal itself need have no actual disclosed value. The system depends only on the people at the bottom of the pyramid believing that something special awaits them at the top. In fact, the real value of this goal must never be revealed. It must appear limitless, and thus capable of rewarding an unlimited number of new seekers.

Most typically, pyramids serve the purposes of ruthless religions and cults hoping to expand their memberships. In many cases, a charismatic leader personifies the ultimate goal. An "awakened being" presents himself as having attained or inherited spiritual perfection, which enables him to transmit some portion of his divinity to his followers. The task for cult members is to journey up the pyramid of commitment and devotion in order to move closer to the idealized but unattainable goal. Often, the way their progress in this quest is judged—and the way they come to feel closer to the cult leader—is by acquiring new members. The hundredth member of a cult can consider himself part of the inner circle only after another thousand people have joined. (Likewise, the hundredth employee of a corporation like Microsoft is considered to be one of its founding fathers once a few thousand other workers have entered the ranks.)

A cult member's unshakable faith and dogged determination in his cause, sometimes even to the point of death, attests to the extraordinary power of the pyramid technique. The pyramid can motivate a group of otherwise normal people to sacrifice everything they hold dear in the name of a higher goal. Thus it was only a matter of time before the pyramid became a tool of business.

Today, multilevel marketing companies like Herbalife, Mary Kay, and Amway incorporate aspects of pyramidal persuasion into their marketing strategies. Although these businesses are capable of actually generating wealth for their salespeople, the techniques they use to solicit and maintain those employee-customers amount to a powerfully coercive selling system. Like in pyramids, the illusion in MLMs is that an individual moves up as he performs the tasks set out for him. The fact is that salespeople only appear to move up in relationship to the newcomers filling in the places lower on the totem pole. As Stephanie learned, to earn and hold one's place, an amateur salesperson must not only sell a certain quantity of merchandise but, more important, maintain a quota of underlings who each are able to sell a certain quantity, too. The people who make the most money are, therefore, not those who sell the most merchandise but those who find other people capable of filling new positions beneath them. A successful multilevel business's best customers are sometimes its own salespeople.

You Can Have It All

In a few cases, the members actually do make money—if they've gotten onboard early enough to benefit from the multitudes who follow later. Multilevel marketers combine a simple arithmetic principle with the psychological pull of the "pyramid top" to draw money out of the hands of the many, into the pockets of the few. Holding it all together is the faulty premise of earning something simply by having faith in one's ability to do so.

"I began my career as a Mary Kay Beauty Consultant in October of 1977," opens one of the testimonials on a Mary Kay salesperson's Web site. "I didn't think I wanted to be a Consultant; never dreamed I would become a Consultant. But, here I am, nineteen years later, a Mary Kay Senior Sales Director and driving my fifth free car from the Company."

It is telling that a person who "didn't think" she wanted to be a consultant now realizes that she really wanted to all along. If only she had known what she wanted in the first place! The motivational style of the Mary Kay company's system helps their sales consultants realize that they don't know what they want, and then replaces their original priorities with a new one: to "have it all."

Pyramid schemes and multilevel marketing businesses are less about selling a product than selling the system itself. Like cults, the most successful multilevel marketing companies use God as their starting point. As Mary Kay Ash explains in her biography, *Mary Kay, You Can Have It All*—a book that amounts to little more than a promotional tool for her sales company—"Today, I can affirm that the growth and success of Mary Kay Cosmetics is a direct result of having taken God as our guide. I believe he blessed our company because its motivation is right."

No matter how many times the absolute goal of "having it all" is repeated, most women first join because they are desperate to escape a difficult situation. Materials for new members (some of which are generated by individual salespeople) feature testimonials that include the painful recounting of divorces, chauvinism in the workplace, and losing loved ones to cancer.

Sadly, many inductees to multilevel marketing systems make very little money. Directors encourage them to buy as large a set of tools and inventory as they can afford, citing the overly optimistic (or at least misapplied) logic that thinking positively makes positive things happen. New recruits often take out high-interest loans to gain entrance, but never successfully sell their merchandise or more memberships. Desperate to pay back their loans, the recruits make extreme efforts to get friends and family to sign up. "I knew if I could get six more people to join, I'd have enough money to quit," one ex-salesperson of an MLM explained to me. "But I couldn't do that to my friends." (Luckily, to fight negative publicity and to distinguish its members from pyramid scheme operators, the Direct Sales Association has instituted a new policy requiring companies to buy back ninety percent of a distributor's inventory if he or she decides to leave.)

Many MLMs help their salespeople overcome the obvious discomfort associated with enlisting their friends. Mary Kay, for example, rationalizes this game of financial musical chairs through a bizarre corollary of "the Golden Rule as a business philosophy." This is where religion, business, and the "pyramid" combine in a dangerously coercive psychological trick.

As far as I can tell, the thinking goes like this: Since this is such a terrific opportunity, you should want your friends to take part in it, too. Yes, they'll experience the same initial discomfort that you are feeling right now, but then they, too, will take the necessary steps to bring others into the company, and everything will be fine. Have enough faith in God and the power of positive thinking to eradicate this doubt! Look above yourself in the company and see how wealthy and happy everyone is. Your weakness now is selfish and betrays a lack of faith in yourself, your company, and God.

Many Mary Kay members admit that they occasionally have misgivings about the organization but that motivational meetings and videotapes help them push through their doubts. As one New Jersey saleswoman rationalized to an *Asbury Park Press* reporter (November 26, 1995), "To become successful in any endeavor, you've got to get out of your comfort zone."

Those who are able to function well outside the comfort zone are rewarded with tokens of the elusive "glowing eye." Mary Kay distributors who earn twelve recruits and "unit wholesale production" of $16,000 within four months get a red Pontiac Grand Am. Those who earn thirty recruits and $65,000 of production within six months win a pink Pontiac Grand Prix, while $100,000 wins the famous pink Mary Kay Cadillac that the distributor can show off to the underlings who earned it for her.

Similarly, successful sales and recruitment earn a woman a higher place in the company. If a consultant can generate enough sales and bring in enough new recruits, she can advance to the level of sales director or national sales director. Mary Kay literature touts that "after a Beauty Consultant advances to a Director, it is her responsibility to provide her sales group—or unit—with ongoing leadership and guidance. The Director earns her position through a combined effort of her proven selling and recruiting skills and the ability to motivate and lead other Beauty Consultants. Currently, more than 8,000 women are Mary Kay Directors." With more than 8,000 at the director level, it's no wonder these women still strive toward becoming national sales directors, who not only command the 8,000 directors but also enjoy private audiences with their charismatic leader, Mary Kay herself.

The hundreds of multilevel marketing companies operating in the United States today all work on similar principles. Amway boasts more than 2.5 million distributors, although only forty-one percent of these are actively trying to sell products or recruit new members, and this lucky and motivated forty-one percent average only $88 per month in gross income, according to research conducted by Albany's *Times Union* in 1997.

More recently, multilevel marketing companies have replaced the faith in God with a New Age faith in the philosophy of the products themselves. Companies selling herbal remedies, water purifiers, and other "natural" products earn their spiritual credentials by creating the illusion that they are working to combat the stresses and pollution of the modern world. Salespeople convince themselves that they are serving the higher purpose of cleaning the environment, or spreading holistic health cures.

As Mort Spivas, who became a distributor for a network marketing firm selling magnetic insoles, explains it, "These products save people's lives." He believes his products were sold only through network marketing because of a conspiracy by the Food and Drug Administration to prevent healing devices from reaching regular retail outlets. As a result, Spivas says, he was selling not just magnets but a way of seeing the world. "And that's worth as much as the magnets themselves."

Multilevel marketing businesses degenerate into outright pyramid schemes as the products or benefits being offered become less and less tangible. Although a majority of the money is made in membership fees and commissions, most MLMs have a genuine product to sell, even if at a noncompetitive price. Less outwardly reputable, fly-by-night multilevel marketing schemes sell nothing more than membership in a get-rich scenario. These Ponzis only promise that if you pay money to the person at the top of the pyramid, eventually you will be at the top of the pyramid yourself, and then other people will send you some money, too.

The transparently greed-oriented Ponzi scheme gets its name from Charles Ponzi, an Italian immigrant and successful Boston investment broker who sought to capitalize on the simple principle of geometric progression. In 1920, he set up an investment scheme that promised "fifty percent profit in forty-five days" for all who invested in his foreign postal coupons. He was able to fulfill his wild guarantees by paying off early investors with the cash he collected from growing hordes of newcomers. He collected more than $9,500,000 in this manner. Within six months, however, Ponzi had run out of new investors from whom he could get the money to pay off those whose coupons had matured. Thousands of people lost their life savings, and Ponzi was sent to prison. His name was forever equated with the pyramid investment game.

The problem inherent in any Ponzi scheme is that eventually the well will run dry. The market will either become oversaturated with product (if there is one), or the bottom of the pyramid will become so big that there are simply not enough people left in the world to buy in. The people at the bottom of the pyramid must lose.

Consider the math. If each member of a pyramid scheme is required to recruit just ten new members, paying $100 each, then by three levels the pyramid will need one thousand new members. Three levels later, new recruits will need to find one million more participants to earn their quota. Three levels more, a billion. Whether the Ponzi scheme involves selling empty promises or real products, the numbers remain the same.

Thus pyramid and Ponzi artists attempt to convince new recruits that they have gotten in on the "ground floor" of a unique income-generating opportunity. The inevitable dilution of potential earnings becomes the motivation to "get in early." The victims' greed outweighs their common sense. When they invariably lose, they justify the disaster: If only they had gotten in on an earlier level, everything would have been different. In a compulsive cycle, they go from one scheme to another, chasing their losses in the hope of getting in earlier than the last time. The population of regular participants has grown so large that it qualifies as a bona fide subculture. The underground world of Ponzi schemes spills out into the classified pages of newspapers and online bulletin boards of the Internet, hoping to draw in more players. Addicts scour the ads and evaluate new schemes with the misdirected fervor of a gambler "calculating" the probability of a roulette wheel. But Ponzi schemes, like Las Vegas craps tables, are suckers' games. Everyone loses but the house.

The Internet has proved a fertile ground for pyramid schemes, and the enforcement agencies charged with regulating them don't have enough resources to track them all down. Countless pieces of junk mail are delivered to the users of America Online every day, offering "unique business opportunities" that are "completely legal." Amazingly, these scams work as intended: They rob people of their money and create huge profits for their originators, all within the letter of the law.

Although it is currently illegal to launch a Ponzi scheme, it is still legal to sell things to people. In other words, you can't simply ask people to send money to someone higher up in a pyramid; they must receive something in return. Internet Ponzis nominally meet this legal requirement by selling "information" in the form of mailing lists, or even just the instructions on how to participate in the Ponzi scheme itself. They sell nothing more than the rules on how to extend the Ponzi. Just as MLMs lead their customers to think of themselves as new "distributors," successful Ponzis lead the participants to believe that they are the new perpetrators.

Many of the infomercials on TV for wealth-building opportunities work in precisely this way. The television viewers pay a few hundred dollars for kits that show them how to generate wealth by placing advertisements in newspapers selling "information." What sort of information are they given to sell? The *same* information—how to place ads in newspapers to generate wealth! More expensive kits include video and audio cassettes with vague and motivational themes. Their purpose is to help would-be Ponzi schemers convince themselves that they're doing nothing wrong and that they owe it to themselves to be on the winning side for a change. Some packages include a list of newspapers and the addresses of their classified advertising departments. (At least someone makes a profit off the scam.)

Other Ponzis invite their prospects to free seminars at local hotels. Using a mixture of showmanship and other influence techniques, the presenters relieve audiences of their hard-earned money by drawing them into the illusion of a business opportunity. The only qualification needed to become a member is to show up at the seminar.

"In fact, you've already taken the first and most critical step forward," explained the welcoming literature for a seminar I attended at an airport hotel. "This may be the most important step you'll ever take in your quest." Once the audience was seated and ready, the hosts made a point of closing and locking the reception-room doors. "That's it!" the host told us. "Nobody else is getting in. You are it!" He wanted to make sure the audience knew that no one else would get in at this level of the pyramid. Then, like a vaudeville hypnotist asking for volunteers, the speaker selected a person from the audience to come up on the stage. He handed him a hundred-dollar bill and said he could keep it. "How does that feel?" he asked, implying that everyone who signed up for the program would have to get used to this feeling of being given money, seemingly for nothing.

The presenter assured his audience that they had, indeed, found an "opportunity too good to be true." He told us of the hundreds of possible business plans we could launch, but never specifically mentioned any one of them. By the end of the seminar, about two-thirds of the audience had signed checks for $599 to participate. What they received was information on how to create a Web site and then use it to launch a business of their own.

Although less dramatic than a live stage show, the Internet is an easier place to launch a Ponzi. Broadcasting a message to thousands of recipients costs almost nothing, and a clever piece of e-mail can seem more personal than a television ad. Internet-style Ponzis usually consist of a message that is disseminated throughout cyberspace. Because the letters that work the best tend to get distributed more widely, Ponzis have developed according to the rules of natural selection. Today's surviving Ponzi letters utilize a wide range of influence techniques.

The subject line of the letter, like all good junk e-mail, exists only to fool the user into opening the message. "$50,000 in 30 Days, Guaranteed!" is a popular one. A more recent ruse is to make the letter look as though it were misdirected. The recipient line may read "Bill," and the subject line will say something like "Get back to me on this today." The entire letter might be in the form of correspondence between two fictional people. The recipient is to believe he is the lucky beneficiary of a computer glitch.

The writer of the e-mail will assume the role of a charismatic leader and will often claim to have either a credentialed history as a lawyer or businessman, or a coincidental stroke of good fortune. The results are kept vague, like "Imagine yourself on a 60-foot yacht." The letter asserts that "your luck has already changed" and that now a small amount of effort must be expended: "It won't work for you if you don't try it!"

A long, confusing series of numbers ends with a simple declaration: "All you need to do is follow the program EXACTLY AS INSTRUCTED."

The products "sold" by most of these Internet-style Ponzis are just lists of e-mail addresses that the participants can use to launch their own Ponzis. It never occurs to the victims that these are probably the very same lists that have been used hundreds of times before, mostly by other Ponzi victims.

The worst of the Ponzi schemes trade on the superstitions of their more paranoid recipients: "Dolon Fairchild received this letter and, not believing it, threw it away. Nine days later he died." Like traditional "magic" chain letters, these Ponzis augment the lure of financial reward with a supernatural punishment for noncompliance. The greedy victim who refuses to acknowledge his own desire for ill-gotten cash can now justify his decision as an act of self-preservation.

Knocking on Heaven's Door

My own brief experience with a pyramid's persuasive tug was the result of a failed relationship with a woman who was deeply involved in a New Age cult led by a Balinese guru. I first met Janet (not her real name) at a theater workshop taught by one of the original members of the Actors Studio. After we had been dating for about two months, Janet began to tell me about another of her teachers—a very spiritual man who was even more inspiring to her than our theater maestro. Although her New Age beliefs had never been an issue, I had always wondered just why they were so important to her. So, at her encouragement, I took advantage of a free "introduction" being offered at a villa that his followers kept for him in Santa Monica.

When I arrived, I noticed that there weren't gongs, incense, or any of the other accoutrements I imagined would fill a New Age ashram. It looked more like the home office of a successful psychiatrist. When the guru himself emerged wearing a Ralph

Lauren suit and Bruno Magli loafers, I felt a bit intimidated yet oddly reassured at the same time. His style wasn't foreign or esoteric enough to set off any alarms. He greeted me with a handshake, and said that Janet had already told him a lot about me. He was looking forward to seeing if I was capable of experiencing "the colors," and brought me into a small room. He then closed the door and asked me to sit down and relax. He waved his hands around, then moved behind me. That's when, to my surprise, swirls of color seemed to emanate from the air. Surely this man had something special, I thought. Either that or he had mastered a terrific magic trick. "Good," he said, as if he had been auditioning me. "You had a great entrance. You could go very far."

After performing free introductions on a number of other newcomers, the soft-spoken spiritual leader gave a lecture by candlelight, using concepts from pop psychology and basic Buddhism. His faithful followers—among them several prominent therapists, businesspeople, and religion professors—nodded along, entranced by his rhythmic cadence. I tried to follow his wandering logic as best as I could, and to keep my cynicism in check. He presented himself as the exclusive doorway to a new level of consciousness and peace. Although it was hard to accept that the Buddha himself had been reincarnated as an Asian pop psychologist, his ability to "create colors" had, according to the respected clientele present, been documented by a number of established scientific institutes. If nothing else, this man seemed to possess some miraculous abilities worthy of exploration.

The guru told me I was a suitable candidate for follow-up "color cleansings," at a cost of $200 each. My girlfriend told me I should be honored to have been approved as a student, and encouraged me to take advantage of this unique opportunity. Only by paying for cleansings would I begin to experience their great benefit. After two or three of these, however, I learned that only after a $2,000 "full-spectrum encounter," in which I was to sleep overnight at the villa-ashram, would I be capable of "melting" the accumulated distortions I had developed over my twenty-six years of unclear living. Luckily, before I moved up to that level of financial commitment, I had a chance to speak to some of the people who had dropped out of the group—most of them women who had paid thousands of dollars over a period of years for what turned out to be ritualized sexual abuse performed by the guru during these overnight retreats.

One young dropout, a philosophy grad student at USC, told me that the guru had brushed his hands against her breasts during her very first cleansing. Afraid it may have simply been an accident, she said nothing about it. Cleansing after cleansing, he made further advances, until she was sure his groping was intentional. When she complained to one of the guru's assistants, she was not believed. Instead, she was immediately brought before the guru, who, alone with the girl, convinced her it was she who slowly seduced him. Then she was brought before the entire cult to be reprimanded for lying, and she eventually recanted her accusation. After this incident, she remained a member for more than a year, rationalizing that she was responsible for temporarily corrupting her teacher's absolute purity.

Other students welcomed his advances and looked forward to nights when they would be chosen to sleep with him. Sometimes as many as three or four women would service the guru at once. Even though most cult members had taken a vow of celibacy, the women still were encouraged to offer their bodies to their teacher so that they could receive the "physical essence" of his energy. The intercourse was never referred to as sex but as sharing a "divine intimacy." Like a child molester preying on his own daughter's need to be loved, the guru made his victims complicit in their molestation. Very often he had sex with students who were already married, so that he could subtly blackmail these women later. In any case, the women who had sex with the guru were forced to convince themselves that they were doing something sacred, which drew them further into the cult; the alternative was just too horrible to confront.

Without revealing to her all the evidence I had gathered, I gently asked Janet if she had engaged in any kind of sexual contact with the teacher, which she vehemently denied. "He doesn't get anything at all from *us*," she insisted. I knew if I pressed too hard, I would lose her completely. I hoped my questions would crack her resolve and lead her to ask a few questions herself. But in a few days she told me of her plans to go on a group retreat with the guru to Hawaii, and she asked if I wanted to come along. I didn't, but neither did I want to leave her so vulnerable to this dangerous man. I felt obliged to tell her everything I knew. She seemed a little shocked—less by what I told her than by the fact that I knew so much and had gone to such pains to research her teacher's darker side. By the next morning, however, after she made a few phone calls to other cult members, she turned on me. "How dare you try to shake my faith!" she cried.

She went on the retreat and moved into the ashram shortly afterward, refusing to take any of my phone calls. I spoke with her parents, who told me they were more concerned about keeping their other daughters out of the cult (Janet's sisters had already experienced sessions) than saving the one already so far in.

Why do cult members allow themselves to be subjected to such brutality and exploitation by their superiors, and, once they reach the higher levels of the organization, why do they perpetuate such atrocities? The answer can be found by looking at other voluntary hazing practiced by less formal social hierarchies, like street gangs and fraternities. These groups have seized upon rites of passage to indoctrinate their members that are just as brutal and humiliating as any cult initiation. The severity of the humiliation inflicted is matched only by the resulting dedication to the group. The more intense the hazing, the more intense the loyalty to the club that dispenses it.

Newspaper headlines are filled with accounts of murders committed by young men as part of their initiation into violent street gangs. At the outset, initiates into street gangs are "beat in" by veterans. They must submit to an intense flurry of kicks and punches by the gang's members for either a specified period of time or until the gang leader has judged that the initiate has taken enough abuse. The Gangster Disciples of Portage, Wisconsin, beat a thirteen-year-old girl for six minutes after she elected to submit to a bruising rather than be "sexed in" by six fifteen-year-old boys. Unlike their urban counterparts, few of these suburban and rural gangs break laws for profit. They don't generally deal drugs for organized crime, nor do they commit armed robberies or muggings. Their most violent actions are directed against their own members and those of rival gangs.

Once the beating-in has been completed, inductees of the most violent gangs are made to perform the next rite of passage, which is to commit murder. While some gangs require the initiate to kill a member of a rival group, most prefer that the initiate pick someone at random. This distinction is important. For effective indoctrination, the requests made to the subject must not always appear to be in the authority's best interest. If a gang leader directs an initiate to kill one of the gang's enemies, the order has a practical purpose. The initiate can rationalize what he has been asked to do as beneficial to someone else. If, on the other hand, he has been asked to commit a random act of violence, the murder simply bestows authority onto the people who commanded him to do it. The intended effect is regression and transference. Moreover, the initiate knows that the sole purpose of the murder he has committed is to secure his own initiation. A human life has been spent on his membership and nothing else.

The painful hazings inflicted by college fraternities during "hell week" initiations work on the same principles. Although most fraternities engage in some form of community service, very few allow such charity to interfere with the senseless humiliation of their members' initiation ceremonies. A study conducted at the University of Washington revealed that only one fraternity related its hell week rituals to any socially meaningful project. The beatings, starvation, exposure to cold, sexual humiliation, and other hazing activities have no discernible purpose other than the degradation and indoctrination of new members.

I interviewed two alumni from an infamous Ivy League secret society that boasts several prominent politicians and businessmen as its members. The initiation ceremony they say they endured requires inductees to lie in a coffin and masturbate in full view of the older members. (Of course, these alumni might simply have been maintaining yet another cult tradition of exaggerating the severity of their hazing rituals.) Obviously, no purpose is served by this sort of self-degradation other than the humiliation of the participants. Submitting to such a harsh trial forces the initiate to justify the inherent value of the group he has joined. It is a retroactive reasoning, as one initiate expressed: "Once you do it, you have to believe it was worth it."

Some initiates come to embrace their hazing so much that they are willing to fight to retain their right to be humiliated. When, in reaction to a hazing death on campus, the president of the University of Southern California attempted to mandate supervision over fraternity initiation, the campus rioted. The steadfastness with which fraternities maintain their violent initiations in the face of extreme pressure to the contrary appears to prove they are a cherished social rite. But why?

Psychologist Robert Cialdini, in his book *Influence: The Psychology of Persuasion,* found an answer in a study conducted in the late 1950s. Women who were forced to "endure a severely embarrassing initiation ceremony in order to gain access to a sex discussion group convinced themselves that their new group and its discussions were extremely valuable, even though [the researchers] had previously rehearsed the other group members to be as 'worthless and uninteresting' as possible." Meanwhile, women who were permitted to join the group with a milder initiation found the experience to be of much less value. In another study, the higher the voltage of electric shock delivered to coeds joining a social group corresponded directly with how interesting and desirable they later perceived the group to be.

Like the long line of people standing outside in the cold as they wait to be let into an exclusive nightclub, the people who suffer through grueling initiations believe their suffering proves the worth of the organization they are joining. No pain, no gain is the underlying logic energizing the art of discipline. A painful, purposeless initiation ritual proves a member's commitment to the group.

After my own exposure to the dark world of a New Age cult came to an end, I had the opportunity to analyze why this man and his group had such an unshakable hold over my girlfriend. My anger and distress led me to investigate other cults in the hope of one day getting to the bottom of why so many seemingly intelligent people get caught up in them. I assembled a vast collection of notes and tapes on cult methodology that sat in a drawer for a long time; try as I might to get them published, no magazines were interested in my findings. They all had run too many similar stories before. Although I undertook the research as a vendetta aimed at exposing these techniques for their poisonous effects, it is painfully ironic that this work never would have seen the light of day if an interested party—in this case a business hoping to turn cult status into a source of revenue—hadn't come along ten years later to solicit the ideas.

In my very first interview with Douglas Atkin, he asked me if I knew anything about cults. He had become fascinated by "cult brands" like Apple computers and Harley-Davidson motorcycles, and he wanted to know how cults got started in the first place. If he could understand the features of real cults, perhaps he could apply the same principles to brands that wanted to achieve cult status. Using the information I had gathered about six different New Age cults in the United States, I presented Atkin's agency with a list of twenty features common to them all. They amount to a primer in pyramid schemes, and they depend on nearly all of the coercive strategies we have examined so far, including hand-to-hand selling, atmospherics, spectacle, transference, hypnosis, and storytelling, combined into a unique and powerfully leveraged system. These are the twenty steps I presented to Douglas Atkin and the Wells BDDP advertising agency.

1. The Goal Every cult has a stated, if vague and metaphorical, goal. Because this goal must serve as the "illuminated eye" of the pyramid, it cannot be attainable. Rather, it is expressed as an abstract idea—like "enlightenment," "aliveness," "endless freedom," "liberation," or "salvation"—which the cult member will enjoy once he has "made it" to the top of the pyramid. Entering the cult means escaping from one's problems, and the goal allows members to rephrase this escape as a positive quest toward a higher spiritual state.

2. A Charismatic Leader All cults—whether spiritual or mundane—have a charismatic figurehead. Charismatic, in this context, means more than simply personable or good-looking. Charisma really boils down to the ability to perform a hypnotic induction. The leader must be someone whose speech, manner, and energy exert inexplicable influence. While some leaders develop these skills through years of research into neuro-linguistic programming and Eriksonian techniques, most don't understand the techniques they are using and have intuited how their gestures, vocal fluctuations, or eye contact can lead followers into a suggestible state of mind.

In religious cults, the leader attains his divine status in one of two ways. The first is by claiming to be the hand-picked successor to the last guru, or a reincarnation of a previous messiah— Buddha, Christ, or Krishna. The second is by claiming to embody an entirely new spiritual force—either to have been born sacred or to have suffered an "awakening" trauma or a sudden "new breeze" of insight. The second method allows leaders much more freedom to improvise their tenets on an as-needed basis, or to prescribe strange methodologies by which their followers can reach the same state of meritorious grace.

3. Sacred Doctrine Most cults have a sacred text or doctrine. Often a cult will adopt an established text, like the Bible or the Koran. Others use a spontaneously revealed doctrine. These are usually "channeled" and transcribed. If the sacred text is based on a scientific or philosophical system that has been invented, the leader can simply write it himself.

4. Divine Coincidence New members must learn of the cult effortlessly, as if by grace. Though membership and advancement should be difficult, discovery must be extremely easy. New members might find a flyer on the subway, a small advertisement in a local paper, or be greeted spontaneously by a devotee on the street. Members often describe how a sacred text literally "fell" off a bookshelf in a store, or how a magazine miraculously opened to a page with an advertisement for the cult.

If the member believes he came to the cult through conscious or rational processes, then he is in a position to take responsibility and credit for his participation. Cults try to avoid this perception because a member should be separated from his sense of willpower in order to be fully indoctrinated.

5. Positive Results Through Commitment While discovery and introduction are almost always free, the newcomer is told that he will experience satisfaction only when he has made a financial or equivalent commitment. At sales meetings for another of the cults I investigated, writing a check was equated with the first step toward changing one's life, and new members reported feeling results the moment they made this commitment. Similarly, a full "transmission" of divine energy from a guru is predicated on an act of surrender by the new devotee, usually in the form of cash.

6. Extraordinary Measures Once a new member has made his initial surrender or contribution to the cult, he is asked to do something that contradicts his judgment. It could be as simple as bowing down to the cult leader, or paying what seems like an exorbitant fee for a workshop or weekend seminar (like $2,000 for an overnight full-spectrum encounter). What's important is that the act goes against the new member's own internal sense of appropriateness. The member must get used to acting against his own values.

7. Member Complicity Once an extraordinary measure is taken, the member is rewarded with complicity in the greater pyramid. One member of the Santa Monica cult confessed to me that immediately following his donation of $2,000 for a full-spectrum encounter, the leader took him for a drink in an expensive bar and then paid the tab with the cult's "charity" money! Sex is used in the same way, allowing the cult leader to make the newly committed member a partner in crime. To get out of the cult after this act of complicity, the member will have to own up to all of the cult's practices as if they were his own.

8. A Cycle of Breaking "Self" After extracting extraordinary measures and complicity, the cult leader exploits the commonly practiced spiritual discipline of self-denial and demands increasingly difficult acts of faith from his followers. Sometimes these requests seem to benefit the cult leader—members are instructed to donate huge sums of money, refuse communication with concerned family members, perform sexual favors, or contribute tremendous time and labor to the cult. Just as often, however, these requests will be completely arbitrary or even against the apparent interests of the cult leader. A member might be asked to give $1,000 to a beggar in the street. One cult member I interviewed was instructed by his guru to quit his investment-banking job and become a waiter, even though doing so meant he had less money to donate to the cult. By interspersing real requests with these random and bizarre instructions, the cult leader can avoid the appearance of self-interest. He also can paralyze his followers' ability to second-guess his actions.

9. Confusion and Transference By alternating self-interested and random demands, the cult leader brings his followers into a state of great confusion—they aren't sure how to please him. Sometimes the leader will reward members who fail to carry out his commands, and punish those who complete them successfully. The CIA suggests using rewards and punishments in a random, illogical manner so that subjects regress into childlike dependence. Similarly, the confused cult member eventually regresses to a childlike state and transfers parental authority to the leader—which is why so many cult leaders insist they be called "Mother" or "Father."

10. Prescriptive Behavior Like any victim of induced regression and transference, once his ability to make decisions has been suspended, the cult member looks to his leader for guidance on how to behave. He longs for direction on what to think, do, and believe. Some cult leaders withhold these instructions, reducing their followers to a state of desperate panic. Others present them with long lists of prescriptions, from exercises and meditations to herbs and bathing rituals. Claire Prophet of Montana distributes computer-generated menus listing exactly what each follower should eat for every meal.

11. The Goal of Inclusion Once transference has been achieved, the elusive stated goal of the pyramid cult is replaced with the much more tangible one of establishing a relationship with the leader. The cult members become, in effect, siblings competing for their parent's approval. The result is a prolonged psychodrama that capitalizes on unresolved issues from the members' own family backgrounds. The power of reliving this dynamic cannot be underestimated. The cult leader orchestrates emotional battles, pitting members against one another as they all seek to develop a "special relationship" with him.

12. Never Expose Uncertainty to Those Lower in the Pyramid By the time a member is this far into a cult, he is required to preserve the illusion of its cohesion and perfection. Since a member's sense of status and nearness to the leader is directly related to how many people are beneath him in the cult hierarchy, he must always make an effort to recruit more members.

A member's stature is directly related to his ability to maintain the appearance of steadfast devotion to the cult. He cannot reveal any lingering doubts about the divinity of the leader lest he lose his own place in the hierarchy to more ardent followers beneath him. Further, expressing doubt to a new member is seen as an act of heresy. Why would someone induce a crisis in a new member unless he were hoping to undermine the cult's efforts to expand? Doubts must be expressed only to a member higher in the organization, who is charged with handling the crises of underlings. In fact, a cult member's very position in the pyramid is defined by his ability to quell the doubts of those beneath him, without being thrown into doubt himself.

13. Never Expose Uncertainty to Those Higher in the Pyramid Eventually, any expression of doubt at all is deemed an offense against the cult. To spread one's misgivings to a higher member is, in effect, a challenge to that member's own resolve. Such expressions can be allowed up to a point, but ultimately the member must learn that he is the source of his own doubts and must overcome crises without spreading his confusion to others. Moving up the pyramid is a competitive game. Confessing one's misgivings to a higher member merely affirms the latter's superior status in the pyramid. If one is to move up, he must show less doubt and more commitment than those above him.

14. The Cult Precludes All Other Commitments One by one, each member's connections with the real world must be reinterpreted as base "attachments" that need to be purged. The member's original religion, job, friends, spouse, and children are less important than his relationship with the cult and its leader. The member must not gain positive reinforcement from anything or anyone outside the cult.

Family and social bonds are reinterpreted as distractions from the higher values the member is adopting. One cult member told me about a "spiritual attack" she experienced when she realized that her daughter's piano recital fell on the same night of the week as an important lecture given by her guru. She chose to attend the latter, telling herself that the crisis was an opportunity for her to demonstrate her dedication to the group over her "mundane relationships." All real-world associations, inevitably and by design, come into conflict with one's commitment to the higher goal.

15. Never Refuse a Request A member may never refuse a request made by the cult leader, or in the name of the cult. To do so is to place some other value ahead of the sanctity of the group. Most college fraternities require that new members accept any request from a fellow brother—not just during their hazing or college years, but for the rest of their lives.

16. All Requests Can Be Challenged A cult member who has made an inappropriately personal or self-interested request in the name of the cult will be challenged and punished. On the other hand, members who are in the leader's favor can get away with asking almost anything of those beneath them.

17. Never Take Action in the Cult Leader's Name The cult leader is free from all responsibility. I once watched as my girlfriend informed her fellows in the New Age cult that the leader had requested she clear the room; she was the only one who was to stay. The others protested. When the leader finally arrived, he claimed he had never made such an order—but that my girlfriend misinterpreted what he had said out of her own selfish desires. She accepted the mistake as her own, even though I tried to make her see how she had been manipulated.

As she explained it to me, to make a request in the cult leader's name is to blame the cult leader for any ill will that might result. To claim that "I divorced my wife because the leader told me to" is to refuse responsibility for one's own actions. Although the leader may have "shown the way," a member divorces his wife or disowns his children because it's the "right thing to do." To use the leader as an excuse is just another way to express doubt.

18. Act Automatically Members must strive to act in accordance with the cult leader's wishes without thinking. The conditioning, confusion, and fear to which the members are subjected result in a set of new behaviors that take the place of what normally might be called intuition or instinct. Once achieved, this automatic behavior is a welcome relief from the constant questioning of one's own actions. Interestingly, many cult members report that from this stage of programming onward, they wake up in the mornings with no memories of their dreams.

19. Witness and Accept the Leader's Faults Once they reach the highest levels of the cult pyramid, members are privy to their leader's darkest actions. My girlfriend's cult leader actually used a battery-powered apparatus to create the illusion of colors. His closest aides know that the miracle is really sleight of hand, but they tell themselves that the leader fakes only *some* of his magic as a way to create healthy and character-building doubt in his followers. "If he did it for real every time," one young man told me, "then it would be too easy to have faith."

Members must also come to terms with the abusive behavior of their leader. After a guru beats or sodomizes a member, the witnesses conclude that the cult leader was embodying their own hostility toward the victim. Indeed, the cult leader is a martyr, helplessly acting on the impure thoughts of his closest followers, demonstrating to them their own dark natures. It is up to the inner-circle members to purge themselves of the base energies that might lead their compassionate hero—a mere vessel—to personify their evil.

20. The Cult Leader Is Perfection The final stage of cult indoctrination is to accept the leader as the perfect center of the universe, from which all else derives. The "fully evolved" cult member thus understands all pain and suffering as resistance to the cult leader's divinity. The leader is the single point of entry for God and perfection in an otherwise imperfect universe.

Once he has achieved such a stature in his followers' minds, the leader can ask them to do anything, even to kill themselves. They already have been trained to go against their own instincts. Thwarting one's natural tendency toward self-preservation becomes a pleasurable, almost fetishistic obsession. As members look for more outrageous ways to break their own attachment to life, suicide emerges as the ultimate act of devotion.

These twenty steps to cult indoctrination are applied most dangerously, perhaps, by religious groups, but are just as prevalent in Ponzis and MLMs. Stephanie's induction to the health-products-distribution system followed the steps precisely: Her goal was to move to a private community; she discovered the publicity flyer through what she felt was an "eerie" coincidence; the company had a charismatic leader; the sacred text was the inspirational sales manual; Stephanie's initial commitment was a burdensome $600; and her first extraordinary measure was to supplement her weekly sales total with her own purchases. As she became more fully indoctrinated, she engaged in complicity by lying about her weekly totals for the benefit of her new prospect. When transference was complete, she became completely dependent on the detailed scripts her supervisor had given her. Finally, when Stephanie knew she was in over her head, she kept the truth even from her superior and accepted that her failure was only her own fault. Some MLMs, cults, and even many established churches hoping to expand their memberships use the same basic steps to indoctrinate members, who go on to solicit new ones.

I later analyzed the attributes common to successful cult brands and found them to be strikingly similar to the attributes of genuine cults.

Cult brands are generally associated with an aspirational goal, which is often stated directly in the product's advertising. For Apple computers, for example, the "Think Different" campaign speaks to an Apple user's desire to defy conformity (conformity being embodied by the ubiquitous Windows operating system) and to blaze his own path in the manner of the company's uniquely defiant billboard heroes—Gandhi, Muhammad Ali, and John Lennon. The personality at the center of Apple computers is its charismatic founder, Steve Jobs, whose own story of defying the prevailing industry logic and forging ahead with a garage-based computer business symbolizes the creative spirit that all Apple users value. The easy entry to Apple is its simple operating system. Most users can remember when they peered over someone's shoulder and got their first glimpse of the user-friendly interface. Those who became members of the Apple cult felt that they, unlike the majority of their peers, had the ability recognize the special value of the brand beyond any of its specific attributes.

The members of such brand cults value the extra measures they must take to maintain the products to which they have dedicated themselves. Much of the software for Apple computers is not readily available, forcing users to find what they need in catalogues from mail-order houses. Others join "user groups" in their communities, from which they download necessary software, with extra effort and determined pride. To become known as a committed member of a consumer cult, the customer must make personal sacrifices for the sake of the brand. For Apple computers, it might mean joining online discussion groups and sharing one's knowledge of the system to users who are having trouble—in effect, serving as unpaid customer-service representatives. Extremely devoted Apple users, who call themselves MacEvangelists, volunteer to demonstrate Apple products at retail stores. They work as salespeople for free.

These "power users" are generally rewarded by the company with complicity in the brand's success. Apple was loyal to its early users and advocates, granting them free memberships in their (now-defunct) online community, as well as developer's materials, free software, and T-shirts. Further, the more people Apple users can convert into "Mac-heads," the easier it will be to find software and compatible accessories.

As the brand grows to mainstream popularity, the inner circle of original users must be rewarded with special offers, advance samples of new products, and information about the company's future that they can share with others and use to demonstrate their status. Longtime customers, like inner-circle cult members, are privy to the company's "secrets." Marketers of Converse sneakers gave free shoes and other items to salespeople and high school athletes who they thought could generate cult appeal for the brand. The inner-circle members of the Apple cult are usually repair people or resellers themselves who have financial incentives to remain true to their brands.

Most of the people who become so closely allied with a particular product eventually come to experience disillusionment with the brand they have learned to promote. But after having expended so much effort and so publicly declaring their allegiance to the brand, they maintain at least the outward appearance of deep loyalty. Many Mac users and developers told me they were deeply distressed by Steve Jobs's decisions to make deals with Microsoft and to prevent other companies from licensing the Mac operating system to use on their own computers. But some of these same loyal users told their customers, clients, and fellow online community members that "Steve Jobs knows best," and chose to support his decisions when confronted by friends or journalists. In this way, they were honoring the last cult rule—The Cult Leader Is Perfection—and thus should never be publicly questioned.

The true inner sanctum of any cult brand is the advertising agency in which the brand is devised. Whether or not they believe in the product—or the campaign—the advertising executives adopt an air of creative know-how. They often pretend to have secret research supporting their conclusions, known only by the creative director. Conspiracy theorists, who believe that advertisers use subliminal messages, base their paranoid musings more on this insiderly behavior than on any real technique.

Businesses and other institutions hoping to exploit pyramid techniques apply them more subtly than do cults or advertising agencies, who can hide behind religious fervor or marketing irony. Still, they depend on the underlying psychological appeal of pyramidal exclusivity and painful initiation.

Irrational Exuberance— The Automated Pyramid

"They will find a way to mess it up," Steve Forbes told a CNBC interviewer toward the end of the 1998 Dow Jones run-up.[1] He had been asked whether the explosive bull market could last indefinitely, as optimistic analysts were predicting, or if an unforeseen force could turn things around for the worse. Who is the "they" to which Forbes was referring, and why would they want to find a way to mess it up?

The stock market provides businesses with a way to raise capital, and investors with a way to secure stakes in growing firms. To buy securities on one of the world's many stock exchanges is to buy shares of ownership in any of the thousands of businesses listed there. Although shares are initially offered directly by the companies themselves, they soon trade in an open market between individuals and investment firms, who bet on the shares' future values. The real value of a stock—its "fundamentals"—is based on the projected earnings of the company and the amount of cash the company will pay out to its shareholders in the form of dividends.

The market value of a stock is something else entirely. In spite of its utilitarian purpose of raising and distributing capital, the stock market also functions—and the most cynical anticapitalists would argue, functions primarily—as a pyramid.

Respected investors and experts at the top of the pyramid buy the issues they want at the lowest price possible. Usually they will pick a stock that has gone out of favor for one reason or another. Their own large purchases bump up the price of the stock a couple of points. Then they issue reports or go on television and make buy recommendations on that same stock, based on the recent turnaround in the price. As investors scramble to match the moves of their favorite analysts, the recommended stock invariably shoots up, increasing the value of the expert's portfolio and adding to his credibility. Once interest has reached a peak and the number of new buyers has reached the saturation point, the original buyers sell their stock to the last round of patsies—the lowest level of the pyramid, usually composed of smaller, individual investors—who are left holding the stock as everyone else sells. Then the price of the stock drops accordingly. With devalued stock in hand, the last investors can find no one to buy it at a price anywhere near what they paid. Then the experts issue sell recommendations, buy in again, and the whole process starts all over.

This entire cycle can take place during a single trading session. "Market makers," midlevel investors who hold large numbers of shares for trading, spread rumors over the Internet about small-cap (not widely held) stocks in order to knock their prices down even a fraction of a point. They buy on the dip and then, as people become aware that the rumor is false, sell at a slightly higher price. An uptick of as little as ¼ point on 10,000 shares yields $2,500. Doing this every day, a small-time player can make $500,000 a year off other people's panic and ignorance. Although these practices are illegal, there are far too many stocks and market makers for regulatory agencies to follow every one of them.

Usually, however, the pyramid scheme takes place over several weeks or months and is orchestrated by an influential analyst or mutual-fund manager from a respected brokerage house. For example, in late 1995 the Securities and Exchange Commission (SEC) investigated Jeffrey Vinik, the manager of what was at the time the largest U.S. stock mutual fund, the $53 billion Fidelity Magellan, for manipulating the market. In his statements on television, Mr. Vinik said he believed that high-technology stocks would be high performers, and that Micron Electronics stock was "still relatively cheap." At the same time, however, Vinik was selling off millions of shares of hi-tech stocks, including a majority of his fund's stake in Micron. The tactic was obvious: Keep investors buying the stock long enough for him to dump it himself.

Attorneys for the plaintiffs argued in the *New York Law Journal* (January 4, 1996) that a fund manager like Vinik, with so much money and influence at his disposal, can turn the motions of the market to his advantage: "They have the ability; that's the key . . . [The fund manager] has tremendous power, huge positions in millions of shares of stock and a variety of market sectors. Thus, what they say will have a tremendous impact . . . and they have the ability to manipulate the market."[2]

People gain this ability through their access not only to funds but to media. It's the fund manager's apparent expertise that fools the many people lower than him on the pyramid. Clever ads for Internet-based discount brokerage houses, where individuals are empowered to make trades through their laptop computers, draw new blood and new money into the game every day. The influx of rookies, confused by market gyrations, complicated tax calculations, and earnings data, transfer authority onto the pundits of CNBC and CNNFN. Investors can tune in at 5:00 A.M. each morning to glean the latest tips and handicaps from their new authority figures, under the illusion that they can beat one another to the trading block.

Once people are committed, as with any pyramid, faith is key. During the bull market, people who spoke bearishly were criticized for trying to hurt the economy by breaking the resolve of the faithful. Naysayers were ridiculed on television as pessimistic killjoys who didn't understand the fundamental principles of the ever-expanding economy. The faithful, on the other hand, were cheered by experts and newscasters alike—just as Stephanie was cheered on by her fellow distributors. When the bull market looked to be topping off in 1997, the normally mild-mannered "Wall Street Week" host Louis Rukeyser assumed the role of a preacher, openly congratulating viewers who kept "the faith."[3]

This faith was buoyed by a new breed of financial experts— the "new economists"—who backed up their bullish rhetoric with a set of enhanced theories that pointed to technology as the source of the pyramid's potential for eternal growth. If *Forbes* was the capitalist's tool, then *Wired* was the technocapitalist's, arguing that the introduction of computers and networking could effectively automate returns on investment, infinitely.

One of the principles the new economists advanced, called "network externalities," demonstrated how, unlike in prior eras, the more pervasive a technology, the more valuable it will become.[4] In the traditional economy, diamonds are valuable because of their scarcity. With new technologies, just the opposite is true. For example, in a world with only one fax machine, fax machines would be worthless. The more common a technology is, the more valuable and necessary it becomes. But this "the more the merrier" philosophy is also at the heart of any good

MLM: The value of a Mary Kay distributorship is directly proportional to the number of downline distributors. Likewise, consumers may get on board a cult brand for one reason, and then hold on despite very rational reasons for jumping ship. The more sacrifices people make to maintain their commitment to a certain brand or technology, the more committed they become. The law of networked externalities begs the question of whether the proliferation of all this technology is a result of consumer demand or market necessity. Who ultimately benefits? Those of us who raise the cash to buy and use the fax machines, the people who make them, or those who invest in their stocks?

Like multilevel marketers, the new economists advise that we push through our doubt and forge ahead. *Wired* assured its readers that a "Long Boom" of economic growth was ahead—but they were just as quick to warn that "all along the way the chorus of naysayers will insist it simply can't be done. We'll need some hefty doses of indefatigable optimism. We'll need an optimistic vision of what the future can be."[5] Sometimes this indefatigable optimism will need to transcend common sense as well.

Realizing that making a pyramid work indefinitely would require a steady influx of new buyers, the Long Boomers pointed to Asia and the need for "open systems," which allow for the entrance of new markets into the scheme. Foreign governments must quit their whining about economic or cultural imperialism and open their doors to free trade. As *Wired* put it: "In a nutshell, the key formula for the coming age is this: Open, good. Closed, bad. Tattoo it on your forehead." They meant this initiation ritual figuratively, of course, but the herd mentality it encourages is crucial for the scheme to continue.

Entrance into a pyramid requires that all comers adopt the same primary yet elusive goal—in this case the technocapitalist vision of infinite economic prosperity for all through network externalities. If we surrender everything to the goal of economic expansion and technological development, we will generate global prosperity. As long as everyone buys in, everyone one will benefit from the economic expansion they, themselves, are fueling. But critics worry that the eye atop this Long Boom pyramid may not prove to be as universal as its proponents suggest.

Baltimore City Paper writer Joab Jackson wondered aloud:

> Equating completely free markets with politically open societies is deceptive. While most agree that politically open societies (such as democracies) are preferable to closed ones (such as Communist regimes and military dictatorships), the superiority of a totally unregulated free market is far from uncontested. For instance, George Soros argued . . . that open markets and open societies are anathema because the former reduce every value held by a culture to its monetary worth.[6]

In other words, as the pyramid requires more economic sustenance, more and more of our ideas and activities become grist for this particular mill. As in any cult, our existing values must be replaced by the priorities of the pyramid—which is why, like cult leaders who force their followers to surrender their earthly ties, the technocapitalists call for less government and less publicly sponsored civic activity. Instead of taxing our every word and deed, they bid on them. Moreover, they hope to use the same technologies that they're selling to automate the process by which our personal values are systematically replaced with market incentives.

Critics are labeled pessimists or Luddites, and blamed for holding back the good and necessary evolution of humanity into the digital age. What we don't realize, however, is that our interpretation of what it means to progress might have been formulated for us by those at the top of the pyramid, who stand to profit from our mindless participation.

As in any pyramid scheme, the need to subscribe newcomers outweighs whatever benefits the products or system might offer. Many MLMs sell distributorships more than cosmetics. Stockbrokers sell hype over fundamentals. Cult members seek new recruits to raise their own positions in the hierarchy. Mac users try to convert their friends in order to increase the value and universal compatibility of their own machines. And techno-utopian economists sell a financial rationale for why expansionist economics can go on forever.

In all these cases, the power of networking—social, economic, and technological—is exploited by people who offer little more than the promise of complicity in the scheme itself. The elusive eye atop the pyramid remains as elusive as ever.

CHAPTER SEVEN

Virtual Marketing

The larger question, of course, is whether
persuasive technology is a good idea at all—especially
when talking about turning a machine as soulless as a
computer into what is essentially a propaganda engine.
—*Denise Caruso*, The New York Times

We sell audience, not content.
—*Jonathan Sacks, general manager of The Hub, America Online*

I really believed the Internet could put an end to coercion.

This was back in 1988, when I was still getting laughed at for suggesting that someday nearly everyone would be using e-mail on a daily basis. My first book on cyberculture was canceled in 1992 because the publisher felt that the Internet would be a passing fad—"like CB radio," an editor explained. Two years later, the book was finally released, but even then the Internet was considered a relatively minor countercultural phenomenon—just some weirdos in San Francisco playing around with computers because they couldn't make friends.

What I knew for sure back then was that the Internet would somehow irrevocably change the way we relate to our media, and to one another. Early signs showed that the change would be immensely positive. People would finally have a medium for communicating freely with one another, instead of merely absorbing the messages of advertisers. At least I was right about the first part.

Early adopters of the Internet, like myself, attempted desperately to gain credibility for what we saw as a revolutionary technology, which meant welcoming, even pitching ourselves to, big business. To be backed by an investment banker—or, in my case, to be hired as a "new media" consultant to a *Fortune* 500 company—proved that we were truly onto something. Such gestures amounted to an acknowledgment from all those folks who had once ridiculed our little Internet society that we were the ones holding the keys to the future.

I used to laugh when the executives to whom I consulted compared the Internet to television. TV is a one-way medium, I told them, while the Internet is two-way—or "one-to-many," as pundits like to say. I remember a consultation I did at Sony, where the VP who took me to lunch kept referring to the Internet as "the next great broadcast technology." I explained to him that what we were dealing with was a community-based medium—people exchanging ideas and making new friends—but he just smiled and ate his sushi. I smugly concluded that big businesses hoping to master the Net didn't stand a chance. They would invest their dollars in building infrastructures that they would never be able to dominate. What had happened to TV just couldn't happen to the Internet.

We both were wrong. TV wasn't the right comparison—but mail and the telephone were. Although the Internet would not provide businesses the means to broadcast their advertising-sponsored entertainment to millions of people all at once, it would allow them to communicate to millions of people, one at a time. It did not extend the reach of broadcast advertising, but it would serve as an inestimably powerful new weapon for direct marketing.

Although most current users missed out on the good old days of the Internet, back in the late 1980s online interaction was as much about sending as receiving. The primitive hardware and slow networks in use at the time dictated that the Internet was limited to text-only transmissions. Users would send e-mail, join in live chat sessions, or participate in asynchronous discussions (exchanges that take place over long periods of time) on bulletin boards and USENET groups. The few of us engaging in this new mode of communication felt lucky, and even sensed that the Internet would bring us a kind of liberation.

One of the reasons the early Internet spurred these utopian visions was that, like ham radio had done in the 1930s, it offered amateurs the opportunity to disseminate their ideas globally, except that now one needed to learn only a few modem string commands instead of Morse code. In any case, the Internet was less about the information being shared and more about contact. It didn't matter whether we were discussing the global economy or "Star Trek"; it was the means of discussion itself that felt so novel. Networked together through wires and computers, the Internet community—and it really felt like a community—was a living cultural experiment.

The intensity of this sensation provoked proclamations as outlandish and naïve as the best psychedelics-inspired rantings of the 1960s. Even Timothy Leary jumped onto the cyberculture bandwagon early, proclaiming that the Internet would transform society more profoundly than LSD had. To some, like cyber pioneer and Grateful Dead lyricist John Barlow, it seemed as if the human race were hardwiring its members together into a single, global brain. He and others waxed on about the Internet as if it were the realization of the Gaia Hypothesis—the notion that all living things are part of one big organism. Many believed that our fledgling communications infrastructure would one day bring about global communication and cooperation on an unimaginable scale. As my first book, *Cyberia,* came out in 1994, I began speaking to universities and other groups about my starry visions of this brave new world of online interaction. Even if these dreams depicted Internet-enhanced society as a tad more fantastic than what it ultimately would look like, they indicated the underlying experience essential to our newfound interconnectivity: We did not feel we were interacting with data, but with one another.

The Internet seemed so "sexy" not because of the pornography that happened to be available online, but because people and their ideas could comingle and mutate. A scientist sharing his new research could be challenged and provoked, and then engage in immediate dialogue with his challengers. A philosopher posing a new theory would be forced to defend it against criticism coming from Hawaii or Helsinki. Nothing was safe, and nothing was sacred—except, perhaps, the premise that everyone shared an equal opportunity to give voice to his or her opinions.

As the Internet grew in popularity, and more and more users discovered how absorbing and rewarding it could be, media conglomerates began to panic at the way interactive channels and constant feedback were eroding their monopoly over the mediaspace. By the mid-1990s, the Internet already had eaten away more than ten percent of the time its users previously spent watching television, and the damage was increasing by the month.

Like covered wagons circling in defense against the onslaught of an untamed, indigenous people, media companies banded together for protection. Viacom bought Blockbuster and Paramount, which in turn bought Simon and Schuster; Disney bought ABC which had already bought Capital Cities; Murdoch's News Corp. bought Fox; General Electric bought NBC; Time Warner bought CNN; and Westinghouse bought CBS. Once consolidated, these companies were braced for battle.

The Battle for Cyberspace

The war to retake the media, signaled by the creation of these corporate behemoths, manifested itself in the trenches as a step-by-step undoing of the processes that had liberated the media in the first place. The effects of the keyboard, the joystick, and the remote control had to be reversed.

While cyber optimists like me were out proclaiming the digital renaissance, other futurists with far better business credentials were busy recontextualizing it for the consumption of Wall Street. As skilled as they were at hyping interactive technology, they still had some tough questions to answer before anyone would invest in their visions. How would anybody, other than the phone companies, make a profit off people merely communicating with one another? Television had commercials, and movies had an admission price. People interacting online were not buying anything, nor were they in the captive or anxious frame of mind that would render them easy targets. They were having fun with one another.

This posed a serious challenge to those who wished to make money online. They could either hope that the anticommercial ethic of the early Internet would fade as more "mainstream" audiences found their way online, or else enact a public-relations campaign designed to speed up that conversion. The slow but steady process by which the Internet was surrendered to commercial use falls somewhere between a real conspiracy and an inevitable, natural shift. The key players certainly knew one another, and often developed their campaigns jointly. But they were merely extending the already awesome power of the market into a new arena. If market forces brought down the Soviet Union and the Berlin Wall, they could surely break through the resistance of a few Internet users.

Their first job was to gain both public acceptance and financial support for the appropriation of cyberspace. They had to convince investors that there was a way to make money online, while showing Netizens that business could make the Internet safer, cheaper, and more fully featured. Who were "they," exactly? In some cases, they were young computer programmers looking for ways to turn their formidable talents into rewarding careers. In other cases, they were well-recognized but underpaid futurists, social theorists, and economics philosophers looking to finally cash in on the many ways they had foreseen the digital age. The rest were marketing gurus who had already used television, the telephone, and direct mail with much success, and sought to extend their reach.

Ironically, perhaps, it was my faith in the liberating powers of cyberspace that made me one of the last people to take such efforts seriously, and to reckon with the Internet's coercive potential. I saw the computer keyboard and mouse as our best weapons in the effort to turn around the mind-numbing impact of traditional media. Just as the remote control had deconstructed the television image and the joystick demystified it, the keyboard and mouse spawned a new generation of do-it-yourself media tacticians. That's why, even as my opinions were being sought by corporations hoping to exploit these technologies for their own ends, I was incapable of seeing where their efforts would lead us.

In the early nineties, I attended several meetings at Harper-Collins (the book company that published *Cyberia*), in which some of the executives running the company's new multimedia division wanted to know how to leverage their vast backlist to gain a foothold on the Internet. Rupert Murdoch's News Corp., which owned HarperCollins, already had an online service called Delphi. Surely there was a way to "synergize" these two subsidiaries, they thought. The question was simply how to go about it. Like most of the New York companies looking to exploit the Internet, HarperCollins and Delphi understood that the main thing they could offer consumers was content. "San Francisco may own the interface," I remember one executive telling me, "but New York owns the content." As long as content meant copywritten texts, of course, he was right. If Harper-Collins could turn the Internet into a distribution channel for its massive storehouse of text, games, and other copywritten materials, it could cash in.

After a year of publishing books in CD-ROM format, however, HarperCollins's executives realized that these computer products were no match for the thrill of live engagement with other human beings on the Net, and, by 1996, had reduced their multimedia division to a token, administrative presence. Countless other companies followed suit. Something had to be done.

Although businesses had failed in their efforts to capitalize on the initial surge in Internet use, the race was on to find a way to make money online. Many different companies, working independently, arrived at a similar strategy. The first step was to reverse the do-it-yourself attitude that the computer keyboard had provoked, and restore the supremacy of commercial content over social contact. The trick would be to change the perception of the Internet as a communications medium to a broadcast medium, which meant convincing users that our interactions with one another were less important than the data we could download and the things we could purchase with our new equipment. Accordingly, the work of futurists like Alvin Toffler and Marshall McLuhan was mined for models and concepts that could reframe our understanding of what was happening to us. That's how Information Age became the label to describe the communications breakthrough. Previously, the users themselves had been the content of the Internet. Now, it would be "information."

In 1995, Nicholas Negroponte, the founder of the corporate-sponsored Media Lab at MIT and a major investor in *Wired* magazine, drew a faulty but calculated distinction between on-line and real-world interaction. He said that in the physical world, we exchange atoms, but that in the online world, we exchange bits—meaning units of information. Negroponte saw us entering an information age, chiefly characterized by the fact that we now would exchange units of data rather than physical objects.

The problem with reducing online interaction to an exchange of bits, and the interactive age to an information age, is that it allows cyberspace to be quantified and, ultimately, commodified. The fact is that the social and emotional substance of an online interaction cannot be described in terms of bits of information. As far as the nomenclature of these cyber theorists was concerned, a social dimension to online transmissions did not exist. The Internet was not something a person engaged with; it was a set of information that could be accessed. And anything that can be accessed can be given a price tag.

The second stage of the transformation was the remystification of the media, which had been demystified by the advent of interactive devices like the joystick and the remote control. *Wired* used busy graphics and wrote in a buzzword-laden style, stoking newcomers' fears that the Internet was technically complex and conceptually daunting. Without proper instruction, users would surely get lost out there. Meanwhile, more mainstream publications like *Time* magazine, themselves threatened by competition from the many news services sprouting up online, ran frightening cover stories about "cyberporn." *The New York Times* reported that innocent people were jeopardizing their health by taking advice from online holistic practitioners, while drive-time radio fed us stories about dangerous computer viruses—items lifted directly from the press releases written by the software companies selling us protection from these evils.

Once the Internet was seen as a danger zone best traveled with the help of experts, it wasn't long before a mediating filter known as World Wide Web became the preferred navigational tool. Unlike bulletin boards or chat rooms, the Web is—for the most part—a read-only medium. It is flat and opaque. You can't see through it to the activities of others. You don't socialize with anyone when you visit a Web site; you read text and look at pictures. This is not interactivity. Like a fake decibel meter at a basketball game where the crowd is led to believe its cheers are actually moving the needle, there's nothing truly participatory about it. Although anyone can publish his ideas on his own Web site—the Web did represent a tremendous leap for self-publishing—the interface is not all that conducive to conversation. But only by compromising its communicative function could the Web's developers turn the Internet into a shopping mall. The sole interactive outlet that remained for most users was the back channel of private e-mail.

Further aiding the effort to remystify new media, designers made the programs necessary to navigate the Web more complex than earlier tools. The original Internet was built and navigated by researchers and university students using "shareware"—software that was distributed and exchanged for free. These simple programs worked on the most primitive computers, and they functioned in a transparently straightforward fashion. Their no-frills designs and freely published code helped users understand how they were put together and allowed anyone to participate in their development and offer enhancements. The original Internet was a "shareware universe," expanded and maintained chiefly by its own participants.

By 1995, Netscape had become a for-profit company, and the "browser wars" were under way. An ethic of free-market competition replaced the era of freewheeling cooperation. As if to rewrite history, many Internet experts and journalists developed a mythology that the Internet was developed not by university researchers but by the United States military. A widely circulated article by cyberpunk author and Global Business Network member Bruce Sterling implied that the Internet was just an extension of the Defense Department's effort to maintain a communications infrastructure in the event of a nuclear war. Although the true history of the Internet, and the military's rather indirect contribution, were later recounted in Katie Hafner and Matthew Lyon's 1997 book *Where Wizards Stay Up Late,* the damage had been done. The Internet would forever be associated with the Cold War arms race, and it's communitarian roots could be discounted more easily. Anyone who wrote articles disagreeing with the folklore of a military-built Internet or the virtues of a competitive marketplace was quickly labeled a "leftist."

As profit-seeking software companies took over where shareware developers left off, programs became correspondingly less efficient and less accessible. The code for software was no longer routinely released to the public for us to modify or improve. Even if it had been, these new programs were much too convoluted for the average user to understand. We were once again at the mercy of the companies from whom we bought our equipment and software. Newer versions of software required newer versions of operating systems, which in turn required newer and more powerful computer chips and increases in RAM (memory).

People who wanted to use the Web were initiated into an endless cycle of upgrades. In a campaign of planned obsolescence that made the 1970s automotive industry's schemes look like child's play, computer manufacturers and software companies conspired to force more and more purchases. Imagine if automobile companies controlled the designs not only of vehicles but of the roads. By changing the kinds of surfaces we drive on, they could force us to buy new kinds of tires, and then new kinds of cars on which those tires fit. Similarly, Microsoft can use proprietary code to develop Internet sites that require new kinds of browsers, browsers that require new kinds of operating systems, and operating systems that require enhanced hardware.

The dominance of the World Wide Web also gave traditional entertainment companies, salespeople, and advertisers an Internet they could at last understand. From now on, the Internet would be treated like the broadcast media they had already mastered. The entertainment industry began to invest heavily in on-line video and music services in the hope of one day being able to charge people money for receiving such goods via the Internet. Salespeople understood that Web sites gave them a way to put their entire catalogs of merchandise online, and that secure credit-card transactions would allow customers to purchase whatever they wanted without leaving their homes. Marketers were delighted by the development of a more tractable mediaspace in which to peddle their wares. They bought space on the most heavily trafficked Web sites for slick "banner" ads—colorful patches begging to be clicked on, diverting Internet users to commercial Web sites.

The third way marketers co-opted the interactive mediaspace was through the manipulation of shortening attention spans. Although online real estate is essentially infinite, the willingness of human beings to sift through it in real time is not. Reviving a term coined by social scientist Herbert Simon in 1971, the new economists announced that we had entered an "attention economy," where the only limiting factor on the business community's ability to earn money online was the number of "eyeball-hours" they could wrest from an Internet user. New methods of attention control—from graphical interfaces to Internet portals—were researched and implemented, targeting the people who had grown used to the freedom of the mouse and remote control. Meanwhile, all this focus on attention spans and resistant youth led to a flurry of news reports about attention deficit disorder, which in turn prompted worried parents to seek medications like Ritalin for their children so that they could compete effectively in the complex and highly accelerated marketplace of the twenty-first century.

The Tactical Database

Early in the summer of 1998, I was invited to join a few other writers, online enthusiasts, and legal activists in the Park Slope, Brooklyn, apartment of *Data Smog* author David Shenk to discuss what had happened to the Internet. It seemed to us that the promise of this interactive mediaspace was fast fading as the concerns of business outweighed those of the people who stood to benefit from its existence.

The result of this and several other such meetings was a document we published online and in *The Nation* called "Technorealism." The two-page proclamation called attention to the fact that the Internet is a public space and that the public therefore has the right to decide how it should be used—in schools, in communities, and in the commercial sector. We felt that most commentary and debate about cyberspace was being dominated by those who saw market forces as the only valid method of defining online culture, and we sought to stake out a new middle ground. We believed it was possible, even necessary, to support the mindful development of cyberculture beyond the priorities set by business interests, which had so far seemed to wreck so many other kinds of human interaction. And we meant to do so without resorting to the fearful, neo-Luddite rhetoric so often heard on the six o'clock news.

The rather moderate document we generated was met with immediate ridicule and disdain. Michael Kinsley, the former *New Republic* editor who was now in Microsoft's employ as editor of their online publishing venture, *Slate,* publicly dismissed the technorealist effort as a self-serving Gen-X whine, but also admitted freely that he had never even bothered to read it. *Wired News* and *The New York Times* interviewed pro-business stalwarts like Esther Dyson for their reactions, and went on to mock the technorealists for our naïveté. Some looked for agendas beneath our words. Were we just trying to promote our own writing careers through a new kind of publicity stunt? Others thought we were simply killjoys or closet Marxists.

Perhaps we had already lost the war. In spite of the fact that over a thousand people had added their electronic signatures to the online document within a week of its being posted, the overwhelming sentiment in the mainstream media was that any attempt to challenge the businesses that, they believed, had paid for the technological infrastructure was futile and misguided. Libertarians and progressives alike had come to believe that cyberspace was no place to enact public policy; it was either a place to do business or one to avoid altogether.

How did the Internet simultaneously come to represent a gold mine of capitalist opportunity and a threat to the American way? Why are the newspaper headlines proclaiming the unlimited earning potential of new online business ventures matched only by equally outrageous claims from cyber cynics about the degrading effects of cyberporn?

The answer lies in the Internet's incredible potential as a means for commerce—a potential that's inevitably come to be both liberating and frightening. It's a medium that on the one hand allows people to exchange ideas and information—and even develop bonds that carry over into the real world—on an unprecedented scale, but on the other hand gives demographic researchers the ability to monitor our actions as never before, down to the individual keystroke. Because this activity is occurring on a computer, it can be analyzed automatically and interpolated into the vast storehouses of data previously collected by demographic specialists. All these demographers needed was a tactical weapon with which to navigate the Internet and draw those keystrokes out of us, and they found it in e-mail.

Like an answering machine that's always on, an e-mail account is always ready to receive correspondence—whether you are online or not. My e-mail privileges on Interport, my access provider, mean merely that I have paid for a mailbox on one of their giant, constantly running computers. I also have the right to dial into that big computer from my home machine, and use it to access other computers and networks on the Internet. These computers, or "servers," hold all the World Wide Web pages, USENET groups, discussion boards, e-mail messages, and other data I might want to access.

Unfortunately, I have no easy way of determining which messages are being sent to me by friends, and which are from companies trying to sell me things. Since all the messages go directly to Interport's computer, I'm not even aware when an advertisement has been stored on my behalf. I won't find out what's been sent to me until I log on to the Internet and ask for my mail. Then, all the messages being stored for me are transferred to my computer, and I get to open them, one at a time.

As anyone who has used an Internet account for a while will tell you, the majority of messages circulating online are the electronic equivalent of junk mail, or what has become known as "spam." Spam has become so pervasive that it has changed the character of our Internet activity. Worse, it has wreaked havoc on the functionality of the Internet itself.

Part of the problem is that the Internet is still so slow that it takes several minutes to download one's mail—minutes that cost money. People who have neglected to check their mail for several days or weeks come to loathe the thought of going back online; they know they will have to sit and wait while dozens of unsolicited offers are downloaded to their machines. Then, they will have to sift through those messages to determine if there's any real mail mixed in among the junk. Those whose e-mail accounts have remained relatively uncluttered so far most likely haven't engaged in much online activity. But, like anyone who has used just one mail-order catalog and soon found his mailbox filled with them can attest, it takes very little for the online marketers to pick up your scent.

Of course, virtual coercion was not born with the computer or the Internet, but with the realization by advertising pioneer Claude Hopkins in 1923 that catalogs and mail solicitation comprise a unique branch of marketing. He called it "scientific advertising," named for the laborious process by which direct-mail practitioners analyze the responses to their mass mailings and then recalibrate their appeals based on past results. Direct-mail campaigns are not generally arrived at through inspiration but through calculation.

Honing their craft in this scientific manner since the 1920s, these nerds of the marketing industry have assimilated every new development in statistics, demography, and, ultimately, computer programming into their campaigns. With increasing sophistication, direct-mail practitioners test their solicitations, analyze results, and target their audiences. As a result, direct mail has grown to account for more than sixty-eight percent of all magazine subscriptions, and twenty-five percent of all charitable contributions.

Before computers, direct-mail marketing wasn't much more sophisticated than any other mass medium in which marketers are forced to treat their entire audience as a single customer. The same letter or catalogue was sent to every prospect, so the techniques that gained the widest currency were ones that appealed to relatively universal emotional triggers. Unlike a human salesman, who can wait until he has made eye contact before introducing himself, the direct-mail marketer has no ability to gauge our feedback until he counts up the total number of responses. He has no way of interacting with us until we send back a response. His ploys, then, are more like those of a trapper than of a hunter. He cannot track us down; he must simply bait his traps and wait for us to notice their existence. Whatever bait worked last time, he'll use again the next.

Beginning in the 1970s, however, direct-mail solicitors teamed up with demographics researchers and consumer-database companies to specifically target the people they wanted to reach. Unlike magazine publishers whose sweepstakes offers use traditional techniques—like fake checks or free gifts—designed to coerce almost any recipient, modern direct-mail specialists have been empowered to create campaigns that are customized to a particular audience. Sometimes this audience is as small as one person.

As early as the 1920s, mail-order businesses began keeping paper-based lists of their customers and selling them to other direct marketers in noncompetitive businesses. These crude mailing lists were tallied by hand and usually contained little more about the prospect than his address and whether or not he had ever purchased anything. When these lists were transferred to computers, they could be combined with other lists and subjected to more statistical analyses. Today, there are companies whose sole purpose is to compile, analyze, and cross-reference data collected by the census bureau, telephone companies, credit bureaus, and retail businesses. Many then exchange their findings with other such companies.

The PRIZM research firm, for example, developed its system of "market segmentation" in 1974. Using what the demographics industry calls "cluster analysis," PRIZM classifies every American neighborhood into forty basic lifestyle segments, or clusters. They then use statistical analysis to look for "links" between customer characteristics and buying behavior. As PRIZM's promotional material explains, their system offers "a definitive battery of consumer data to fine-tune the PRIZM Clusters for behavioral discrimination."[1]

In processing data from the 1980 U.S. census, PRIZM took every variable in the database (ethnicity, housing, social rank, urbanization) and used computer-generated feedback loops to analyze and compare them to other data recorded elsewhere (new-car sales, magazine subscriptions, real estate transactions, and direct-mail responses). From this data, they were able to determine the linkages between a particular demographic cluster and its members' likelihoods of buying a car, house, or magazine subscription—as well as what brands and what types of marketing they were likely to respond to. PRIZM makes it clear that their system "explains, predicts, and targets consumer behavior."

Other firms, like Donnelley Marketing Information Services, obtain student rosters, voter registrations, and lists of children's-book buyers, and also send questionnaires to 45 million households. From this data, the firm compiles its widely used Donnelley Quality Index, known as the DQI^2. This database contains individual listings for tens of millions of consumer households. If you bought this book, your family profile is probably in there.

Countless other companies with whom we do business regularly supply our purchasing behavior to these master lists in exchange for other sets of information. Our credit-card purchases, as well as our responses to the offers sent along with our monthly bills, are all used to predict our future behavior. Many such offers, particularly those for free life-insurance policies and credit-card loss-protection services, exist solely for the information they provide marketing companies when we fill out the requisite questionnaire. Other offers are designed to tell which "hot buttons"—marketing scenarios or psychological appeals—we respond to most readily. Once the credit-card company has determined that a particular household has responded to an advertisement for a free credit card with a higher interest rate, say, instead of one with a higher annual fee and a lower interest rate, it can share this information with a telephone company, which will pitch a long-distance offer accordingly.

As a result, today's direct-mail training manual looks more like a math textbook than like a primer on marketing. Aspiring direct marketers learn statistical techniques—regression analysis, the linear probability model, discriminant analysis, and segmentation modeling—long before they are taught how to write a single line of a direct-mail letter.

Francine Edelman is one of the leading practitioners of the new, database-heavy style of direct marketing—probably because she takes a practical, nonjudgmental approach to her work and has adjusted adeptly to the changes that computers have brought to her industry. "When I first got into the direct end of the business," she tells me from her office in New York's Soho district, "it was a lot more tactical: Get an offer out, and get it out to everybody. Throw it up against the wall and see what sticks. And over the years it has evolved and become very sophisticated and a lot more strategic, because you really have to get down very deep into your customer base and understand their psyche. What are the hot buttons that are going to make them respond?"

Although it's fascinating to come up with theories explaining why a particular hot button causes a group of individuals to respond the way they do, direct marketers like Edelman care less about explaining causes than listening to the effects. It's enough to track the correlation between the style of an appeal and its effectiveness in producing a response. Such an ethic is what allows Edelman's firm, Rapp Collins, to claim it can offer "one-to-one marketing on a mass scale." Their access to databases and correlative analysis gives them the tools to craft direct-mail appeals customized for every individual who receives them.

Explaining how this analysis would translate into a pitch for a phone company, Edelman spells out the customized approach: "We would write, 'Dear Doug: We know you currently have caller ID, call waiting deluxe, and three-way calling, and we have a great plan for you. For one low monthly rate, you can get your local service, all these services, plus up to twenty more.'" By tailoring the pitch to the individual customer profile, Edelman says, "you are able to deliver relevant offers to the right people."

Such extreme personalization of direct mail didn't always work. Edelman confessed that "when we first started getting into all of this customization and segmentation, and being very specific with people, there was a fear that it would come across as being too Big Brotherish: 'We know all this about you.'" Edelman says that today, most of us have grown accustomed to the fact that our purchases, our income levels, and even our telephone-calling patterns are now part of the marketer's database.

When marketers began applying direct-mail techniques to telephone solicitation, consumers responded with even more fear and resistance. Unlike direct mail, telephone solicitations demand our immediate attention, whether or not we are in any condition to effectively parry the telemarketer's coercive strikes. By the 1980s, most Americans were already regarding the telephone as an enemy—especially between the hours of 5:00 and 7:00 P.M., when telemarketers know we are most likely to be at home eating dinner.

In an effort to reclaim the power of the telephone, telemarketers initiated the same two-prong strategy that Internet marketers would use ten years later. First, they exploited the advantages of databases, automation, and tracking to create scripts that target each prospect with unparalleled specificity. Second, they embarked on a public-relations campaign to make us less resistant to their use of the telephone system as a marketing tool.

Like hand-to-hand coercion, telemarketing allows the caller to gauge our moment-to-moment reactions to his pitch. Telemarketers extensively test their sales scripts: Every time we reject one of their pleas, they record our response and then measure the effectiveness of one of several different retorts that have been scripted ahead of time. In this manner, they can offer rebuttals targeted to almost every objection imaginable.

Project Sunrise Winback, a telemarketing campaign developed by Rapp Collins to help BellSouth win back customers who had switched to other local carriers, used a branching script that automated this process. The scripts for Project Sunrise Winback varied depending on the region and demographic being targeted. In most cases, the caller began with a simple greeting, followed by, "In reviewing our records, it has come to our attention that you have decided to try another local toll-service carrier. Is this correct?" If the respondent answered yes, then the marketer attempted to identify the nature of the prospect's dissatisfaction with BellSouth: "May I ask what was the primary reason that prompted you to switch companies?"

The customer's response to this question was broken down into eight possible categories, each with its own follow-up script: (1) lower rates; (2) better service; (3) additional services; (4) reward programs; (5) use long distance for discounts on local toll service; (6) other; (7) related or socially connected with competitor; (8) ten cents per minute.

People who answered "better service," for example, were told, "It is interesting that you mentioned service, because Bell-South believes in and strives to provide the best service in Kentucky . . ." Understanding that people who value customer service also tend to value a company's local affiliation, the scriptwriters were sure to include a reference to the state where the prospect lived. Those who answered "long-distance discounts," however, were given a no-nonsense spiel: "Ma'am, Bell-South gives you everyday fair prices. That way the savings go in your pocket and not to discounts on products you may not want or need anyway."

The scripts for such telemarketing campaigns go on for dozens of pages, branching out into ever more specific and meticulously researched responses. Eventually, we either allow ourselves to be talked into accepting the telemarketer's pitch, or we hang up the phone. In the latter case, the precise path we took through the script is put into our personal profile in the company database, so that new countermeasures may be devised and incorporated into the next script we are subjected to.

Our growing annoyance with these scripted calls has led the corporations dependent on telemarketing to create television commercials designed to change our perception of the technique. Countless advertisements with friendly-faced telemarketers wearing hi-tech headgear and speaking confidentially with grateful consumers fill the airwaves. Joanna Kalliches, a creative director at Rapp Collins, reveals the underlying agenda of such campaigns.

When MCI launched their Friends & Family program, they were a small operation, and they were going to rely solely on outbound telemarketing. To predispose you to talk to these people on the phone, they launched a series of commercials that featured their MCI telemarketers, who looked like buddies, basically. It was a group of guys kidding around with each other, with the headsets on, calling each other by name, talking about this new program. Now all that advertising was doing was putting a face to a voice, so when they called people cold to sell them MCI, people were like, "Oh, are you Charlie? Are you Bob?" They used psychology and the mindset of the people they were calling to say, "We are just like you, we are not thin, not models, not overly handsome—we are just everyday people."

Most important, the campaign was aimed at shrouding a mechanized, computer-generated, and psychographically tuned script in the cloak of simulated humanity.

The Electronic Squeegee Men

As an interactive environment, a World Wide Web site can be more carefully scripted than a telemarketing campaign. Each click of the mouse brings the prospect to a new set of pitches and "advertorial" designed to herd him toward the "buy" button. In real time, a Web site can adjust itself to the recorded propensities of an individual visitor based on his e-mail address, prior visits, and previous behaviors. It is a self-customizing sales environment.

Likewise, e-mail gives direct marketers almost all the advantages of junk mail without the high costs of postage and paper. Spam is crafted to elicit a maximum response, then blasted out to literally millions of people at once. In this way, Internet marketers have largely recapitulated the arms race in which direct marketers like Rapp Collins have been engaged.

Their first challenge, like any direct-mail marketer's, was to get people to open and read the advertising messages at all. Luckily, most e-mail programs display the name of the message's sender and a brief "subject" line, indicating the message's content. For a time, then, most junk mail was pretty easy to identify and discard without ever being opened.

Advertisers quickly responded by imitating the appearance of real mail. Like direct marketers who disguise their envelopes as important correspondence, many spam advertisers now use names like Heather or System Administrator as a return address, and a subject line that implies a history of correspondence— "One more thing," or "Urgent news about your account."

The e-mail arms race began in earnest when Internet mail programs and online services offered their users the option of creating lists of people from whom they would like to receive mail and automatically discarding messages from anyone else. The problem with this strategy was that it became impossible for you to discriminate between unwanted messages from advertisers and a message from your niece in Akron who had just gotten an account on America Online and whose name hadn't yet been added to your list. With this shield in place, you certainly couldn't meet anyone new.

In a more advanced strategy, Internet service providers began helping their subscribers fight back with filtering programs designed specifically to recognize and delete junk mail by identifying the return address. America Online developed one of the better ones and was so successful at filtering offenders that an Internet marketing firm called Cyber Promotions actually sued the company for infringement of their First Amendment rights. A U.S. district judge wisely concluded that AOL, a private business, is allowed to block whatever it wishes on behalf of its members. These programs work by filtering all mail from servers known to be thoroughfares for spam.

Crafty spammers developed countermeasures for this defense, too. To mask their original addresses—and thus circumvent filtration programs—they have hacked their way into the Internet's protocol for passing mail from server to server. They use a "third-party host"—meaning basically any non-spam related service provider—as a relay for their mail, and pass undetected through the filter. It is the very openness of the Internet's e-mail system that makes it ripe for such abuse.

Implementing yet another countermeasure in this escalating electronic war, most service providers have reengineered their systems and closed themselves off to all relayed mail. Now they only send out mail that originates from within their own system. But this additional checkpoint—like a military blockade on a highway known to be used by terrorists—prevents normal users from relaying messages, too. Before service providers began denying third-party relays, I was able to access my e-mail from any node in the world. If I logged in on a friend's computer in Spain, for example, a few simple keystrokes allowed me to send or receive e-mail through my home account in New York. Today, if I want to send e-mail from a location outside my home area, I must make a long-distance call and dial directly into my own network. These changes are very much like those implemented by the U.S. Postal Service in the wake of the Unabomber's mailed explosives. Packages weighing more than a pound no longer may be placed in mailboxes but must be brought all the way to a post office, where security cameras photograph every patron.

These third-party blockades affect me, of course, only because I don't happen to be a subscriber to one of the two or three largest Internet access providers in the world, such as America

Online or IBM, who have the resources to offer dial-in access from hundreds of different cities. (Either that, or use one of the advertising-supported mail services offered on the World Wide Web.) The final result of the arms race in cyberspace is that customers wanting freedom and flexibility of use must abandon their allegiances to local companies and subscribe through multinational corporations. The Internet itself no longer can provide a truly global connection. Instead, we must depend increasingly on private corporations and their own international computer networks to meet our communications needs.

The more we feel the need to be protected in cyberspace, the more leverage large companies will have in influencing our behavior. As we surrender our browsers and mail programs to ever more advanced forms of filtration, we become more dependent on service providers who have made deals with large, respected conglomerates. As the Internet becomes swamped with messages from companies we've never heard of, and then "enhanced" with digital locks, verifiable e-mail addresses, and other security measures, we find ourselves edging toward trusted brand names and institutions. The more dangerous the online world looks, the more we gravitate toward the familiar, and the more those already trusted businesses are able to monopolize cyberspace.

In 1991, for example, the Lotus corporation developed a CD-ROM called MarketPlace, a database of personal information for about 120 million people in more than 30 million households, which was compiled by Equifax, a leading credit-reporting agency. The product, which was to sell for $695, was aimed at small businesses and individuals who can't afford the fees for tremendous databases owned by companies like PRIZM and Donnelley. MarketPlace was conceived as a retail product, and so Lotus openly publicized it. Internet users and consumer-advocacy groups launched a countercampaign aimed at fighting a product they saw as intrusive and a violation of privacy.

After receiving more than 30,000 written, telephoned, and e-mailed complaints, Lotus decided to scrap the project, and consumer advocates celebrated their victory. In reality, all they succeeded in doing was allowing wealthy *Fortune* 500 companies to maintain their lock on demographic research. Small businesses, nonprofit organizations, and individuals were the only ones shut out, while for these larger companies it meant business as usual.

In cases like this, well-meaning advocates struggle to regulate how companies use the information we've given them voluntarily. They do almost nothing to curtail the use of information that we don't even know we are providing. Our activities online and the software we use to browse through the World Wide Web leave a trail of information about us everywhere we go. Some sites can even procure information about our behavior long after we've left them.

Internet advertisers have reacted to our constant griping with a new policy of rewarding individuals for their voluntary attention to spam and online advertising. Seth Godin, the founder of a leading Internet direct-marketing firm, Yoyodyne, dubbed this innovation "permission marketing." The new technique works, in Godin's words, "to turn strangers into friends, and friends into customers." The idea is to elicit prospects' permission to market to them, either by offering a discount, by giving them a gift, or simply by promising them courtesy and attention. When the technique works, the target doesn't feel put upon. Once a dialogue is initiated, the prospect is slowly drawn into the sales pitch. As Godin puts it in his book *Permission Marketing,* "The idea is to have a mutually beneficial dialogue, and the more you tell people about what to expect, the greater the anticipation you'll be able to create. That's important as you work to leverage it."[2]

Some marketing companies, like one called Cybergold, pay

users twenty-five cents for opening e-mail advertisements, and between fifty cents and a dollar for visiting a Web site to read promotional material or play a game designed to advocate its clients' products. Firms from telephone companies to brokerage houses, desperate for a way to market on the Internet without looking sleazy, now use these pay-the-customer advertising services. As one brokerage house public relations manager explained to me at an Internet industry luncheon, "It provides us with tightly defined target markets of willing recipients at a significantly lower cost than direct mail." And, in theory, a significantly lower hostility rate.

Another marketing company, Eyegive, pays a charity of your choice if you agree to receive and peruse large advertising messages on your Internet browser's "start" page. You fill out a number of forms indicating your personal preferences and demographic information, and they automatically send you advertisements every time you log on to the Internet. For every ad you read, a small donation is made to the charity you've selected. The company's press releases claim that participating sponsors will benefit from the "halo effect" associated with cause-related marketing "because their messages are presented in a positive context." But this sort of voluntary submission to advertising messages is more like paying a squeegee man a dollar after he's washed your window. We are paying for the privilege of not getting mugged, and end up telling ourselves that we've kept a criminal off the streets.

Mice in a Maze: Pacing and Leading Online

Although a lot of thinking goes into the designs of the Internet's more coercive utilities, once they are actually implemented they don't require any thought at all. Marketers can sit back while their programs take care of everything. If flashing a red banner makes us click on a promotion, our response will be noted and the red banner will be used again. The research, analysis, and implementation of the Web's influence techniques are absolutely automated. The psychologist's pacing and leading is replaced by the machine's input and output. What works is repeated; what doesn't work is altered until it does work. The keys to influencing human behavior are tested on a trial-and-error basis. With tens of millions of people online making countless mouse clicks every day, such techniques are quickly achieving a nearly surgical precision.

The banner ad has evolved into its present form through just this sort of automated analysis. Banner-advertising companies constantly test new methods of getting us to "click through" their rectangular swatches of color to the Web site for the company or product being sold. A higher click-through rate means a successful new technique. Ads with animation, for example, have been shown to increase the user-response rate by twenty-five percent.[3] Tracking technology allows banner-ad companies to customize the advertisements each person sees. A Web site can detect the city or server through which a user is accessing the Internet, as well as his e-mail address. This information is transmitted to the Web server by our browsers. Small, invisible markers planted by marketers onto our own hard drives can transmit much more information about us, too.

DoubleClick, the industry leader in online banner advertising, has developed an advanced set of detection devices, which allows the company to offer advertising customized to an individual computer user. As their promotional literature explains, "DoubleClick allows you to target specific industry codes by content affinity, browser, system type, geography, and time of day. By taking advantage of the Web's ability to deliver targeted ad messages, you can create stronger, more personal relationships with your customers." When they were trying to win Toyota's online advertising business, DoubleClick launched a banner campaign that directly targeted the automaker's employees. Whenever a Toyota worker accessed a Web site in DoubleClick's network of domains, the banner ad was immediately customized to welcome this member of the Toyota family. DoubleClick won the automaker's business. Although the technology for putting an individual user's name within a banner ad on the Web exists today, most of us are not yet conditioned to respond favorably to such a highly personalized approach.

Many Internet users have found ways to cope with the banner ad. Shareware sites offer software that effectively filters banner ads without compromising other Web content. Web surfers have also grown familiar with the locations and shapes of most banner ads, making it easier for them to ignore all but the most intrusive and distracting compositions. In response, the most advanced Internet marketers have abandoned the billboard approach to online marketing and instead have resorted to turning our own Web browsers into tools of surveillance.

When you visit a Web site, the people running that site often have the opportunity to capture and store your e-mail address. They can also determine exactly which pages you look at, how long you look at them, and which buttons, links, or pictures you click on. When I used the Web to buy a plane ticket for a talk I was giving in Australia back in 1997, I wasn't surprised when I received spam from two different companies offering tour and hotel packages at my destination. As of this writing, lawyers and consumer advocates are debating whether SABRE, an online ticketing network, should be free to sell information about its customers to other companies. According to the Federal Privacy Act of 1974, they do. Only the government is restricted from collecting and transferring personal data. Business is specifically exempted.

Some Web sites go one step further and install tiny files called "cookies" directly onto our computers, which can be used to identify us whenever we access a particular page. In fact, a cookie is capable of recording everything we do at a Web site, so that when we return, a profile of our previous actions and reactions comes along with us. Therefore a Web site can adapt itself to appeal to our established patterns of behavior. It amounts to an automated and involuntary form of the customer survey.

A group of hackers called Cult of the Dead Cow has created viruses that demonstrate how cookies can be used to deliver *continuous* supplies of information about us over the Internet. Once installed, such a cookie can search our computers' hard drives and monitor our keystrokes, even when we are not connected to the Internet. As soon as we log back on to the Internet, the cookie relays all this information back to its programmer, invisibly.

Most Web browsers now give users the option of removing or refusing cookies, but unfortunately are unable to distinguish between helpful and hurtful cookies automatically. To refuse them all would be to disable some extremely useful functions of Internet sites. A cookie can create a list of our financial investments, for example, so that every time we log on to a stock-market site we can view a personalized chart with instant quotes. An airline-reservations site can use a cookie to store our seating preferences or dietary restrictions. A bulletin-board site can keep track of which conversations we have participated in, and where we left them off. Utilized ethically, cookies are a powerful enhancement to the Internet's functionality. Although it's technically possible to refuse some cookies and accept others, they are used so commonly that we would be forced to evaluate the merits of individual cookies every time we explore a new link.

Much of the information that cookies gather and transmit about us is ultimately bought and sold, and this has become a big business. The online service from which we purchase travel tickets might have a relationship with, say, another company that sells books. If we visit the book site after buying a ticket to Maui, we will be welcomed with a list of books about traveling in Hawaii. Both companies, working in concert, can access the same cookie. And if while attempting to purchase one of those books our credit card reaches its limit, we'll receive e-mail from another company offering to restore our credit rating, and so on. The relationships between these companies is often undisclosed, as the legality of such information transfers has yet to be established.

Industry spokespeople and the magazines in which they advertise argue that the collection and marketing of our personal data will lead to a more customized experience of the Internet. When data about our personal preferences is bought and sold, the logic goes, then more companies will direct us to what we like. If every site you visit already knows you are a forty-year-old woman with an income between $60,000 and $80,000 a year, you will not be bothered with ads directed to fourteen-year-old boys. If your profile indicates you like chocolate, water sports, and classic cars, and also shows you do not respond to junk mail but do tend to buy products online after reading articles about them, commercial sites that have access to this information will present you with articles about the products that are of interest to you. It's as if the Internet has the power to customize itself to your desires. A consumer's paradise.

But an Internet run by commercial interests means more than just customized banner ads and spam. It is a world more contained and controllable than a theme park, where the techniques of influence can be embedded in every frame and button. Microsoft has an entire department dedicated to "Decision Theory and Adaptive Systems"—the study of how human beings relate to data and interfaces. Although much of the department's work is geared toward creating more user-friendly interfaces, my contacts at the company claim the much-shrouded division's true purpose is to determine the decision points in online behavior and how to manipulate them effectively.

The field of pacing and leading through computers has been dubbed "captology" by B. J. Fogg, a Sun Microsystems researcher who studies the effects of interfaces on human behavior. Like a travel map provided by the AAA, complete with instructions on where to stop for food and accommodations, the interfaces and software we use can direct our actions and even our purchasing decisions. The display on GTE's Airfone screen—nestled into the headrest of the seat in front of you on the plane—flashes messages suggesting you check your voice mail or call home. Theoretically, a cellular-phone display screen could be programmed to do the same thing—a technique that could be augmented by the phone company's database of your most frequent calls.

A screensaver program available online for certain Hewlett-Packard color printers encourages the purchase of more HP products. As technology critic Denise Caruso reported in her *New York Times* column,

> The virtual pet for the computer desktop encourages users to make multiple original copies on the printer instead of duplicating the original printout on a color copier. This, in turn, keeps them buying more of Hewlett's color inks. . . . The larger question, of course, is whether persuasive technology is a good idea at all—especially when talking about turning a machine as soulless as a computer into what is essentially a propaganda engine.[4]

Today, we don't even have to venture onto a computer to be drawn into closed systems of electronic coercion. A best-selling book called *The One to One Future* instructs marketers how to customize direct marketing in order to create the same kinds of consumption loops. For example, in the one-to-one future that the authors envision, all of our retail purchases will be recorded in a series of personal databanks. A "diet data bank" would use the UPC bar codes scanned at the checkout line to record our supermarket purchases. Diet-conscious customers could be identified through their patterns of consumption, and even given their own portable scanners. With these devices in hand, they could stroll through the aisles, scan the UPC bar codes on different packages, and read a computerized display of the products' nutritional content. Of course, the store would also accumulate a complete record of every product that the customer evaluated, in what order, for how long, and whether he chose to buy it.

This designer consumption would amount to a nearly hermetic feedback loop between each consumer and his marketers—a form of pacing and leading where the customer's taste is mirrored and then slowly led toward progressively more extreme manifestations of itself. It is a recipe for technologically induced obsessive-compulsive behavior, as our desires are repeatedly amplified and then fed back to us. The one-to-one future differs from the marketing we're subjected to today only in its speed and specificity.

Perhaps this process is easier to comprehend when it happens in reverse. Shopping channels on cable television feature hosts whose dialogues and presentations may appear bizarre to unaccustomed viewers. Actually, their odd, mechanical behavior is shaped moment-to-moment by the rate of telephone purchases. As anyone who has watched one of these channels knows, the number of items sold is continuously tallied in a small box in one corner of the screen—partly to add a sense of urgency to the sales pitch, but mostly, since the number is displayed on a monitor in the studio, so the host making the pitch can determine how his tone, language, and style of delivery are influencing the number of sales. If speaking faster makes the number increase more rapidly, he will maintain his accelerated rate of speech, as long as it keeps working. In this way, the host becomes a kind of automaton, stuck in a feedback loop where his only goal is to make that number increase.

The MovieFone Syndrome

Like the host on a shopping channel, the people turning media into an electronic marketplace aren't fully conscious of what they're doing. By using the Internet to automate their business models, they have combined the force of the market with the power of the computer to amplify the blind effects of each. Commercial media seems to have taken on a life of its own, dedicated to selling more goods to more and more people in less and less time. Although human beings set the whole process in motion, it's as if once they built the engine, they abandoned the throttle and all the other controls to the machine itself. It has been running on automatic ever since.

As the average consumer becomes a cog in this media machine, he finds himself succumbing to the pressures of the inevitable network externalities that emerge. Our slow acceptance of a commercial Internet was just such a process.

Call it the MovieFone syndrome. At first, the telephone ticket service seemed like a terrific convenience. It was novel and fun. Instead of waiting on long lines at the box office, we could find out show schedules and secure our seats ahead of time, all from a touch-tone phone for just a few dollars per ticket. Once a critical mass of moviegoers signed on to this technology, however, refusing to use the service and pay the extra charge meant the strong possibility that our movie selections might be sold out.

Anyone who couldn't find a way to get to the theater well before show time was gently forced to buy the tickets through the service, whatever the cost. Now some telephone ticket services allow callers to reserve the seats they will sit in, effectively creating a new class of moviegoer. Those who wish to have good seats—or, in some cases, any seats at all—must pay the additional charge. What began as a convenience quickly became a necessity—and a way to bring the price of a movie ticket above ten dollars.

The MovieFone syndrome demonstrates the darker side of network externalities—the economic principle that shows how a technology's value increases with its wide acceptance. Something that begins as a novelty, like a telephone ticket service or a version of an Internet browser or even a kind of direct-marketing technique, soon becomes so widely accepted that those who don't partake begin to lose their ability to enjoy, to engage in, and to discriminate between the things society has to offer. People who don't learn to use the money machine at the bank are penalized with a reduced number of live tellers and longer lines. People who don't opt for the expense of cable television miss their local sports teams' broadcasts. And similarly, those who don't participate in the world of online commerce may be risking financial and cultural obsolescence.

Take Microsoft's online commercial strategy, sidewalk.com. Ostensibly a guide to restaurants, movies, and other attractions in America's major cities, the online service is designed to become a "point of purchase" for these forms of entertainment. Users click through friendly databases of information until they find the restaurant they want to go to, and then make their reservations online. In some cases, users will pay a small service charge, while in others the restaurant or business may pay Microsoft directly for the publicity and exposure to new customers.

Since Microsoft makes the dominant Web browsing software,

many of the features of their Sidewalk site take advantage of their own proprietary software, or of membership in their proprietary online service. As more users take advantage of the convenience of the service, the law of network externalities will come into effect, making the service—as well as the software necessary for accessing it—more valuable. Of course, the software will eventually need to be upgraded, as will the computers to run that software. Consumers will spend more time and energy paying for new equipment and software, then learning how to operate it, just so that they can participate in the same sorts of activities they did before.

And the people who can't afford all this? They'll either be left out of the loop completely or choose to take advantage of the many free and discount online services currently being offered. Of course, these free Internet packages require that the user sit through commercials and promotions. The poor pay for their access by submitting to more marketing. Those better off, meanwhile, pay cash for the privilege of commercial-free commerce.

Once Microsoft begins to offer electronic forms of currency and credit—projects on which the company is currently working—the cycle will be complete. We are dependent on the software, the machines, and the monetary scheme in order to participate in our culture, and the company providing it to us takes a profit at each level. Because Microsoft and its competitors are private companies, accountable to no one (unless they are found to have broken laws), the consumers have no recourse. Although, in theory, we can "vote with our dollars," we risk isolation or worse. Buying computers with alternative, incompatible operating systems cuts us off from the network. Unless we jump off together, in large enough numbers, our protests hurt no one but ourselves.

What began as an egalitarian set of channels quickly became a direct feeding tube for advertisements and a self-contained environment for automated commerce. In an attempt to limit the abuse of the networks by con artists and relentless marketers, Internet service providers implemented new technical protocols that restricted the open functioning of the Internet, which ultimately sent Netizens to the closed communities of large commercial providers with their own business agendas. Mainstream media outlets, surviving on the revenue from hi-tech advertisers and their own parent corporations' new-media subsidiaries, lead the public relations effort by spinning this disaster as a Long Boom for big business. After all, the global economy itself, banking on the future prosperity of expanding hi-tech markets, is depending on it. Like well-trained propagandists, they warn of the dangers of noncompliance, the horrors that await those who refuse protection, and the glorious future for all who get with the program.

The current direction of Internet technology promises a further calcification of its interactive abilities. Amped-up processing speed and modem baud rates do nothing more for communication than speed things up. They do, however, allow for the development of an increasingly TV-like Internet, making the Sony executive's dream of the Web as a broadcast medium a reality. As we buy bigger computers and faster modems, we simply expedite the arrival of set-top computers and interactive television.

The only obstacle I've seen to the implementation of Web-enhanced TV—known as "convergence media"—is the cable-television industry's fear that once we have Internet access on our televisions, we might choose to tune in to noncommercial Web sites or, worse, interact with other users instead of watching the major networks' programming. When I consulted to a subsidiary of TCI about developing content for their @Home broadband cable network—a fully interactive set of TV channels through which viewers can play games and make purchases—the executives' chief concern was how to steer viewers to their own content and away from everyone else's.

It was the prospect that the Internet would end up being just another theater of operations for the media wars that provoked my colleagues and me to publish the Technorealism document. Most of us had been using the Internet for years but had found we just weren't enjoying it anymore. Nowhere could we find people championing the technology without also pushing what had become the party line of corporate capitalism. Our aim was to correct the many myths dominating discussions of new media, without giving up on the Internet's still-unrealized promise as a tool for communication. Perhaps a set of policies could be developed that returned the expansion and use of these networks to public or even civic control. When my friend who writes about technology for *Time* magazine found out I had signed on to the Technorealism document, he was aghast. "I reserve judgment," he said in our first phone conversation after the document's publication, "but I think you're crazy to put your name on that thing."

Still, no matter how dark things have seemed, I can't help but be optimistic about where this evolution of virtual coercion may ultimately take us. Perhaps the thousands of signatures on the document are an indication that I'm not alone in my disillusionment about how these technologies are being used, and how little control we seem to have over them.

And, of course, I never would have thought to write about the techniques of coercion in the first place had I not witnessed them being practiced by a machine. I don't know if I ever would have come to grips with my own participation in their development if I hadn't seen them applied so aggressively in the electronic marketplace. Like watching a time-elapsed scene from Godfrey Reggio's hypnotic documentary *Koyaanisqatsi,* where the daily motions of a chaotic city suddenly make rhythmic sense, experiencing the warp-drive cycles of computer-automated coercion provides a new kind of perspective on a very old art.

In the worst case, by pacing and leading ourselves into abject despair, we may force ourselves to find remedies more profound than Prozac. We may choose to take the time to distinguish between what we're told and what we really want. We might even find a way to think for ourselves.

Buyer's Remorse

By the time she finally dropped out of her health-products distribution network, Stephanie had brought her family into serious debt, and she was committed to getting them out. As a telephone customer-support operator for a computer retailer, she now earns about twenty percent more per week than she spends in additional care for her younger two children. Her job has proved anything but rewarding. In spite of the friendly materials she received from the human resources department, she has found her work environment extremely constricting.

Her superiors randomly monitor the telephone calls she answers, and the time she dedicates to each one is logged by computer. Every call on which she spends more than two minutes earns her a negative mark. Each time she offers to send a repairman or exchange a part under warranty, she receives the equivalent of two negative marks. She has been provided with scripts to read that she believes were designed to make the unhappy customer assume he has broken the computer himself, or violated his warranty in some way. If she goes "off script," however, she is reprimanded.

Stephanie got terribly depressed. She was diagnosed with work-related anxiety and given a prescription for the drug Inderal—a blood pressure medication which is also used for performance anxiety because it steadies the racing heart rate and trembling hands of the nervous actor or musician. Although the drug did nothing for her depression, her anxious performance on the phones has improved.

Stephanie's home life has deteriorated, too. She used to bring her family to a Unitarian church on Sunday, which she found very rewarding. Now, because Sunday is the only day both she and her husband have off, they go to a warehouse shopping "club" instead. Stephanie, guilty about how little time she spends with her children, compensates by letting them pull items off the shelves for themselves, figuring she has enough overtime pay coming to fit the extra toys and candy into her budget. Meanwhile, she finds herself buying prepared foods at higher prices than she paid for raw foods at the grocery store. Still, she is grateful for the convenience.

Stephanie and her husband have considered working fewer hours, but watching the violence on the local news and "NYPD Blue" keeps them both aspiring to the day they can afford a small house in one of the private neighborhoods springing up outside Houston. Their exhaustion at the end of their day—more than their fear of crime—keeps them watching the TV rather than going out with neighbors.

I consider Stephanie a friend. Before she left Los Angeles and moved to Texas, she taught me more about theater history than I had learned in three years at graduate school. She is an extremely bright woman. But every few months, when I speak to her on the phone, I'm saddened by what I hear. Her voice is flat, and her aspirations are few. She speaks in clichés, and doesn't offer much of a defense when I try to challenge the decisions she has made. It now seems to me that Stephanie, like so many other victims of today's coercive tactics, no longer realizes that she is actively pursuing the goals presented to her by influence professionals.

I lost touch with Mort Spivas about a year ago, after he joined a spiritual group in New Mexico. The last time we spoke, he told me that he realized his engagement with the magnet company, though lucrative, was just another version of the same old heartless salesmanship that had led to his earlier breakdown. By dedicating himself to a fully awakened master with "deep insights" and "unquestionable integrity," Spivas hoped he would finally purge himself of his desire to profit at others' expense. When I questioned his teacher's stance on sex (abstinence) and engagement in popular culture (to be avoided at all costs), Mort politely told me that it would be best for us not to talk again until he felt more secure in his new life.

Douglas Atkin left Wells BDDP to become a partner at a smaller, boutique agency that values his artistic vision. There, he devises campaigns he hopes will entertain and even enlighten audiences, rather than just sell them products and services they don't need. He is continuing his research into cults and chaos math, and working hard to make his clients understand the value of such seemingly esoteric endeavors. I have continued consulting to Atkin but can't help questioning the application of my counsel.

What part am I playing in the coercive cycle? It's hard for me, or for any of us, to tell. Stephanie leads computer customers to believe that they have broken their machines—and feels so guilty about it that she needs to be drugged. But all she wants is to erase the debt caused by having fallen prey to a multilevel marketing system. Mort sincerely wants to make amends to himself and God for the years of psychological tricks he played on his customers. Can he possibly accomplish these goals by spending his savings to live in a Santa Fe ashram and his time attempting to secure new members? Douglas Atkin genuinely hopes to raise the level of television media. Can he ever successfully transform the advertising budgets of major corporations into media campaigns that make people think for themselves? Even if he does, how long will those corporations pay for it?

Just as I was finishing this book, I went out to San Francisco to participate on a panel about kids and media, a fund-raiser for a new museum. As long as I was in the Bay Area, I figured I'd take advantage of an open invitation to address the staff of Cheskin Research, one of the world's leading market-research firms.

Although located in a bland Redwood Shores corporate park, the atmosphere at Cheskin is playful, open-minded, and sincere. This is the kind of place where young interns are allowed to spend an afternoon sharing their feelings about the color yellow—and where that discussion will be earnestly applied to a research study. At Cheskin's helm is Davis Masten, a stylish, mid-forties entrepreneur who had worked on Atari's original game consoles and Microsoft's interface and marketing strategies.

I spoke to about fifty researchers assembled in a large triangular conference room, sharing what I know about the ways people relate to marketing and new media, and peppering my talk with suggestions about how to create less coercive campaigns. I encouraged them to examine whether the products they were charged with marketing had any redeeming social values, and to highlight those qualities in their strategies. I explained how marketing that depends on the audience's insecurity or low self-esteem will tend to have diminishing returns as the targets learn to resent the people making them feel so terrible.

Afterward, Davis and I hopped into his black BMW sports car

and headed for his Redwood Hills home to meet his wife, who is a scientist, and two of her colleagues whom I had long admired. *This will be a great night,* I thought as we raced with the top down toward the beautiful sunset.

I was awestruck by the landscape through which we drove: mile after mile of lush estates, each more exquisitely appointed than the last.

"Who lives in these places?" I asked, wondering what these people could have possibly done to acquire such an opulent lifestyle.

"Palo Alto computer executives," Davis shouted over the revving engine. "A lot of 49'ers," he added, referring to the San Francisco football team.

I couldn't help thinking how nice such a lifestyle must be. I imagined living in one of these houses with my future family, sending my kids to the best private schools, and owning a sports car like Masten's. How many marketing consults would I have to do to get this wealthy? Could I get a job at Cheskin Research? What could I say to Davis that would make him consider me?

Here I was, finishing a book on the devastating social cost of coercive strategies, yet I was ready to sell my soul in order to acquire property that probably wouldn't do much to add any real value to my experience of life. Nevertheless, I felt inferior—like a professional failure—and longed to have the kind of life that Masten had created for himself by perpetuating the very consumption-based value system that was making me feel so worthless to begin with.

And Davis is a terrific guy. He's as progressive and well-principled as the best of us. If he's earning a bit of extra money, so what? It gives him the ability to shield his family from the perils and uncertainty of modern life. He has worked hard for his security and peace of mind. I wanted some of that, too.

Why did I want it? If I had anyone to blame, it wasn't Masten

or his neighbors but a society that has become completely ob-
sessed with consumption, and my own readiness to participate
in its endless churn. These are the only spoils of the coercive
arms race: So many of our corporate and personal resources
have been surrendered to the battle that it seems the only way to
avoid coercion is to join in the arms race ourselves.

As a result, our new religion is to become more plugged-in, in
whatever way possible, to the way the world works. The purpose of life is to buy and sell things, or even ideas. But like any
compulsive behavior, our buying and selling merely spurs the
need to buy and sell more. There's always a better house, computer, or school district, if only we can make enough money to
move to that next level. Just as the trailer-park resident aspires
to a bigger TV, the Soho aesthete aspires to enter the finest art
gallery with the authority, and purse, of a true sophisticate. We
are what we buy, and we can always buy better. And the more
we buy, the more we fund the development of coercive techniques that compel us to buy still more.

Likewise, there's always a more lucrative job, a bigger office, a
higher title, or a position of greater authority, if only we can
make enough sales, please enough clients, or win enough con-
verts to advance. Just as the Mary Kay distributor strives to sign
on more underlings so that she can make it to the next level of
her company, the McDonald's marketing consultant struggles to
invent new stadium promotions that, if successful, will earn him
a promotion or a raise.

The true outcome of the arms race is that it makes the coercer
and coercee indistinguishable. We are all coercers, and we are all
coerced. Ultimately, there is no "they." The corporate executive
who demands more effective advertising from Atkin is only responding to the shareholders of his company, many of whom
comprise the very audience to which Atkin's ads will be directed.
It's as if we have surrendered to a set of systems that coerce us as

society. As a result, we are suffering a collective confusion: a culture-wide inability to make choices in a rational way.

Coercion is much more debilitating than persuasion or even influence. Persuasion is simply an attempt to steer someone's thinking by using logic. Influence is the act of applying readily discernible pressure: I want you to do this; I have power over you, so do it. Coercion seeks to stymie our rational processes in order to make us act against—or, at the very least, without—our better judgment. Once immersed in a coercive system, we act without conscious control. We act automatically, from a place that has little to do with reason.

What's wrong with acting from the gut? Nothing, if it really is our gut. Under normal circumstances, the intuition and emotions are as good at weighing the pros and cons of a decision as the intellect. But in a coercive environment, our gut is just another access panel to our control knobs. We respond to emotional cues devised by the agents of consumption. We react on a visceral level—the way I did to the beautiful homes of Redwood Hills—from a place of fear and insecurity.

This easily provoked confusion, coupled with our weary sense of paranoia, merely compels us to buy and sell more, by any means necessary, in the hope of finally alleviating our despair. And our ruthless commerce is no longer limited to products but now includes lifestyles, political candidates, morality, and even religions. The further our coercive environment paralyzes our judgment, the more we depend on the metrics established for us by other people and institutions to gauge our progress. Everywhere we look—from the media to politics to the world of finance—we encounter systems devised to suspend our common sense and confirm our greatest fear: that we need to do more in order to just be.

Our best minds struggle to develop philosophies that can somehow frame this accelerating frenzy as an extension of democracy. Besides being mathematically suspect, the Long Boom new economic theories deserve a cultural critique as well. Even if they are correct and enhanced open markets can bring hi-tech products to everyone in the world who wants them, since when have we decided that the supreme and inalienable human right is the mindless production and consumption these devices stimulate? Will this be America's legacy?

The real effect of the law of network externalities is that it establishes the priorities by which we live. It does not enhance the freedom of the individual at all. Rather, once enough people have bought into a certain (often subtly oppressive) system, the rest of us must buy in as well or risk losing our connections to everyone else and our access to the activities we value. Network externalities set the terms by which our highly networked society defines participation and success.

And how can this participation, and the incremental successes with which it rewards us, yield any lasting satisfaction? It can't, because the systems in which we are participating are designed merely to stimulate more of the same. We can't be allowed any satisfaction, because feeling good about ourselves and our relationships with one another thwarts the operating principles of the coercive cycle. We feel the need to participate in it only when we are keeping up with the Joneses—not when we are enjoying their company. Real friendships quiet the aspirational jitters that lead us to reach for our Visa cards at the slightest prompting.

The only way out is to accept the fact that we all are to blame for our collective predicament. This cult of consumption requires our complicity. We affect a posture of satisfaction in order to fool one another and ourselves that we have achieved some measure of detachment from the game. Secretly, we pray that we will find the true peace we are looking for when we have moved up just one more level toward the top. We ache to find a plateau with sure footing.

This ache—this sense of constant misgiving—may just be our best hope for escape. Although it is the key to the coercer's art—the very self-doubt that he mines in order to provoke our compliance—it is a voice that emanates from within ourselves, not from some external cultural imperative. "They" do not own that voice—*we* do. And listening to it offers us the best indication of whether we are moving toward or away from a more enriching experience of life. We shouldn't seek to quiet it with mindless acquiescence to the first external command we hear; we should use it.

Rather than suppress the sense of hopeless desperation this voice evokes, we should amplify it. It is responsible for our pangs of conscience—those moments of clarity, of "buyer's remorse," when we realize that we are on an endless treadmill. That weekend of depression that Spivas endured after coercing the old couple from the Bronx to buy a bed beyond their means was, perhaps, the most clearheaded two days of his life. The day Stephanie turned to a health professional to combat her depression was prompted by the same healthy remorse that led my group of Internet enthusiasts to write the technorealism document, Hank to reject his Promise Keepers oath, Howard Rubenstein to adopt a public-relations strategy based on truth, and a stadium filled with Jets fans to boo the McDonald's representatives off the field.

We all have such moments of remorse—both as coercers and as the coerced. The sense of panic we feel when we get lost in the shopping mall can just as easily be a cue to pause as it is a trigger to act. So, too, can the pang of guilt about pressuring a customer to make a purchase serve as an opportunity to relent. It's precisely during these moments—when we're thrown off balance—that we need to stay still. They are the moments when we are most vulnerable to coercion, yet also when we are most prepared to make a change that will arrest the self-defeating cycle in which we are trapped. We can always come back and buy that TV tomorrow. We have the prerogative to stop, to think, and to disengage.

By no means does this mindfulness preclude full participation in the best that our society has to offer. Nor is it any excuse to retreat to the hills and adopt a fortress mentality of home schooling and survivalist isolation. For as long as there are people willing to find meaningful ways to relate, there will be opportunities to do so. New forms of social gatherings—from raves to Internet discussion groups—are emerging every day, each of which offers the chance to enact meaningful change.

Around the world, I find more and more people willing to take the often difficult steps necessary to reclaiming the society we surrendered to the arms race. Information-technology specialists are forming collectives to develop computer operating systems with "open code" that can be augmented by anyone who has a mind to do so. Sports fans are abandoning the oppressive atmosphere of corporate-sponsored spectacle for the genuine excitement of local, high school, and minor league games.

Activist groups like Adbusters sponsor "buy nothing" days, while progressive churches launch charity campaigns and soup kitchens in an effort to divorce commerce from the spirit of holiday giving. Young people fed up with the cost and exclusivity of nightclubs and concerts are turning to smaller, private gatherings in one another's homes, or, when public officials permit, to free festivals. Church and temple socials and evening classes are burgeoning as singles look for mates based on their spiritual outlooks rather than their professional affiliations.

Media-literacy resources are popping up on the Internet and as part of public-school curriculums, designed to educate children about the manipulative power of advertisements and commercial programming. Independent political parties and unaffiliated candidates are fast gaining ground on their Republican and Democratic counterparts, winning enough votes in local contests to earn lines on ballots and sway elections on issues of genuine importance to their supporters.

Each of these initiatives is spurred on by the very same voice questioning the purchases we make, the deception we practice, and the sacrifices we endure to remain in the coercion game. For just as easily as that voice can compel us to act against our better nature, so, too, can it inspire us to build the kinds of structures that make positive impacts on society at large.

There is no "they" who can reverse this process without our consent and participation. For without our complicity, they are powerless. Without us, they don't exist.

BIBLIOGRAPHY

Books

Aaker, David A. *Building Strong Brands*. New York: The Free Press, 1996.

Ash, Mary Kay. *Mary Kay, You Can Have It All*. Rocklin, CA: Prima Publishing, 1995.

Barna, George. *How to Increase Giving in Your Church*. Ventura, CA: Regal Books, 1997.

Bixler, Susan. *The Professional Image: The Total Program for Marketing Yourself Visually*. New York: Perigee Books, 1984.

Block, Tamara Brezen, and William A. Robinson, editors. *The Dartnell Sales Promotion Handbook*. 8th ed. Chicago: Dartnell Corporation, 1994.

Braswell, Kermit L. *Step by Step: A Financial Campaign for Your Church*. Nashville: Abington Press, 1995.

Carnegie, Dale. *How to Win Friends and Influence People*. 1936. Reprint. New York: Pocket Books, 1982.

Chomsky, Noam. *Necessary Illusions: Thought Control in Democratic Societies*. Boston: South End Press, 1989.

Cialdini, Robert B. *Influence: The Psychology of Persuasion*. New York: William Morrow, 1993.

Crossen, Cynthia. *Tainted Truth: The Manipulation of Fact in America*. New York: Simon and Schuster, 1994.

Delmar, Ken. *Winning Moves: The Body Language of Selling.* New York: Warner Books, 1984.

Dilts, Robert, John Grinder, Richard Bandler, and Judith DeLozier. *The Study of the Structure of Subjective Experience.* Neuro-linguistic Programming, vol. 1. Cupertino, CA: Meta Publications, 1980.

Fletcher, Tana, and Julia Rockler. *Getting Publicity: A Do-It-Yourself Guide for Small Business and Non-Profit Groups.* Vancouver, BC, Canada: Self Counsel Press, 1995.

Garreau, Joel. *Edge City: Life on the New Frontier.* New York: Doubleday, 1991.

Godin, Seth. *Permission Marketing.* New York: Simon & Schuster, in press.

Goldman, Robert. *Reading Ads Socially.* London: Routledge, 1992.

Goldman, Robert, and Stephen Papson. *Sign Wars: The Cluttered Landscape of Advertising.* New York: Guilford Press, 1996.

Hafner, Katie, and Matthew Lyon. *Where Wizards Stay Up Late.* New York: Simon & Schuster, 1996.

Hawken, Paul. *The Ecology of Commerce: A Declaration of Sustainability.* New York: HarperBusiness, 1993.

Huxtable, Ada Louise. *The Unreal America: Architecture and Illusion.* New York: W. W. Norton, 1997.

Kelly, Kevin. *New Rules for the New Economy.* New York: Viking, 1998.

Knight, Sue. *NLP at Work.* London: Nicholas Brealey Publishing, 1995.

Kobs, Jim. *Profitable Direct Marketing.* Chicago: NTC Business Books, 1993.

Leach, William. *Land of Desire: Merchants, Power, and the Rise of a New American Culture.* New York: Pantheon, 1993.

Ogilvy, David. *Ogilvy on Advertising.* New York: Vintage Books, 1983.

O'Hanlon, William Hudson. *Taproots: Underlying Principles of Milton Erickson's Therapy and Hypnosis.* New York: W. W. Norton, 1987.

Packard, Vance Oakley. *The Hidden Persuaders.* New York: D. McKay Co., 1957.

Peppers, Don, and Martha Rogers. *The One to One Future: Building Relationships One Customer at a Time.* 1993. Reprint. New York: Doubleday, 1997.

Poderis, Tony. *It's a Great Day to Fund-Raise!* New York: FundAmerica Press, 1997.

Porterfield, James D. *Teleselling: A Self-Teaching Guide.* New York: John Wiley and Sons, 1985.

Ries, Al, and Jack Trout. *Positioning: The Battle for Your Mind.* New York: McGraw Hill, 1986.

Shenk, David. *Data Smog: Surviving the Information Glut.* San Francisco: HarperSanFrancisco, 1997.

Shepard, David. *The New Direct Marketing: How to Implement a Profit-Driven Database Marketing Strategy.* New York: Irwin Professional Publishing, 1990.

Silva, José. *The Silva Mind Control Method.* New York: Pocket Books, 1978.

Simpson, Christopher. *Science of Coercion: Communication Research and Psychological Warfare, 1945–1960.* New York: Oxford University Press, 1994.

Singer, Margaret Thaler. *Cults in Our Midst.* San Francisco: Jossey-Bass, 1995.

Sowell, Thomas. *Conquests and Cultures: An International History.* New York: Basic Books, 1998.

Speer, Albert. *Inside the Third Reich: Memoirs.* Translated by Richard and Clara Winston. New York: Macmillan, 1970.

Stauber, John, and Sheldon Rampton. *Toxic Sludge is Good for You!: Lies, Damn Lies, and the Public Relations Industry.* Monroe, ME: Common Courage Press, 1995.

Sutton, Remar. *Don't Get Taken Every Time: The Insider's Guide to Buying Your Next Car.* New York: Viking, 1982.

Articles

Athitakis, Mark. "U2's Golden Parachute." *Express* (East Bay), June 27, 1997.

Bencivega, Dominci. "Opinion or Deception: Fund Manager Accused of Market Manipulation." *New York Law Journal,* January 4, 1996.

Bennet, James. "The Media Business: Coors to Introduce Specialty Beers." *The New York Times,* September 18, 1995.

Block, Peter H., Nancy M. Ridgway, and Scott A. Dawson. "The Shopping Mall as Consumer Habitat." *Journal of Retailing,* March 22, 1994.

Brandweek staff. "Number Crunching, Hollywood Style." *Brandweek,* October 6, 1997.

Carey, James. "Casino Boom Aids Designer's New Focus." *Hotel and Motel Management,* November 6, 1995.

Carlisle, John. "Public Relationships: Hill & Knowlton, Robert Gray, and the CIA." *Covert Action Quarterly,* Spring 1993.

Caruso, Denise. "Knowing When You're Being Seduced by Powerful Persuasive Techniques." *The New York Times,* December 29, 1997.

Cassidy, John. "Bear Headed." *The New Yorker,* July 28, 1997.

Chomsky, Noam. "Media Control: The Spectacular Achievements of Propaganda." Westfield, NJ: Open Magazine Pamphlet Series, 1991.

Crenson, Matt. "Scent of Cookies Brings out Best in Shoppers." *Las Vegas Review-Journal,* October 14, 1996.

Davis, James D. "Promises to Keep." *Sun-Sentinel* (Fort Lauderdale), July 30, 1995.

Dearlove, Des. "A Breath of Lemon-Scented Air." *The Times* (London), April 3, 1997.

Eddy, Kristin. "Making Sense of Scents." *Atlanta Constitution,* December 18, 1996.

Faust, Fred. "Fit for Service: Employee Uniforms Play a Key Role When Casinos Are Styling Their Image." *St. Louis Post-Dispatch,* July 26, 1993.

Freeman, Paul. "Hitting High Notes in Marketainment Business." *Puget Sound Business Journal,* June 27, 1997.

Gallagher, Pam. "In the Pink." *Asbury Park Press,* November 26, 1995.

Goldberger, Paul. "The Store Strikes Back." *The New York Times,* April 6, 1997.

Gorman, Christine. "Doctors' Dilemma." *Time,* August 25, 1997.

Hermes, Will. "Lollapalooza, Coral Sky Amphitheater, West Palm Beach, Florida, June 25, 1997." *Spin,* September, 1997.

Hirsch, Alan R., and S. E. Gay. "The Effect of Ambient Olfactory Stimuli on the Evaluation of a Common Consumer Product." Paper presented at the Thirteenth Annual Meeting of the Association of Chemoreception Sciences, April 1991.

Jackson, Joab. "The Great Wired Conspiracy?" *Baltimore City Paper,* February 11, 1997.

Knight, Jenny. "They'll Be Dancing in the Aisles." *The Independent* (London), September 19, 1996.

Kotler, Philip. "Atmospherics as a Marketing Tool." *Journal of Retailing,* vol. 49, no. 4, Winter 1973–1974.

Leonhardt, David, with Kathleen Kerwin. "Hey Kid, Buy This!" *Business Week,* June 30, 1997.

Loepp, Don. "Creating Curricula: Do It Right." *Plastics News,* November 6, 1995.

McCue, Janet. "New Scent Stirs Positive Vibes." *The Plain Dealer,* September 28, 1995.

Morgan, Carol, and Doron Levy. "Why We Kick the Tires." *Brandweek,* September 29, 1997.

Orenstein, David. "Many Dream, Few Make It." *The Times Union* (Albany), August 17, 1997.

Pareles, Jon. "Lollapalooza's Recycled Hormones: Rebellion by the Numbers." *The New York Times,* July 14, 1997.

Radowitz, John von. "Bills That Cause a Stink." *Press Association Newsfile,* October 25, 1991.

Ringle, Ken. "Smithsonian: The Greatest of the Mall." *The Washington Post,* August 10, 1996.

Rooney, Francix C. "Sex, Wine, and Sitars: Shoe Fashion for the Groovy Male." *Journal of Footwear Management,* Spring 1970.

Sandomir, Richard. "Marv Albert Marches Deeper into the Mud." *The New York Times,* November 19, 1997.

Schwartz, Peter, and Peter Leydon. "The Long Boom." *Wired,* July 1997.

Simon, Jeff. "TV Topics." *Buffalo News,* November 23, 1997.

Spangenberg, Eric R., et al. "Improving the Store Environment: Do Olfactory Cues Affect Evaluations and Behaviors?" *Journal of Marketing,* Spring 1996.

Stodghill, Ron II. "God of Our Fathers." *Time,* October 6, 1997.

Syphus, Taylor. "Music Hits the Right Chords for Businesses." *The Salt Lake Tribune,* September 8, 1996.

Venturi, Robert. "The Psychology of Money." *Psychology Today,* March 1995.

Whiteson, Leon. "Pei Masterpiece: Too Elegant Here?" *Los Angeles Times,* October 22, 1989.

Web Sites and Other Sources

Adbusters. http://www.adbusters.org.

Central Intelligence Agency. *Counter Intelligence Study Manual* LN 324-91.

Federal Trade Commission Decisions, Complaint against AMREP Corporation, Docket 9018, Final order, November 2, 1983.

Gifford, Bill. "They're Playing Our Songs." *Feed Magazine,* October 1995. http://www.feedmag.com/95.10gifford/95.10gifford1.html.

Junkbusters. A complete antitelemarketing script, and information on how to combat direct-mail practitioners. http://www.junkbusters.com.

"Kubark Counterintelligence Interrogation" manual, released through the Freedom of Information Act. http://www.parascope.com.

Mary Kay. http://www.marykay.com.

Mike Kay's Peak Power Seminars. http://www.mikekay.com.

National Public Radio. "Morning Edition," February 13, 1996.

State of Missouri vs. Direct American Marketers, et al. Thirteenth Judicial Circuit, Division III. Case no. 96CC066114. March 1997, pp. 315–20; 701–8.

United Colors of Benetton, "Customer Service and Sales Training."

Watson, Peter. *War on the Mind: The Military Uses and Abuses of Psychology,* excerpted at Psywar Terror Tactics Web site. http://www.parascope.com.

NOTES

Chapter One: Hand-to-Hand

1. Central Intelligence Agency, "Kubark Counterintelligence Interrogation" manual, CIA classified publication, July 1963. Obtained through the Freedom of Information Act in 1997, and distributed on the Internet at http://www.parascope.com.
2. "Mike Kay's Peak Power Seminars," tape one, "Overall Approach."
3. Remar Sutton, *Don't Get Taken Every Time: The Insider's Guide to Buying Your Next Car* (New York: Viking, 1982), p. 9.
4. United Colors of Benetton, "Customer Service and Sales Training," p. 13.
5. Federal Trade Commission Decisions, Complaint against AMREP Corporation, Docket 9018, Final order, November 2, 1983.
6. Ken Delmar, *Winning Moves: The Body Language of Selling* (New York: Warner Books, 1984), p. 56.
7. Robert Dilts et al., *The Study of the Structure of Subjective Experience,* Neuro-linguistic Programming, vol. 1 (Cupertino, CA: Meta Publications, 1980), p. 81.

Chapter Two: Atmospherics

1. Paul Goldberger, "The Store Strikes Back," *The New York Times,* April 6, 1997.

2. "In Style: Nike Marries Brand and Retail," *Chain Store Age,* March 1, 1997.

3. Leon Whiteson, "Pei Masterpiece: Too Elegant Here?" *Los Angeles Times,* October 22, 1989.

4. William Leach, *Land of Desire: Merchants, Power, and the Rise of a New American Culture* (New York: Pantheon, 1993).

5. Ibid.

6. Ada Louise Huxtable, *The Unreal America: Architecture and Illusion* (New York: W. W. Norton, 1997).

7. Philip Kotler, "Atmospherics as a Marketing Tool," *Journal of Retailing,* vol. 49, no. 4, Winter 1973–1974.

8. Francix C. Rooney, "Sex, Wine, and Sitars: Shoe Fashion for the Groovy Male," *Journal of Footwear Management,* Spring 1970, p. 22.

9. Peter H. Block et al., "The Shopping Mall as Consumer Habitat," *Journal of Retailing,* March 22, 1994.

10. Leach, *Land of Desire,* pp. 60–65.

11. Ibid.

12. James Carey, "Casino Boom Aids Designer's New Focus," *Hotel and Motel Management,* November 6, 1995.

13. Garreau, Joel, *Edge City: Life on the New Frontier* (New York: Doubleday, 1991), p. 51.

14. See the extensive investigative research in Bill Gifford, "They're Playing Our Songs," *Feed Magazine,* October 1995, http://www.feedmag.com/95.10gifford/95.10gifford1.html.

15. David Hargreaves, in "They'll Be Dancing in the Aisles," by Jenny Knight, *The Independent* (London), September 19, 1996.

16. Paul Freeman, "Hitting High Notes in Marketainment Business," *Puget Sound Business Journal,* June 27, 1997.

17. "Personality and Social Psychology Bulletin," as quoted in "Scent of Cookies Brings out Best in Shoppers," by Matt Crenson, *Las Vegas Review-Journal,* October 14, 1996.

18. Alan R. Hirsch and S. E. Gay, "The Effect of Ambient Olfactory Stimuli on the Evaluation of a Common Consumer Product," Paper

presented at the Thirteenth Annual Meeting of the Association of Chemoreception Sciences, April 1991.

19. Des Dearlove, "A Breath of Lemon-Scented Air," *The Times* (London), April 3, 1997.

Chapter Three: Spectacle

1. Albert Speer, *Inside the Third Reich: Memoirs,* trans. Richard and Clara Winston (New York: Macmillan, 1970).

2. Ron Stodghill II, "God of Our Fathers," *Time,* October 6, 1997.

3. James D. Davis, "Promises to Keep." *Sun Sentinel* (Fort Lauderdale), July 30, 1995.

4. Robert Hilburn, "U2 Unleashes a Beast: The 'Pop Mart' Tour," *The Seattle Times,* May 4, 1997.

5. Mark Athitakis, "U2's Golden Parachute," *Express* (East Bay), June 27, 1997.

6. Jon Pareles, "Lollapalooza's Recycled Hormones: Rebellion by the Numbers," *The New York Times,* July 14, 1997.

7. Will Hermes, "Lollapalooza, Coral Sky Amphitheater, West Palm Beach, Florida, June 25, 1997," *Spin,* September 1997.

Chapter Four: Public Relations

1. Peter Watson, *War on the Mind: The Military Uses and Abuses of Psychology,* excerpted at Psywar Terror Tactics Web site, linked through http://www.parascope.com.

2. Central Intelligence Agency, *Counter Intelligence Study Manual* LN 324-91, released through the Freedom of Information Act, and available from the National Archives.

3. John Carlisle, "Public Relationships: Hill & Knowlton, Robert Gray, and the CIA," *Covert Action Quarterly,* Spring 1993.

4. Noam Chomsky, "Media Control: The Spectacular Achievements of Propaganda" (Westfield, NJ: Open Magazine Pamphlet Series, 1991).

5. John Stauber and Sheldon Rampton, *Toxic Sludge Is Good for You!: Lies, Damn Lies, and the Public Relations Industry* (Monroe, ME: Common Courage Press, 1995), p. 105.

6. Cynthia Crossen, *Tainted Truth: The Manipulation of Fact in America* (New York: Simon & Schuster, 1994).

7. Christine Gorman, "Doctors' Dilemma," *Time,* August 25, 1997.

8. Don Loepp, "Creating Curricula: Do It Right," *Plastics News,* November 6, 1995.

9. Jeff Simon, "TV Topics," *Buffalo News,* November 23, 1997.

10. Howard Rubenstein, "Marv Albert Marches Deeper into the Mud," by Richard Sandomir, *The New York Times,* November 19, 1997.

Chapter Five: Advertising

1. David Ogilvy, *Ogilvy on Advertising* (New York: Vintage, 1983).

2. *Brandweek* staff, "Number Crunching, Hollywood Style," *Brandweek,* October 6, 1997.

3. David Leonhardt, with Kathleen Kerwin, "Hey Kid, Buy This!" *Business Week,* June 30, 1997.

4. Jim Schroer, quoted in "Why We Kick the Tires," by Carol Morgan and Doron Levy, *Brandweek,* September 29, 1997.

5. "On Advertising," *The New York Times,* August 14, 1998.

Chapter Six: Pyramids

1. Steve Forbes, interviewed on "CNBC News," July 31, 1997.

2. Glen DeValerio, partner at Berman, DeValerio & Pease, in "Opin-

ion or Deception: Fund Manager Accused of Market Manipulation," by Dominci Bencivega, *New York Law Journal,* January 4, 1996.

3. Quoted in "Bear Headed," by John Cassidy, *The New Yorker,* July 28, 1997.

4. Kevin Kelly, *New Rules for the New Economy* (New York: Viking, 1998).

5. Peter Schwartz and Peter Leydon, "The Long Boom," *Wired,* July 1997.

6. Joab Jackson, "The Great Wired Conspiracy?" *Baltimore City Paper,* February 11, 1997.

Chapter Seven: Virtual Marketing

1. PRIZM promotional materials.

2. Seth Godin, *Permission Marketing* (New York: Simon & Schuster, in press).

3. DoubleClick promotional materials.

4. Denise Caruso, "Knowing When You're Being Seduced by Powerful Persuasive Techniques," *The New York Times,* December 29, 1997.

ABOUT THE AUTHOR

Douglas Rushkoff is the author of *Playing the Future, Cyberia, Media Virus,* and the novel *Ecstasy Club.* He is a commentator for NPR's "All Things Considered," a columnist for *The New York Times* syndicate and a regular contributor to *Time, Paper,* and *The Guardian.* He lectures and consults about media around the world and is Professor of Virtual Culture at New York University. He lives in New York City.